To Monica
Best wishes from The
Alan Greenberg

CONFESSIONS OF A
GOVERNMENT MAN

How to Succeed in Any Bureaucracy

ALAN L. GREENBERG

© 2010 Alan L. Greenberg
All Rights Reserved.

No part of this publication may be reproduced, stored in a retrieval system, or transmitted, in any form or by any means, electronic, mechanical, photocopying, recording, or other-wise, without the written permission of the author.

First published by Dog Ear Publishing
4010 W. 86th Street, Ste H
Indianapolis, IN 46268
www.dogearpublishing.net

ISBN: 978-160844-342-0

This book is printed on acid-free paper.

Printed in the United States of America

For the careerists

CONTENTS

PART FOUR
THE TWILIGHT YEARS

ACKNOWLEDGEMENTS

First, I have to thank my wife Sheila, children Roberta and Barry, their spouses, Steve and Allie, and my grandchildren Lauren, Joshua, Emma and Matthew for their indulgence. This project took away quality retirement time which could have been spent with them.

A heartfelt thank you to all of the wonderful and dedicated people with whom I had the pleasure of working during a most rewarding career.

I would like to acknowledge former associates, David Almaleh, Alan Berman, Paul Chistolini, Robert Collegio, Andy Gerardi, Bill Jenkins, Diane Marinacci, Renee Miscione, Joe Moravec, Ed Spitzer, Brian Tait, and Michele Vanden Broek, among others, for helping me recall some of these tales. A special thanks to good friends Barry Becher, Carla Heymsfeld and Jennifer Heno for the advisory services on style and form. Thank you to my editor, Grace Lichtenstein, for laboriously correcting my grammar, punctuation and excess verbiage.

In preparing for this venture I read books by others essaying their past. A word of gratitude to authors Anthony Bourdain, David Sedaris, Michael Lewis, David Hanson, and Richard Yancey for their ability to successfully apply humor to subjects that others might take just a bit too seriously.

INTRODUCTION

This book is for anyone who has worked for, against or with a bureaucracy.

My ascent to the top rung of the ladder of government careerists was not meteoric. It was gradual with many bumps in the road. I owe my relatively successful finish to a combination of skill, luck, timing and more than anything, bulldog perseverance. In my opinion, perseverance and a generous sense of humor are among the most important ingredients to success in any large organization.

Miraculously, I survived to retirement eligibility and beyond. During that time I encountered a lot. If I were to stretch every line of bull I heard or read end to end, it would extend from Coney Island to Pismo Beach.

This book is a compilation of events and words of wisdom accumulated over a near-four-decade career as a humble servant of the people. Some of the wisdom came from the most unexpected of sources.

The anecdotes are based on personal experience. In the interest of protecting confidential information and people's privacy, names of the living were changed, with the exception of elected officials, federal judges, well known people and those situations in which the real name was an integral part of the story. I specifically included the real names of several high level White House appointed GSA officials who I thought made significant contributions to the organization. This group includes Terrence C. Golden, David J. Barram, Stephen A. Perry, Robert A. Peck and F. Joseph Moravec. I also mention two of my colleagues, Edward A. Feiner and Alan M. Berman. All other living GSA names are fictitious. Where I felt it necessary I changed, or interchanged, personal histories and characteristics. In addition, certain events were altered in time, place and description so as to limit any potential embarrassment to particular individuals, including myself.

Some of my "rules" are not original. I try to give credit to known sources. If I cite a "rule" as original and it has previously been published elsewhere it is purely coincidental.

This work is intended as a motivational tool to convey some of my personal business strategies and beliefs, but equally to entertain. I would like to demonstrate that the government can be friendly and that key decisions are made by real people in real life situations.

When I spoke to groups, during and after my career, to test material for the book, I explained that I had family and X-rated versions of my speech. I stated that "if I offend anyone along the way please tell your friends." The book version is somewhere in between, because without the salty expressions a few of the anecdotes would lose their effectiveness.

This is not a "tell-all" book although I possess enough information to do so. Unfortunately, if I did that too many people would be banging at my door to get a piece of me.

I had the privilege of rubbing elbows at the highest levels of government and industry and meeting some terrific people along the way. Although I poke a bit of fun at some personalities and show just a little disdain for the agendas of certain politically motivated people of questionable intentions and qualifications, I have the utmost respect for those who choose public service as a career.

To me, humor has always been an integral part of a successful work experience and often was closer to truth than fiction. The best textbook for understanding and surviving the bureaucracy is *Parkinson's Law*. The good professor, when he wrote his book in 1957, was spoofing the British system of government, but many of his theories are valid today. I cannot count the number of times I spent endless hours on utter nonsense while at the same time issues with a far greater order of magnitude were rammed through the system for the sake of political expediency.

I hope you enjoy my romp through a unique career and I hope you can take away some strategy which will help you achieve your own career objectives. Most of all I hope you will chuckle.

PART ONE

The Big Picture

CHAPTER 1

I Wish I Had the Kind of Job You Think I Have

My retirement party was almost like a mob funeral with all of the proper respects being paid, except that the guest of honor was still alive.

There are two great things about reaching a lofty status in any organization, and being with that same organization during five decades. For one, people tend to laugh at your jokes with more frequency. Being the boss might have something to do with that. Secondly, when you have been around as long as I had been, you can get up in front of a group of people, mutter any kind of incoherent nonsense, and people will think you are some sort of a genius.

I loved my career, but without a sense of humor I never would have made it. Nothing was ever quite what it seemed to be. As in any political arena, you had to look beyond the surface to get the real details. I often think of the words of an esteemed former colleague who, like me, was a senior manager. "Consider me the government's proctologist. I look at everything from the worst possible angle."

But there comes a time in life when you get signals that it's time to slow down and plan for changes. Smell the roses, as scholars have said. With this in mind, it's good to think about retirement before the laws of nature take the decision out of your hands. As a lifetime New Yorker and a workaholic, I never really thought about how the end will come. Then with almost thirty-nine years of public service behind me, much of which was spent in high-profile positions, the hints came quickly.

I was getting tired, and I developed an attitude that every day spent *out* of the office adds a day to the end of my life. With that in mind I traveled to boondoggle conferences that I would never otherwise consider attending. This was not a good sign.

When I contracted a case of what I called "Florida blood," I realized that the end was near. When this malady sets in you act and feel like a Florida condo resident (something like Seinfeld's parents) without actually being there. Your body gets chilled easily, making it uncomfortable to commute on those wintry New York days and you get hungry for dinner around four in the afternoon. Worse yet, you think about dinner choices while eating breakfast; you forget the meaning of color coordinated clothing; and you incessantly clip coupons. Fortunately I recognized this condition in the early stages.

*   *   *

I often wondered what life would have been like if my career had been closer to some people's perception of those of us in the public sector. True, I was tenured *government worker*, but if I was a fat, dumb, and happy bureaucrat, which is how many people stereotype us, then how come I left for work before dawn and returned after dusk? When other people were playing, I and many like me spent countless hours working the home computer, cell phone, BlackBerry or just pouring through an endless mountain of paper, much of which ultimately bore my signature. I'm not a drinking man because if I had a drink every time I felt a little stress I would need a liver transplant. There were a few instances, however, when I got off my evening train and phoned ahead for my wife to stir a cool piña colada.

Perceptions aside, the reality is that during my lengthy career I had been to more intriguing places, met more influential people, and committed more money than most people do in a lifetime. I also met my share of flakes, eccentrics and pompous windbags, some of whom I wouldn't trust to fold a chair for me. If I sought a post-retirement career as a Hollywood casting agent, I would set up in the lobby of the federal building where I spent my working life.

But this is not about me. It is for the good of the people.

The inspiration for this undertaking came from a few real time applications of my many rules for understanding and succeeding in the bureaucracy or the corporate jungle. In no particular order of preference, the most important axioms are "always keep a sense of humor," "learn from everyone," and "dogged perseverance." Lurking in the background is one more all encompassing truism, "never trust a politician."

I had a lot of fun but I was serious about my work and I used humor as an antidote to pressure.

*   *   *

We have all heard stories about teachers who provide a lasting impression on their students. One of my more inspiring teachers was

Miss Rich, my ninth grade math teacher in Montauk Junior High School, located in the Boro Park Section of Brooklyn.

I had just passed the test for admission to Stuyvesant High School, one of New York's premier schools for math and science. As a youngster I actually considered engineering as a career. The day after the test results were announced a handful of classmates were beaming over their accomplishment when we walked into Miss Rich's math class to continue learning about figuring the circumference of a Spalding rubber ball. When the class began, Miss Rich looked in my direction and in her firm voice announced to me and the entire class, "Greenberg, do you *really* think you're smart enough to go to Stuyvesant?" Talk about building someone's confidence.

Actually she was prophetic. I was not good in math and I would likely not have succeeded in engineering school. Instead I went to Erasmus Hall High School, the oldest public high school in America and continued on to Baruch College which was the business school of the City College of New York, a public college which offered qualified New York City residents an excellent free education.

I owe it to Miss Rich for bringing to my attention at an early age that if I am to succeed in the world it would be because of hustle, grit and savvy rather than brilliance.

Growing up in Brooklyn in a working class environment didn't hurt my development. Hustle and street smarts were a good substitute for what was lacking in Ivy League credentials. From the age of thirteen until my first full time job I had hustled for my spending money with part time jobs. Western Union boy; delivery person for the grocer, butcher and cleaner; truck loader; bookkeeper's assistant for a bra company; bank messenger; retail clerk; busboy and waiter; and shill at a Coney Island game stand, among other positions.

The modest beginnings contributed to what became intolerance for bureaucratic, political and legal bullshit. This gave me less than passing scores when it came to tact but I found that over time, having the unique ability to pick the flyshit from the pepper served me well.

*   *   *

The first real test of maintaining a positive attitude in business came shortly after college during my pre-government, time to find myself, stage in life. I was working for a third rate business equipment company trying to market their inferior product. Under the best of circumstances, I would not have succeeded in selling umbrellas in a rainstorm, so this was a challenge. One day my boss, an intellectual in a world of sharks, called me into his office for personal counseling. "Alan, think of every problem as an opportunity." This idea was to be a lifelong personal motivational tool. Unfortunately, at that point, my *problem* was that he was firing me and the *opportunity* was to find a new career where I will actually make a living. Everything worked out, but to this day I still consider every problem an opportunity for improvement.

Fast-forward thirty nine years. I ended my government career as the senior regional official of the Public Buildings Service, U.S. General Services Administration in New York. I was responsible for management of a billion dollar real estate and construction program. As a member of the Senior Executive Service of the federal government, I had achieved an elite level that less than one half of one percent of career federal employees reach. In the corporate world, I would be the equivalent of a regional vice president, or a "big-ass suit from the top floor." My title had been Assistant Regional Administrator, Public Buildings Service, but in reality I was nobody's assistant. That was the protocol. Assistant regional administrators ("ARA"), for the various components of GSA, were career people. The boss, appropriately titled Regional Administrator ("RA"), was always a political appointee. The ARA handled the business elements and provided continuity of programs. The RA got photographed by the press and made sure the current president got credit for initiatives of the prior administration.

The job I held has since reverted to a prior title, *regional commissioner*. Had the change been made during my tenure I would have played that title up big, especially when I made restaurant reservations. "The *commissioner* would like a table."

One single distinction of my career was that I was the first ARA in New York in the 55 year history of GSA to actually *retire* from the job. Others had left by transfer, demotion, resignation or death. In other regions they also left by indictment.

The first inkling of a post-retirement career as an author and speaker came three months before my scheduled departure. I had journeyed to Buffalo, New York, a place where I spent a lot of time during my career and might have influenced the downtown skyline, past, present and future.

This particular trip was more ceremonial than substance, as are many meetings when you reach an exalted level in government. The purpose was to meet with tenant representatives in a 35-year-old asbestos-filled federal building and explain GSA's plan to phase out the building. It was a friendly audience, many of whom I had met before. They already knew and bought into the GSA proposal to vacate the old building and acquire quality leased office space so my visit was strictly protocol. Most mass audiences I addressed over the years would have preferred to run me out of town.

Our project manager for this undertaking was a very capable young man named Ken Thompson who had been based in upstate New York and had earned the respect of GSA's customers. When Ken introduced me to the audience he referred to me as a 38-year veteran with GSA, a good guy, a self-styled comedian, a snappy dresser and "a general fun guy to have around." Never once did he mention any of my alleged accomplishments enroute to and during my tenure as top person in the northeast. At that point I realized that I might have missed my calling in life. Thanks, Ken, for reminding me to always keep a sense of humor. When I actually retired I changed my goal from selling my knowledge to the highest bidder to devoting my remaining productive years to being "a general fun guy."

*   *   *

It seems like only yesterday, but when I came to GSA in 1965 I was a baby-faced recruit who got carded in bars for drinking eligibility. When I retired a lifetime later I still got proofed, but this time it was in the movies for the senior discount. In between, there was a career filled with memorable experiences.

On the day I reported to GSA I was welcomed as warmly as if I had horseshit on my shoes. My first boss was a branch chief named Alex. He was like legendary football coach Vince Lombardi. When a reporter asked one of Lombardi's top players whether the coach gave special treatment to his stars the player said, "Vince treats us all alike. Like pigs." That could also be said of Alex. On my first day, Alex gave me two pieces of wisdom to last a lifetime. "We're surrounded by thieves and liars," was his take on his peers, employees, superiors, customers and anyone else who had the pleasure of doing business with him. His other mantra was "All politicians are whores." This was a lesson that I was to learn many times over in my career, perhaps a bit more diplomatically but there was always that silent barrier between careerists and political appointees or elected officials.

I owe Alex a debt of gratitude for what he taught me about the work ethic and for providing me with an endless supply of great quotations. He never took the diplomatic approach. I remember attending a meeting in which we were trying to convince high level military people that our scheme for housing a major Department of the Army communications component was the best deal for the government. At that point in history, GSA was more of a regulating agency than a service agency so we had captive customers. We were a provider of necessity, not choice. After a frustrating session in which Alex wouldn't give an inch, one of the military reps, named Sylvester, said to him, "You don't understand. This is what my *general* wants."

Intimidation tactics never got the better of Alex. He calmly turned all 140 pounds of himself to Sylvester, pointed his finger at Sylvester's polyester jacket, and as his face got redder and voice slowly rose, said. "What! Your *general* wants it! Well *fuck* your general! When he drops his drawers his balls are no bigger than mine!"

I used variations of that quote frequently.

Other than Alex, almost every man I met that first day was named John or Jim. Their last names seemed all to be Murphy, Kelly or Lynch. The ladies were all Mary or Betty; they had Wonder Woman eyeglasses, teased hair and pounded Underwood or Smith-Corona manual typewriters.

I received my share of advice from crusty veterans. Before settling in, an old-timer named John, who must have been at least forty years old, introduced himself, offered a hearty handshake, and said to me, "Son, let me give you a bit of advice. Get yourself another job." More than forty years have elapsed and I'm not sure of whether I should have taken his advice or not.

Apparently I was a willing listener, or too frightened to disrespect my elders. This senior person filled me with his personal quirks, much of which concerned a deteriorating domestic situation. Among the details of his life, which I did not have a need to know, was his confession that "My wife says having sex with me is like brushing her teeth."

*   *   *

I've dealt with elected officials and political appointees at many levels. Some had more ability than others and some were less ruthless. Some were indeed very nice. But one thing was always true. The political agenda in Government will supersede good business practices and any personal or humane considerations, unless there is something to gain politically. In a dispute situation, a careerist can never win a battle with a politician because the support at the top will always be in favor of the politician.

This polarization is always an issue among senior career managers. No matter how capable you might be and how often you prove yourself, when a new administration comes in, you start proving yourself all over again. After ninety days in office, a political appointee in a senior management position has the power to unravel the most respected of careers. The dockets of the Equal Employment Opportunity Commission ("EEOC"), Federal Labor Relations Authority ("FLRA"), Merit Systems Protection Board ("MSPB") and the federal courts are filled with disputes and records of extensive settlement payouts as a result of this.

While administrations change in the White House every four or eight years, at a local level it is more frequent. The relationship of careerists and political appointees can be described with every cliché in the book: oil and water; Hatfield and McCoy; Red Sox and Yankees. They're natural opposites. Careerists understand and accept the system, but on the local level, many high level political appointees come in with self generated fanfare and actually think they earned their position. More often than not, their sole qualification is to be well connected. To paraphrase an oft-used sports analogy, they woke up on third base and thought they hit a triple.

*   *   *

In the years leading up to my exit I always maintained the position that, unlike many careerists, I would not retire on my eligibility date and I would not set a target date. I will know when I'm ready. Drink no wine before its time.

For federal employees, the end focus is on what is affectionately called the KMA date, the KMA being "Kiss My Ass." This is the eligibility date for retirement, ideally at the fifty-fifth birthday with thirty years' service. When I reached my KMA date I was not ready to retire. Fifty-five is young, I still had plenty of energy and I enjoyed my work. I walked around with a bureaucratic swagger consistent with a tenured job and my phone was not ringing off the hook with offers from private industry.

When I finally made the decision, it was because I was facing the number one item on my list of The Top Ten Indicators that it is Time to Retire. The top indicator was "When your boss is younger than your children." It was now time. My case of Florida blood was just a side effect.

My boss was Young Bruce, a youthful but well seasoned and effective political appointee. Bruce was the third political boss I had in my first two years as top regional stripe. After only a couple of years in his job, Young Bruce had made his mark and was moving on to a position in Washington. Young Tiffany, another political appointee, would replace him. Bruce worked his way up the political ladder in the

Republican administration of New York City government, worked a few political campaigns and had an unsuccessful run for New York State Assembly. Tiffany worked in daddy's business. The fact that daddy worked a few Bush campaigns and was on a first name basis with several influential senators didn't hurt. Without that genetic happenstance, she might have been an account executive at a cosmetics firm instead of the head of a high profile real estate and construction operation, an industry in which she had little knowledge. This was noted by *The New York Times* on its op-ed page. I had kids older than both Bruce and Tiffany so I decided it was time to go gracefully. After almost four years in this stressful final assignment, things were unraveling and I was a physical and emotional wreck. When I walked out the door I had hemorrhoids that were older than my newest boss.

*   *   *

I would love to say that when I was selected for my final high management position back in the year 2000, that I was the brightest, most experienced and most logical choice for the job. The reality was that I was the last man standing. Maybe I didn't deserve the job but the way I figure it, I have arthritis and I don't deserve that either, so I happily accepted the job.

Late in the Clinton administration the political boss in the region was a fellow I'll refer to as Louisiana Clem, although some called him "Happy Hour Harry." Clem was a Good Ole Boy political hanger-on who had been heavily involved in southern politics. Nobody knew what he had on whom to be rewarded with his high profile, high responsibility position. He was of marginal ability and brought personal baggage to the job. At the same time, another party loyalist and an extremely capable executive had been the commissioner of Public Buildings Service in Washington. The episode that led to my predecessor's downfall and my ascent to the throne was an example of how political blood is thicker than water.

Matty D, who I succeeded, had been the assistant regional administrator in the region for ten years, an amazing streak of longevity considering the risks of the job. He was also a friend and a decent person. When Clem came along Matty reached the point of no longer being able to execute flawed commands and actually made references to his boss's making critical decisions, or more often non-decisions, while not fully coherent.

The inevitable confrontation ensued. Clem wanted Matty out. Matty took his case to the commissioner who always respected his ability. The commissioner, in typical political fashion, waffled and wavered but didn't support Matty, who was then exiled to a make-work job in Washington. The agency was further embarrassed by the subsequent actions of Clem, with the notable exception of selecting me as Matt's successor. Clem distinguished himself by a series of critical no-shows, protocol slights, conducting business out of a local pub and receiving sensitive government faxes at a Seven-Eleven because his home phone was disconnected. As if that weren't problematic enough, Citibank, which had the contract for government Visa cards refused to issue him one because of his credit history. He was mercifully relieved of his duties when George W. Bush was elected. The last I heard, he was giving airboat tours along the Louisiana bayous.

Because Matty D had his loyalists in New York, he suggested that any of his managers who were eligible ought to apply for his now vacant senior executive job, to make it difficult for the administration to bring in an outsider that wouldn't be loyal to the New York staff. As it turned out, I was the only in-house candidate who was eligible, interested and willing to go through the application process. It was a crapshoot. If I was selected and it didn't work out I would retire or take an easy job in purgatory for a while. I was retirement eligible and had planned to do so soon anyway. This would give me an added lease on my career and beef up my pension. I welcomed the opportunity to go out on top.

I applied for the top job just to break balls. Now my name was in gold letters on the executive suite door. The fun was about to begin.

I quickly found out that the best parts of the job were that people were always aiming to please and I was empowered to make things happen. I also found that former associates, who retired and went to work for contractors, affectionately called "Beltway Bandits," reappear, like a bad dream. Some that I hardly knew during their working years were over me like flies at a barbeque, glad-handing and passing out business cards, trying to peddle their purported influence. It rarely worked.

*   *   *

I began collecting witticisms from many sources as a youngster. I often told my children and my employees to never disregard the sage utterances of non-scholars. Like the famous Yogi Berraisms, there is logic behind what initially seems absurd.

An early piece of advice came to me from a baseball coach during my high school years. "You can't make chicken salad out of chicken shit," was his way of telling me that I will never be a third baseman. Not original, but it stung nevertheless and stuck in my memory for future application. Another wise man who offered his advice in a helpful manner was an army KP sergeant who observed how inefficiently I peeled potatoes. It was taking too long and a lot of hungry troops would be showing up to eat. "Boy, you gotta work the work; you can't let the work work you." Initially I said to myself that I was being lectured to by an idiot, which was what most college educated military people thought of the lifers. Damned if he wasn't right. It took time to sink in but it made sense. I was not peeling with the right technique and it would take me two hours to do a one-hour job. The military had a machine in the kitchen, which could have reduced this to a ten-minute operation, but that was lost on everybody.

Over the years I kept notes of these expressions, or *rules* as I like to call them. Along the way I added a few of my own. I also recorded anecdotal events, quirky personalities, twisted uses of the English language ("This contract has not been *gratified*."), bureaucratic expressions ("level of comfort" is the bureaucratic equivalent of, "Yes, I absolutely concur, but if you are wrong, I never really said that I agreed with you."), acronyms (Try to figure the meaning of FIST, MARS and CONUS), and other factoids.

Comedian George Burns referred to his wife Gracie Allen's observations as "illogical logic." I've seen much of this. For instance, the affirmative action activist who said to me, "I know that six percent of these contracts (He meant contract *dollars*.) has to go to women. That's one in six." Or a bidder on a contract who said, "I'm cutting ten percent from both of these jobs. That's twenty percent."

At least he was honest. We had a contractor who was plea bargaining a potential multiple fraud and bribery conviction. To assure credit for time served he asked the assistant United States attorney to recommend that sentencing be "concurrent and *radioactive*."

Then there was the fellow who worked for me who wrote up his findings about potential locations to lease with a classic description. "I exposed myself to another building. It was an elevated building with the front door on the side." In reading through that convoluted logic I never quite determined whether he meant that the building had an elevator or it was on stilts and what part of him was exposed. Based upon the rest of his description I assumed it didn't matter anyway.

CHAPTER 2

Look Before You Light

Of all the memories of my years of service nothing stands out more than the cast of characters I've had the good fortune, or misfortune, to encounter.

A broad overview can be found in the nicknames, most of which were based on personalities or other individual characteristics. All of them play a role in these memoirs, directly or indirectly. In most cases they were just being themselves.

I was initially hired by a distinguished gentleman known as the "Poet Laureate of GSA" or the "Briarcliff Bard." He had a mane of flowing white hair and would intersperse his pep talks to street savvy New Yorkers with excerpts from Shakespearean sonnets. I previously mentioned his right hand assistant, Alex, who was as crude as the Bard was poetic. Together they were the good cop-bad cop type, although not by design.

The Bard retired shortly after I came on board. He was succeeded as division director by the most unforgettable character I ever met, the cigar chomping *"Symphony"* Sid Beckett. Sid wore a Columbo-like rumpled raincoat and dandruff flakes adorned his pinstriped suit, which he donned over white wool socks. I always said he was a snappy dresser above the ankles. Sid was so consumed by his cigars in the pre-no smoking days of public buildings that more than once he lit up his trash can by dumping the lighted stubble into the pile of paper. Sid collected cigar bands both as a hobby and to ultimately redeem them for useless prizes. After a shopping bag of his precious possessions disappeared from his office he demanded an FBI investigation of the missing bands, barking that someone took them because "they recognized the value."

Among GSA veterans, Sid stories provided never ending happy hour talk of the old days. Everyone claims to have been there when he pulled the grizzle of a cigar butt out of his jacket pocket and asked for a light, only to realize that it was already lit.

Sid would never be accused of being a fashion plate. With his bald top and stringy side hairs he bore a strong resemblance to Bert

Lahr in "The Wizard of Oz," or, for those who remember him, comedian Ed Wynn. He walked about with cigar ashes on his shirt or tie to complement the dandruff. One of his employees complained one day, "That well-groomed Mr. Sid told me I need a haircut."

For all of his quirks, Sid was a brilliant individual. He held a law degree from Cornell University, where he excelled academically and in several varsity sports. He had the misfortune, however, of coming of age during the Great Depression and never lost that frugal mentality. His first job out of law school was as a prison guard in the Atlanta Penitentiary (His alternate nickname was "The Warden."). He eventually found his way to GSA, where he had a major role in developing the federal real estate manuals.

Sid had many idiosyncrasies, the most conversation-worthy being his absolute inability to remember names. It didn't matter if you met him this morning or worked for him for twenty years, he still could not remember your name. The closest he ever came to my name was *Goldberg*.

In my early career most of the working stiffs sat at plain wooden desks lined up in long rows in a big, noisy, open office. The managers had cubicles in the front and around the perimeter. Sid, being the boss, had a large corner office which was at least 100 feet from my work station. When Sid needed something, or someone, he had a habit of charging out of his office, cigar ashes flying about, and then walking towards the person he needed while pointing in the general direction of his mark and attempting to talk. Not remembering the name, the one-sided conversation started with a very loud, "Uh, uh, uh....!" while he was approaching. Without looking up, you knew where he was going and his mood by the quantity and inflection of the "*uh's.*"

Sid's defense mechanism for his transgressions on names was that he would substitute a physical description or one's nationality for the name. In today's climate he would not get past the first day without an EEO complaint. When talking in the third person he would say, "Get me, uh, uh, *Whatshisname*, the *Chinaman*." It was not unusual for him to refer to someone as *the rabbi, the schvartza, Chiquita* or *Pedro*. There was the person he knew as *No Neck* and the two gentlemen of contrasting height to whom he referred to as *The Long and the Short of It*.

Symphony was relentless in his frugality, not only for himself but in his counseling of others on how to stretch a buck. There was a method behind this madness because those of us who traveled for the company had to get by on allowances far below industry standards.

He was doing this for our own good. For my very first business trip to our nation's capital Sid suggested that I save a few bucks by staying in his favorite hotel which offered rooms at a special government rate, with *bath down the hall.* "You don't have to take a shower every day anyway," he counseled.

Sid told us where to eat to get best value and *how* to eat to stretch out a limited budget. We received a flat travel amount in those days, regardless of what we spent, so when we traveled by road he even suggested that we sleep in the car to save money and then shower and shave in the federal building in the morning. In Puerto Rico where we sometimes ventured because it was, for some inexplicable reason, part of our region, Sid knew where all the nightly manager's cocktail parties were held, which served as a substitute for paying for a dinner.

There was one predictable quirk about Sid. Every year, on the afternoon of April 14th, he would hustle from his office, and head in the general direction of the bullpen. He would mutter a few *uh, uhs* at nobody in particular, puff a little smoke from his cheroot and then ask if anyone had a blank Form 1040. Sid never did his taxes before the night before the due date.

Sid deserves special recognition because he was truly a Godfather to me and a mentor in my career.

* * *

There were many other characters, some of whom appear prominently in these memoirs.

There was Frosty, the Fat Man, Lucky, Big D, the Iratollah, the Chief, Big Ed, and Sonny Boy.

We had royalty amongst us. There was the Queen of Kings, the Princess of Darkness, the Duke of Earl, Earl the Pearl, Pearl the Earl, the Black Pearl and the Duke of Hurl.

Let's not forget the Senator from South Carolina, the Baron, the Sheriff, the Colonel, the Constable, Cowboy and the Judge. There was Bigfoot, Skin Tight and the Austin Strangler.

As time and my career marched on we had John Boy, Quick, Slick and Fast Eddie, Uneven Steven, Alfred E. Neuman, Bozo and Khrushchev. There was the ever popular RAM, GOD (Gerhard Oskar Doernhof), and Sam the Sham.

In no particular order, there was the Bulldog, the Hawk, Shark, Albany Fox, Miller the Driller, Lighthead, Twilight, Ever-ready Freddie, Slime and Nate the Snake.

There was also Matty D and Joey D, TJ, ET, BT and PC. We had Stretch, Tiny, Large Lewis and Shorty, Captain Video and Houdini. Houdini was my onetime budget chief who had a habit of making things disappear and reappear at the most inopportune times.

Who can ever forget Clean Gene, Sporty Morty, Dirty Harry, the Master of Disaster, Top Dollar, Stormin' Norman, Dollar Bill, "Sledge" Hammer, Dizzy Lizzy, Uncle Miltie, the Flower, Tallulah, Pittsburgh Pat, Shotgun, Fred the Furrier, Cyrus the Virus, Meyer the Buyer, Mouth of the South and the Old Grey Mare.

We had "Then Came" Brunson, "Crash" Helmut, Junior, Joe Junior, Junior Joe and Lady Rambo.

Lady Rambo was a demure young woman with a correct Westchester County upbringing. She had a degree from a proper university but times were not great for recent graduates and she had been working in a flower shop serving customers with names like Muffy and Skip. A year after her employ with us as a leasing specialist trainee, she took on the demeanor and vocabulary of a sailor. This was a success story for us.

Our cast included politicians, artsy types, scholars, bureaucrats, strong-arms and every day petty thieves. There were quirky personalities, such as the Silent Man, whom I didn't hear speak for ten years and who broke his silence at the most inopportune time, or the guy who insisted on coding all telephone messages he took by alphabetizing the spelling of names. Thus my name became Aaln and my close associates were Addiv and Hjno. The initiator of all of this wordplay was a fellow named Adderw. This is the same guy who insisted upon referring to geographic locations by their airport codes. Headquarters became DCA, and he worked on big projects in EWR and BUF and eventually requested a transfer to his hometown ORD.

CHAPTER 3

Laughter on the 21st Floor

I came to the government shortly after college. I had successfully completed what was then called the Federal Service Entrance Examination. It was never my intention to make a career of it but being right out of school and draft eligible, without an engineering or technical degree and no discernable skills to show for my four years in a business college, it seemed like a good idea. My plan was to stay until my military obligation was over. I already knew that if I were drafted or enlisted, the law guaranteed my job when I return. Signing up with the feds meant that I would always be able to eat, at least hamburgers.

As things turned out, I did my army time and returned unscathed to GSA. It was a combination of luck and fortuitous timing that kept me stateside and out of Vietnam.

Coming to GSA was a significant event in my life. It was the start of a long and satisfying career. Being thrust into a position of importance, which required hard decisions and accountability, after a very brief break-in period, was a major boost to my confidence level. I had the opportunity to take initiatives. I credit GSA and my first GSA boss, as well as my wife, for bringing me out of a lifelong shell.

Besides for the introduction to my first tyrannical boss, Alex, and my new colleague who insisted upon telling me about his marital woes, I would be inundated with technical and philosophical advice during my impressionable early days in the work force. Fortunately I was independent enough not to listen to most.

I was hired as a realty trainee, to learn the business of leasing real property for the government and managing projects to prepare the space for occupancy. The regulatory and procedural aspect of it became far more important than the business and technical part.

All of the serfs sat in a big, open office with tile floors, a plaster ceiling, and rotary telephones which resonated through the entire floor. Voices carried so you knew everyone's business and pleasures.

Our office was in an old building on Church Street in lower Manhattan. It was the last building demolished for the construction of the World Trade Center. We had a first hand view of the early site clearing and excavation. We also had a magnificent view of cruise ships entering and leaving New York's harbor daily. Some people were so preoccupied with the ships that they forgot why they were in the office.

From my vantage point on the twenty first floor I observed the early construction phases of the World Trade Center, I watched the beginnings of the landfill west of Manhattan which became Battery Park City and I even saw the slow redevelopment of the Jersey City riverfront across the Hudson. While doing this I encountered one of the most unusual blends of personalities that you could ever hope to meet. It was at this point that I concluded that if I was going to survive in government the most important qualification would be a sense of humor.

Alex's secretary was a matronly woman named Mary Dolan, with thirty years of government service behind her and a loyalty to her boss consistent with the male dominance of the era.

Mary's allegiance to Alex included her self-proclaimed task of being his eyes and ears. Among the duties she enjoyed the most was her charge of the daily attendance sheets. She neatly mimeographed a list of all employees in alphabetical order. Each evening before leaving she removed one sheet from the stack in her desk and placed it on a clipboard on an old wooden mini-table near her desk. In the upper right hand corner she would hand-write the date. After NAME, the other columns were headed IN, OUT and REMARKS. Every morning, as the staff arrived, each would initial and indicate an arrival time. Our working hours were 8:30 AM to 5:00 PM with no variances. Everyone was expected to arrive not later than 8:30 AM, with a five minute grace period, or be considered late and under obligation to submit a Standard Form 71-Request for Leave, for one hour of annual leave. Mary took it upon herself, at precisely 8:35 AM each morning, to walk over to the table, scan for missing signatures and draw a red line across any unsigned NAME spaces to prevent back-timing by late arriving staff. At 8:45 she would bring the list to Alex so he could intimidate the late-comers by forcing them to come into his cubicle to sign the sheet.

This was my first experience with a power play in government. Mary loved her role as enforcer and it became a real cat and mouse game for the old-timers and habitual latecomers to outwit her. Sometimes there would be a tug of war at the sign-in table when Mary was in the act of red-lining the sheets. Often, the late arriving employee would lunge at the table like a third baseman going after a hot line drive, just before the 8:35 mark.

Sitting diagonally opposite Mary was another Mary, secretary to the Poet Laureate. Her primary role in life was to stroll to the outer window at 8:45 AM each morning, gaze outside and predict the weather for the remainder of the day. She would then tell all her calculation of the number of months, days and hours until her retirement. This scenario would be repeated at precisely 4:45 PM when we would get the evening forecast followed by a sigh and, "Oh well, another day and a half's work for a day's pay." Nobody had much of a clue as to what she did in between the two weather forecasts. The Bard, being more of an artiste than a taskmaster, did little to change the situation.

I was surrounded by an interesting crew.

My immediate first line supervisor and on the job coach was a guy named Beefsteak Charlie, who was a clone of Alex. Charlie regarded all customers as well as any GSA employee outside of his area as the opponent, not to be trusted. Consequently, our mission was more a matter of harassment and prevention of any progress than it was to serve our clientele. Since our customers had no choice but to come to GSA for their space and furniture needs it became a power trip for the diminutive Charlie to assert his authority. He regarded all expenditures a personal affront and considered it his responsibility to squeeze every government agency into the smallest quantity and poorest quality space to save the taxpayers' money.

Sitting at a desk between me and the window with the view was "Pittsburgh" Pat Grogan, a/k/a the Baron, a senior technician with personal delusions of grandeur. It was Pat's good fortune to have found his way to government, which has a lengthy due process to fire anyone for incompetence. He would not have lasted one week in a profit-making organization.

He acquired the Pittsburgh Pat handle when he managed to milk a project to complete space layouts for a new Pittsburgh federal building and courthouse to the extent that it cost the government dearly due to delayed and incomprehensible submissions. Pat took a drafting course at the old Delehanty Institute and now prized himself as a great architect. He was extremely critical of every real architect, claiming that his own experience in business and life was far more beneficial than their education at places like Pratt Institute or Cooper Union.

In reality, Pat's prior experience was working on the Alaska pipeline. While he would have liked us to believe that he was instru-

mental in the design and construction of major portions of this
endeavor, the common belief in the office was that he was a grease
monkey and gopher.

There were two consistencies in Patrick's behavior pattern. One
was that every time a new employee came on board he would but-
tonhole them, question them, make disparaging remarks about their
education and finally offer to show them the ropes. Charlie would
forewarn every newbie to use discretion about where they sought
advice.

The other sure thing was that every morning, after Pat arrived
for work fashionably fifteen minutes late and after he and Mary
engaged in a little tete a tete with the time sheets, he would settle in at
his desk which he would meticulously clean the night before, and pick
a debate with the person at the desk on the other side of me.

Morrison J. Bothwell II, my neighbor to the right, was a distinguished looking southern gentleman in his sixties. His best years were
behind him and the government was his retirement career, or at least
a place to spend his daytime hours. Morrison had white hair, a large
belly and wore vested suits with a pocket watch, giving him an aura
of aristocracy. People called him Murray for short, which bothered
him although he never made a real fuss over it. The name Murray
made him sound like a common New Yorker rather than the polished
southern gentleman which he perceived himself to be. He was referred
to by Charlie and Alex as the Judge or the Senator from South Carolina.

Every morning he and Pat would find something to argue
about. Lyndon Johnson's handling of the Vietnam War one day;
which pushcart had the best coffee the next day. It didn't matter, as
long as they had something to debate. They all ended the same way.
Murray would have enough of this and simply bark back, "Pat,
you're nuts." Patrick would seethe but the argument would be over
for another day.

The best debates were over the professional capabilities of the
office personnel. Patrick had the least formal education but professed
to be the best technician around. Every time Alex pressed him for
completion of a task or a simple answer Pat would say that he was a
professional and should not be rushed. Alex's reply was that Forty-
Second Street (which was notorious for it's sleaze at the time) was
filled with professionals.

Morrison's best comeback line to Pat came during a discussion
about the relative merits of some of the prominent design firms of the
day. Pat claimed that a major firm, Designs for Business, which

rejected him for employment several times, was incompetent and that he could professionalize the operation. Murray's reply was, "Pat, the only way they'll let you into D for B is if you carried a mop." This was good for the office because the two of them didn't speak for about a month after that.

Sitting nearby was another realty technician, Wilson P. Thorn who was a hyper, beer drinking, chain smoking one hundred percent American of great ability but questionable ambition. He sported a pompadour which must have been six inches high and he kept his blond hair in place with a quart of toxic hair tonic. Willie universally disliked everyone and was not ashamed to say it. He had a law degree but thankfully never practiced law, in or out of government, even though he introduced himself at meetings as the government's attorney. He hated attorneys, which is probably not such a bad thing. He disliked the Irish (drink too much), the Jews (said they were all con-artists), African-Americans (or Negroes as they were known then), Italians (thought they were all criminals) and Indians (too many Indian doctors). He endlessly knocked the Roman Catholic Church, the medical profession, and the bar association (which refused to admit him). Almost every name he ever uttered was preceded by the words "that idiot," or followed by, "asshole that he is."

Thorn's belly hung over his belt buckle, yet he supplemented his daily diet with a formidable dose of Hershey bars, donuts from the coffee wagon and custard from the local Carvel or equivalent. Although some of us gently suggested that the stomach cramps he often suffered might have been related to his dietary habits, he adamantly denied this. Years later, his careless lifestyle came back to haunt him. He was forced to undergo major abdominal surgery. Of course he blamed his incompetent physician for allowing this to happen.

Will also was predictable in his daily behavior. He would arrive late and blame the Marys for a conspiracy to hide the attendance sheets. He would then call the head of the typing pool, Betty, a total incompetent because she couldn't read his handwriting and her people, especially "those colored typists from Alabama" would be chastised for constantly making errors typing his letters. He would complain that the janitorial staff stole candy bars from his desk, that Lyndon Johnson was an idiot, that the Mayor of New York should be impeached (or worse) because the subway was late and that Pittsburgh Pat, whom he refused to acknowledge, was a non-productive disruption to the office. At least he got that right. After shuffling a few papers and rewriting a two page letter five times he would go for lunch.

When GSA relocated to the new federal building at 26 Federal Plaza, Thorn, who also considered himself a historian, decided he wanted to personally walk every street in an ever widening perimeter around the office to check out all of the old buildings. He would start his lunch hour with a candy bar at the desk for energy and then begin his walk. In due time he covered all of the streets of Soho, Chinatown and Tribeca, before expanding to Noho, Wall Street and the Lower East Side. He then returned to the office with a custard cup in hand to show everybody the street map that he had been marking. This passion eventually ended when he covered most of the walkable area, but more important, he found it more satisfying to glutton himself in Chinatown almost daily, rather than the walks which gave him a bit of exercise.

I eventually became Wilson's boss so I had to pay closer attention to his idiosyncrasies and work avoidance habits. One scheme he had going, which took me a while to discover, was that he would routinely leave a pair of glasses on his desk and a sport jacket hanging on the hook alongside, creating the illusion that he was nearby somewhere. When I would look for him my secretary would return from the search and say that he was "away from his desk" which was true but in reality he was twenty miles from his desk, having quietly slipped out of the office and gone home.

*   *   *

The most erratic yet enjoyable character in the office in my early years had been a contemporary of mine. Paolo Rossini was an intelligent and reasonably hardworking person, at least from 8:30 AM to 5:00 PM, and not one minute longer. Paolo did essentially the same work that I did, the difference being that I handled upstate New York as a trainee and he handled part of New York City.

Paolo's downfall came in part as a result of his refusal to work one second beyond five o'clock, lift a pencil before eight thirty in the morning or exert one bit of energy during his designated lunch hour or coffee interludes. This irritated both Alex and Symphony Sid to no end. Alex used to say that if they pay you to work to five it wouldn't hurt to work ten minutes longer.

He would add that if you were meeting with a customer out of town and you were done by noon, instead of taking the one o'clock bus back from Albany, you should pay some impromptu visits to other occupants of the federal building. He didn't do this in the interest of customer service, but more to police the government agencies to be sure they weren't occupying five square feet more than their handbook entitlement.

Paolo had other quirks that would drive Sid and Alex berserk. He frequently performed in amateur opera companies and would sing arias at his desk. He preferred to be addressed as "Don Paolo" because of his operatic interests and talents. Paolo would come to the office with hair dyed blonde one day and as his whims or opera roles dictated would at times sport a beard or moustache, both of which were frowned upon in the conservative workplace of the mid-sixties.

Paolo's ultimate slide was attributable to his penchant for practical jokes and his love of the ladies. In the sixties, if one had a spouse but consorted with consenting adults of the opposite sex, even if it was just as a lunch companion, it was adulterous in the minds of the traditionalists.

Alex had values about as traditional as they get and didn't appreciate Paolo's antics, especially his friendship with a certain young secretary named Mary who worked in another division. She was considerably younger than the other secretaries named Mary. I don't know whether Alex had a moral issue or just a fear that the friendship may result in revealing business secrets and give Alex's rival a competitive edge.

Paolo was incessantly on the phone with this woman. Because several people shared phone numbers at the time and nobody heard of caller ID, whenever the phone rang Paolo would lunge to answer it in a feeble attempt to keep this relationship private. He wasn't doing a good job of it and since the friendship had gone far beyond lunches at the Automat, Paolo was now looking over his shoulder. There were a few who didn't appreciate his playboy style so he had to prevent anyone from revealing these peccadilloes to his bosses or, worse yet, his spouse, as if they didn't already know.

One day Alex and Sid left the office to attend a meeting in Newark. The way to go is to take the PATH line, then known as the Hudson Tubes, from a terminal right beneath our building on the future World Trade Center site. Before leaving they needed some information from Paolo, who was nowhere to be found. They strolled out of the building and into the station and proceeded towards the stairway to the train platform. Enroute they passed a small coffee shop with windows facing the promenade.

When Alex and Sid, who were both sticklers for rigid office behavior, spotted Paolo and Mary in the illuminated window smiling and holding hands over coffee and Danish, Paolo's career with GSA was as good as over.

This was 1966 and Alex had the authority to fire him for being AWOL. Although Paolo drove Alex crazy at times, deep down Alex liked him and didn't want to hurt his career. He just wanted him far away. The compromise was the implicit understanding that he would find another job and there will be no bad references.

I learned that the surest way to get rid of someone was to give them favorable ratings and good references. As I moved up the management ladder, I was finessed by this technique a few times so I was always wary of exceptional ratings

Paolo eventually departed for greener pastures but not without leaving a legacy behind. Besides his unpredictable behavior, his practical jokes didn't spare anybody.

Paolo would unscrew the mouthpiece of the old Ma Bell phones, stuff cardboard over the voice input and then replace the mouthpiece. In that manner, no matter how loud the speaker shouted into the phone the response from the other end was, "Huh? What? I can't hear you!" He loved to do this with some of the old timers who originally came to the government with a letter of recommendation from the local party chairman. He generally did it concurrently with placing a phone message, emulating Mary's handwriting, to call a local Congressman.

Then there were the plastic turds left at the office entrance and, of course, the photos of *Playboy* bunnies which he would inconspicuously slip into people's work papers before they went to an appointment so that they would surface unexpectedly during the meeting. He enjoyed seeing people make excuses when the photos would appear right in the middle of a presentation.

By far, the target of most of his one-on-one pranks was one "Large Lewis" Levine, a senior leasing specialist and future branch chief with whom Paolo worked on many New York projects.

There was the time the two of them were riding up a crowded elevator in midtown Manhattan when Paolo inexplicably turned to a startled Large Lewis and shouted for all to hear, "No, I will *not* go with you to your apartment!" Lewis was of the dimension and strength that he could have broken Paolo's wrists in one motion but chose to write off the incident to immaturity, figuring that if he laid a hand on the perpetrator with any malice it would be he who would be more likely to be disciplined.

Then there was the day Lewis was driving a standard issue government Plymouth sedan along Queens Boulevard. Paolo sat in the passenger seat observing the surroundings and singing "Nessun Dorma," which irritated Lewis almost as much as having to read his inter-office memos. When Lewis glanced Paolo's way again, he noticed him tossing sheets of paper from a small notepad out the window. With his left hand at the wheel he grabbed the pad with his right hand. There were a few more sheets to be tossed, on which Paolo had written, "I'm being kidnapped by a pervert."

Paolo had exceeded his boundaries with this one. When they stopped for a light in Woodside, with six lanes of traffic around them, Lewis calmly told his passenger, "Out of the fuckin' car!" An argument ensued before Paolo realized that the Large One wasn't joking and could probably cripple him with one swipe. Lewis then reverted to his military police training and applied the old pinch above the elbow with a gentle shove towards the door. "Out!"

The virtuoso exited the vehicle, bolted across two lanes about to resume movement after a light change and came to a halt on the island separating the main road from the service lanes.

There are a few unwritten rules in life and both Lewis and Paolo respected them. You settle differences yourselves and don't go running to the bosses with complaints or excuses. We've all heard the expression, "Don't get mad. Get even."

It didn't take long for Paolo to get even.

Despite Lewis' bulk, he was very sprightly and was an early daily arrival in the office. He compensated for this with a catnap or two during the day. Nobody got particularly upset when they heard loud snoring from his cubicle. It was nap time and he would soon awaken with new energy, kind of like a greyhound given a dose of espresso.

Paolo noticed that Lewis would leave his cubicle for a morning nature call about 9:30 AM every day. He used his time in the stall to scan the day's racing entries and occasionally would nap for a few minutes. Paolo had previously picked up on the snoring behind the stall door. He waited for his spot.

On this particular morning Paolo observed his mark, paper under his arm, heading to the corridor. He allowed five minutes before going into the windowless men's room unobserved. As expected, he heard the snoring. The *Morning Telegraph*, the city's authoritative racing paper, was on the floor, folded by his feet. Lew used to say, "It's great that the *Telegraph* comes out early enough for me to take to the crapper in the morning."

"Lewie, you there?" he whispered, hoping to get no response. There was silence, except for the snoring.

Paolo quietly tiptoed to the exit door, shut the light and exited, leaving the large one sitting on the pot with his pants at his ankles, asleep and in total darkness. He reached in his back pocket and unfolded the pre-printed letter size paper which read OUT OF ORDER and neatly tucked it into the crevice between the jamb and the door. To prevent any immediate retribution, he headed downstairs to the beanery for morning coffee with Mary.

It's anyone guess as to how Lewis reacted when he awakened in the dark. Although nobody ever admitted to the practical joke, Lewis had a pretty good idea of the culprit and was ready to resort to a physical confrontation had it not been for the embarrassing consequences if the details of the caper were revealed.

The whole issue became moot when Paolo sipped coffee with Mary, oblivious to the fact the Alex and Sid would soon pass by.

I was not immune to Large Lewis' idiosyncrasies.

Lew had an aversion to flying. That was not good because he did a lot of leasing work in the Buffalo, New York area, which had a heavy federal presence. The drive from Long Island to Buffalo could not have been fun.

I was scheduled to accompany him for learning purposes to Buffalo for meetings with potential lessors to the government. As I was to find out later, Lewis had already made his selection, hinted to the prospective bidders as to what their final offers should be and already set up a construction schedule from the date of award. Little wonder that we had a concentration of leases from one property owner, a prominent Niagara Falls undertaker.

Lew was burdened with a neophyte on this trip but he was not about to go out of his way. He commanded that we would drive to Buffalo and still arrive in time for a 10:30 AM Monday meeting. I was to meet him at the off ramp at the Cross Bay Parkway exit of the Belt Parkway in Queens, not all that far from JFK Airport. The rendezvous time was two o'clock in the morning. "Be there or I'll go without you."

I took a taxi from Forest Hills to the intersection of Cross Bay Parkway and the Belt and instructed the driver to let me out near the off ramp. He shook his head as I paid him and with my suitcase, walked a few feet into the off ramp as if I was going to the highway to hitchhike. It was mid-February so I wouldn't have lasted long.

At precisely 2:00 AM a government vehicle sped up the off ramp and screeched to a halt. "Get in!"

We then got back on the highway. Lew drove non-stop for the next three hours until we were outside Albany, New York. At 5:00 AM Lew decided, "Let's take a look at the Federal Highway Administration space. It's right off the exit." In the darkness of night, Lew aimed our headlights into the windows of an almost completed new building to do our version of a construction progress inspection.

By 5:02 AM we were surrounded by state troopers who had pulled up with their sirens blasting.

No harm done. We explained our mission as super dedicated servants of the people and we were on our way. Lew consented to let me drive for a while. He napped from Albany to Troy, about twenty minutes, and then read the morning paper we picked up at a rest stop. By Utica he was back at the wheel and we were in Buffalo by ten.

Two quick meetings in Buffalo with property owners and then off to Niagara Falls for another meeting with his favorite lessor, which included a proper lunch overlooking the American side of the Falls. This was followed by a tour of potential sites for a new branch office for the Social Security Administration, which was academic because Lew had already decided on which site he would recommend.

By four in the afternoon we were back in Buffalo for a meeting with the GSA area manager, which was less of a meeting and more of a social call to catch up about family, friends and former associates.

At 5:30 PM we finally arrived at our downtown hotel. Rest at last.

Not so soon. "Meet me in the lobby in twenty minutes," Lew ordered.

When the clock struck six we were in the car again. This time we drove east on the New York State Thruway to Batavia, New York, home of Batavia Downs trotting track. To my surprise, there were our Niagara Falls potential landlords, greeting us in the track's restaurant. We had another proper meal, with suitable beverages, and enjoyed ten races.

Back in the car and back to Buffalo. By 1:00 AM we were in the hotel. I was exhausted. This 300 pound hulk of a man had been up for more than twenty-four hours, save for the Albany catnap; he had driven about five hundred miles; ate like he had multiple colons and was still ready to go. I went upstairs, took a leak and fell on the bed in a heap, fully clothed. The next thing I remember was being awakened by the phone at 7:00 AM. "Where the hell are you? We've got work to do."

The second day of this excellent adventure was not quite as taxing. In the morning we visited some government leases on Delaware

Avenue just to review compliance with maintenance clauses in the contract. In the afternoon we did a little exploring on the main streets of downtown Buffalo to try to find a new storefront location for the consolidated military recruitment offices.

After a few passes up Main Street and along Delaware Avenue Lew stopped in front of an obviously familiar location. He gazed up the block, said "Ah, there's no space here. Let's go shoot pool."

We went upstairs and that's what we did for the rest of the afternoon.

*   *   *

Another memorable character I encountered in my early career was one Alfred E. Neuman. This was his real name save perhaps for the middle initial. Nobody was ever so deserving of that name. He had no physical similarity to the *Mad Magazine* character of the same name but his propensity for getting into difficulty or creating a problem which someone else had to solve was amazing. Alfred was in the twilight of his career when I first met him. The word was that at one time, he was rather sharp. But time and life's events had caused the change. There was some talk that he had a stroke or breakdown that also impaired his mental capabilities but that was never validated.

Al was actually a very nice guy and never meant any harm to anyone. Unfortunately he was no longer able to think quickly or write crisply and he was unable to cope with the slightest amount of pressure. He could not make the most elementary business decisions on his own. He was rather fidgety and would drop things or accidentally push desktop paraphernalia to the floor if he had to make a sudden movement, such as to respond to his approaching boss. When the bosses asked him the simplest of questions, such as "Al, what time is it?" he would break into a sweat and his bald head would turn beet red. If the chief asked him how much space Social Security Administration occupied in Scranton, Pennsylvania, Al would go into an absolute panic. It was a bit cruel but some people used his faults as a source of pleasure. Boss Alex took satisfaction in humiliating him in front of others.

After he retired there was no end to the Al Neuman stories. There were few people in the office who weren't victimized in one way or another by Al's transgressions.

As I mentioned, our office consisted of long rows of desks occupied by the serfs. The supervisors inhabited the perimeter cubicles and offices. Alfred was midway down. It wasn't too long before I learned that when Al Neuman was at his desk one should never walk between him and the desk behind.

Whenever someone approached him, whether it was for business, to chat, or simply to pass by, Al would instinctively tense up and roll back on his chair until it hit the desk behind. If anyone was walking behind him he would just roll right into them but the biggest damage would come if the approacher and the chair attempted to traverse the same space at the same time. It was a male dominated office at the time and many sets of gonads, including my own, came close to being permanently immobilized by Al Neuman and his chair.

There is good that comes from everything. One of our co-workers, Gentleman Jim McClanahan, had a serious drinking problem. He became a recovering alcoholic when struck by Al Neuman's chair. After a double martini lunch, Jim walked back to the office and headed on the shortest path to his desk. Had this been before lunch he would have been alert enough to steer clear of Al, but instead he took the Neuman route. As if signaled by a silent alarm, when Jim approached Al sprung back, striking Jim in the family jewels. When he reached down to grab his bundle he tripped over the extended legs of Al's rolling desk chair, went flying across the next aisle like he was diving into the end zone and landed on the tile floor after first hitting his head on the trash can of the neighboring desk.

Between the concussion and the dislocated hip, Jim spent two weeks in the hospital followed by a month of in-patient physical therapy. During this time he was often heavily medicated and naturally was prevented from any consumption of spirits. When he finally left and came back to work he had found religion and a new purpose to life and never again had the need to imbibe. To the day he died more than twenty years later Jim credited Al Neuman's clumsiness with prolonging his life.

Al just had a knack for getting into trouble. Alex sent him to Reading, Pennsylvania to meet its mayor and discuss the current and anticipated federal presence. At the time, Pennsylvania was part of our region and Alfred covered projects in that state, but Alex would only entrust him to smaller jobs. He fortunately never found his way to Philadelphia, Pittsburgh or even Harrisburg. Most of his work involved small field offices for Social Security Administration, Internal Revenue Service or Selective Service System (the old Draft Board) in places like Johnstown or Altoona.

In Reading, after meeting the mayor he was to gather spatial requirements of the agencies in order to consolidate them into a single leased location. At the time, the word *collocate* was a buzzword in

GSA in that the commissioner thought there was some economies to be gained by reducing the number of leases. The more likely scenario was that the real estate development industry saw a bonanza here and lobbied GSA to institute a co-location policy to create activity.

Before Al's brief visit was over and he got on the Greyhound to come back home he created enough havoc to test the mettle of even the best political strategists and publicists.

The first problem came when Al filed his expense report. Al submitted a travel voucher for an overnight stay that included a hotel charge many times the allowable per diem rate. The boss questioned this. Turns out that Al, unknowingly, checked into a local hotel that was the town brothel and the daily rate he thought he was getting was the posted *hourly* rate for a quickie. Al was oblivious to all of this.

This was before faxes and e-mail so it took a day or two before the copy of the *Reading Eagle*, with our Alfred E. Neuman's picture on the front page over the caption, "Federal Official Promises New Reading Courthouse," to reach Alex's desk.

Despite Alex's gruff nature, he rarely lost his composure, but in this case he went totally bonkers. He bolted out of his cubicle like a bronco with the straps a little too tight around his nuts and came to a halt at Al's work station. He slammed *The Eagle* down on Neuman's desk, being careful to avoid near-castration when Alfred jumped and his chair echoed a loud thud against the neighboring desk. Al's dome turned beet red, and he stuttered more "homina, homina, hominas," than Ralph Kramden ever did. Alex didn't want his explanation because, like everything else out of Al's mouth, it would have made no sense at all. Al tried to explain that he was under such pressure and he did nothing more than nod his head to indicate he heard the mayor's question. Unfortunately, his nod had been noticed by a reporter. Now GSA had every congressman in Pennsylvania asking why Reading was getting a building and their district was not, except of course the representative from Reading, who thought he struck gold for the next election and was already issuing statements taking credit for Reading's good fortune.

Like everything else, this too passed and Al settled back to counting desks in small field offices, with strict instructions to refer all questions more complex than the time of day back to the regional office. As much as Alex would have momentarily wanted to fire him (Due process would make this a two year project, which would likely fail at the end.), he accepted that Al was part of the family and required care and nurturing, just like a slow-thinking brother.

One would think that Alfred would have learned his lessons, but he continued to attract trouble, mainly because of his own insecurities.

There was a day when a group of six of us decided to celebrate a birthday by taking the birthday boy to lunch at the Nassau Grill, a local titty bar that catered to Wall Streeters on expense accounts. In return for the privilege of being squeezed into a table, breathing beer-scented air and consuming overpriced hamburgers the patrons were able to observe a few overweight "artists" shake their boobs to the tune of "House of the Rising Sun" or a similar sixties ditty.

When we left the luncheon, for some reason which to this day I cannot explain, we entered an adjoining establishment which practiced its First Amendment rights by offering a wide variety of adult books, games and other accoutrements for sale or short-term viewing. We stayed there all of about three minutes. Upon reaching the door to exit, who is entering? It was none other than our very own Alfred E. Neuman. Seizing on an opportunity to again embarrass Mr. Neuman, one of our group, Ricardo Ricco, said in a loud voice, "Al Neuman! What the hell are you doing here?" If people didn't know Al's name when he entered, they sure did now. Neuman's head again turned crimson. This time his panic was genuine because it was personal, and not a government gaffe for which he could not be held personally responsible.

One of our other luncheon party members observed the action and Neuman's nervousness so he added fuel to the fire by saying. "Neuman, I didn't know you hung out here. Man, wait until Alex finds out."

A few "*homina, hominas*" later Neuman darted out the door and headed back to the office. While he was traversing the six blocks he must have thought of numerous scenarios as his explanation for patronizing X-rated bookstores. Neuman should have known that nobody intended to hurt him but as usual, his propensity for the wrong moves took over.

The first thing he did was to run to Alex's office to explain that he only went in the store because he saw *us* there first. This was a complete fabrication because when Ricco gave him his grand "Hello," Neuman was totally startled.

Needless to say, Alex seized upon this opportunity to compound Alfred's misery. "Why would a man of your age and responsibility want to go into a peep show, Mr. Neuman?"

By the time we returned from our extended lunch Neuman was back at his desk in a cold sweat. He explained to us that he went to

Alex and told him the story of how and why he was where he was. Of course this was entirely unnecessary because we would have never dropped the dime on Al. First, we liked him and second, if we said anything about Al, it would have been a confession of our own transgressions.

For the next six months, every time Al screwed something up, Alex would approach him in view of his neighboring coworkers and say something like, "Mr. Neuman, if you spent more time with your work and less time in adult book stores, perhaps you wouldn't make these errors."

Al Neuman retired only a few years into my career. Later, as an experienced manager, I always said that there is wisdom to be gained from everybody and people deserve respect regardless of their position. At his retirement dinner Al actually gave a very eloquent speech during which he said something like, "There is a time for everything..." He went on with a few examples which I don't recall but concluded with, "..and now it is time to retire."

I always remembered these words. As I approached retirement eligibility many years later I said to myself and anyone else who dared to ask that I would never pre-set my retirement date, as many federal careerists do. I've seen people start counting the days five years before their KMA date. I maintained that I would know when it was time, and I knew it was time when my new boss was younger than my children. In my own retirement speech I paraphrased Mr. Neuman by saying, "I just want you to know that for the record I really don't want to retire, and I'm not being forced to retire, but deep in my heart I know it's *time* to retire." I was thinking of giving Al Neuman credit for that line but unfortunately there was nobody at my retirement party who would have remembered him. They would have wondered how I knew the "What, me worry?" boy.

CHAPTER 4

Rules of the Rogue

Over and over during my career I talked about "Greenberg's Rules." My associates were sick of hearing that they violated a Greenberg rule or that this event falls under one of Greenberg's rules. Notwithstanding this ill-advised resistance, few can doubt that the rules were accurate, like the laws of nature, and that they offered important guidance for success in our organization.

I would often incorporate a few of my rules into management presentations, using what I called the Columbo analogy. For those not familiar with Peter Falk's *Columbo* character on television, when you watch the great detective in action, you already know who committed the murder so you just have to sit back and enjoy Colombo's pursuit of the culprit. Likewise, in my presentations, right up front I discuss my key points, so the audience can then relax and hopefully enjoy the rest of the presentation with no need for copious notes. For this reason I am sharing my key principles early so as you read through the volume you can enjoy the anecdotal examples of how these principles are cogs in the wheel of success.

The rules are part Parkinson (or at least what the Professor might have created if he worked in today's environment), part Greenberg and part sources unknown, but mainly a compilation of what is guaranteed to happen in a large organization controlled by an even larger and more dysfunctional organization, which in this case happens to be the United States Congress.

As for Columbo, he provided me with much wisdom. One thought is to never underestimate anyone, especially your adversary. I can still see Columbo in the shabby raincoat, cigar in hand, looking at someone and saying, "You know, I've been in this business so long that when something is wrong, the nose tells me so." In management, I found that your gut instinct often is the most accurate and you can just sense when something is not right, or when you are being handed a line of crap.

The *S H L E P* Analogy

S H L E P is an acronym to help people remember my foremost principles of success and survival in the jungle. *SHLEP* is a Yiddish word meaning, as a verb, *to carry,* and as a noun it is slang for someone with a weak mind but strong body. A Jewish mother might lament by saying, "My daughter is marrying a *shlep*." Of course, to a Jewish mother, anything less than a lawyer or doctor is a *shlep.*

The significance here is not the meaning of the word, but to remember the letters. Sense of Humor, Learn from Everyone, and Perseverance.

Sense of humor is self-explanatory. I've pushed that throughout my career. One's life work should be fun, not drudgery. There is no harm at laughing at yourself and occasionally poking good-natured fun at others or the organization.

My own sense of humor probably originated during my youth, as a defense mechanism to compensate for a lot of instability. As an adult, humor became a way of life.

Learn from everyone is a concept which is more difficult to get across. One does not have to be lettered to impart wisdom. Some of the more interesting words of advice I have heard came from places like the sports world, the military and the downtrodden. I already gave you the *work the work* example from the military. There are many more.

One of the great motivating speeches from my days in uniform came from another sergeant. This headstrong careerist said the right words, softly, at the right time.

The platoon was gathered on an outdoor bleacher, sitting close together in a perfect symmetrical alignment, although there was plenty of room to spread out. Being comfortable would not have been *in a military manner.* It was a hot day and the lecture was sure to be boring.

"Now *gentlemens* (sic)," began the sergeant. "It behooves you to pay close attention. In fact, if anyone falls asleep during this class, the guys on either side of him will get KP." Needless to say, everyone remained upright, even if they didn't pay close attention. The shoving matches were inevitable when some of the troops objected to their neighbors' constantly sticking elbows in their ribs.

A witticism that I heard as a youth and that I still used as a teamwork builder came from, of all sources, a dishwasher in a hotel where I spent a summer waiting on tables. Dishwashers and other maintenance type people were referred to collectively as *the rummies* and were exploited by the resort owners. This toothless and red-faced down and outer was engaged in a debate with some of the college student waiters over, shall we say, delegation of duties. His response was something like, "Hey, we(sic) all workin' for the same house." This was a lesson learned often, when I would find myself in a position of dealing with conflicting agendas within my own government agency. I would use my old associate's quote, but just as often when my patience was tested to the limit I would get up and shout, "What the hell are we doing here? The name of the game is to get the job done, not to put together the prettiest file!" I usually got my message across.

"We all working for the same house." I can't count how many times I've used this expression, substituting government for house – with better grammar of course.

The point here is that it's the final goal that counts. We were all working for the same government. If the mission is to complete construction on time, then everything else is secondary. The contract didn't have to be perfect in form. If the Small Business goals aren't met exactly or in every category it doesn't mean the project is a failure. And finally, there is risk in everything we do. Pre-occupying ourselves with insulation from frivolous litigation is a sure way to fail.

Accept wisdom from all sources.

My last point is always *perseverance*. There will invariably be setbacks in the road but the goals can be achieved by staying focused. My own career was a perfect example. My head was beaten down so many times that often I had to zip down my fly to eat. When I went into my final assignment as the top chop in the northeast it was basically because I lived the longest. There was no secret to that. I admit it and I offer no apology. I had applied for the very same senior executive position three times over a period of twelve years before being selected at an age when most government careerists are already retired.

Perseverance often comes, not from learning, but from one's roots. In my case, the early years had a major influence on my future style. Growing up under very modest conditions in Brooklyn had a lasting impact. When I was five years old my mother died of breast cancer, leaving my father, at age forty-six, to care for a young one but desperately needing to work his usual six day week. For years I bounced from place to place. At eight years old I traveled the New York City subways alone in order to stay in a school near my original home, to which I eventually returned.

As an only child in an ever changing personal environment it was no surprise that I was a loner. On the positive side, I quickly learned to think and act independently.

My scrappiness came from frequent underdog status. With a non-traditional family situation I didn't always fit in socially. Being poor left me out of a lot of activities. I was slight of build, so I wasn't a good athlete but I loved the competition. I made up for deficiencies with hustle, much the way I later did in business. When I played basketball I was the tenth man on a ten man team and played two minutes a game if I was lucky, but I looked forward to those two minutes. In softball, I was usually stuck at the catching position but I loved it because I was in on every pitch. It might have been an omen because catchers are the leaders of the defense. When I played hockey it was understandable that I would have loved to have been a goalie but the skill level wasn't there. Instead, I played defense, artfully throwing my diminutive body in front of oncoming shooters who outweighed me, or blocking their shots with a helmetless and sparsely padded body.

More than fifty years after my mother's passing I was a cancer victim myself. I was the picture of health when told I had prostate cancer. My first reaction to the doc was, "There goes my winter marathon." The fact that I had a condition which could have killed me didn't hit until a few hours later. All I could think of was missing the anticipated marathon.

All turned out well. I've been cancer free for more than ten years. As for the marathon I missed, I quickly was back in the game. Guinness doesn't keep records in this category but if they did I probably would have set one for running a full marathon one hundred and eleven days after invasive cancer surgery. By the time I retired from marathon running I had fifty to my credit.

Runners have been known to persevere, almost to a fault.

Rules of the Rogue – The First Ten

Ten: Nobody ever calls to tell you everything is OK.

If there was ever a principle which is true 99.9 per cent of the time this was it. Working for GSA was like working for the gas company in that nobody *ever* calls to tell you everything is fine. When people call you with flattery or idle chatter, the other shoe will surely drop.

In my lectures I work my way into this principle by playing a short piece from an old 1950's *Honeymooners'* episode with Jackie

Gleason and Audrey Meadows. In this particular episode, Alice Kramden, played by Meadows, is trying to convince her bombastic and penny pinching husband Ralph, that it is time they modernized and purchased their first television. When Ralph comes home from his bus driving job, she greets him with his slippers, a warm smile, uncharacteristic flattery and an unexpected hot meal. Ralph knows something is up. Eventually, when "my Ralphie" is content and relaxed she says, "Oh, Ralphie, by the way..."

That's as far as she gets. Ralph jumps up, slams his beefy hand on the table and shouts, "AH, HA! By the way! There had to be a 'by the way!' I knew something was up. OK, Alice, what is it? Is your mother coming over?"

Remember that when the sweet talk ends, the "by the way" is sure to come. It could be a request for special or expedited handling – nothing wrong with that. But then again it could also be a request to help find a job for a ne'er do well nephew, a request for a meeting (translated to a sales pitch) because "My boss is in town and would love to meet you," or a request for a special allocation of a precious parking space. I've been asked if I could get people Broadway show tickets or entry into the New York City Marathon as a "by the way." I once even helped arrange a proper burial for an employee at the request of an estranged husband.

Treating a "by the way" call is another matter. As a manager you have to exercise a degree of diplomacy, and being in a political environment, you have to be aware of sensitivities, especially when dealing with people who can exert influence over you personally or over the success of your mission. I usually relied on fact. If it was reasonable and didn't violate any law or policy I would offer to help. If it was ridiculous and guaranteed to come back to haunt me I would simply cite facts and decline. Then there is always the bureaucratic, "We'll get back to you," and hope it goes away in the meantime or the petitioner gets his or her satisfaction elsewhere.

Nine: In a bureaucracy, where you sit is where you stand.

I heard this from a one time boss of mine who had been reassigned to New York against his will. At his first staff meeting, on his first day in New York, he announced, "I don't want to be here and I hate New York." It went downhill from there.

There is less of this stovepipe attitude in GSA now than there had been years ago, but internal rivalries and conflicting agendas still exist in any large organization. Anyone with a position of responsibility in a bureaucracy can tell horror stories about how internal regulations or procedures can actually inhibit the mission of the organization. I've been at too many meetings where minutia or special agendas sidetracked progress.

I had the privilege of being the Project Executive for the high profile billion-dollar Foley Square construction project in New York. This project consisted of the buildings now known as the Daniel Patrick Moynihan U.S. Courthouse at 500 Pearl Street, and the Ted Weiss Federal Building at 290 Broadway. The project was a success and after it was completed, when people would ask me which negotiations were the toughest, I would usually say GSA first, even though I worked for GSA. The City of New York was second, and the contractors a distant third. When you dealt with contractors, there were no hidden agendas. They wanted to complete the project as soon as possible, show a profit and move on.

My pet peeve in the realm of conflicting agendas has always been procurement preference goals. This is a very commendable program, offering special incentives to minority-owned and small businesses in federal construction. I have seen instances where very successful projects were deemed to be failures by our PPG gurus because *one portion* of the goals was not met although the overall goals are met. As an example, an on-time and on-budget construction project (rare) such as Foley Square, would in some circles be considered a failure because the percentage of woman-owned business contract dollars aren't met, even though the overall small and minority business goals are met and substantially exceeded. You then end up spending excessive time explaining this away to serious faced advocates who are oblivious to the fact that the project was a major success story. Yet, if the project had massive cost overruns but the percentage of contract dollars which went to small and minority businesses was above target, the project would be a success in the eyes of some procurement preference advocates.

There are many more examples: those whose job it is to see that you have the perfect contract, even though nobody would sign it; safety officials who rather than using a common sense risk assessment to mitigate a problem, create major havoc over a triviality, such as a stair rail being one eighth inch higher than code; or those environmental enthusiasts whose sole contribution to the pre-planning of a $500 million project is to assure that there will be a bicycle rack outside. These are a few of many real life examples that where you sit is where you stand.

Eight: There is nothing so clear and logical that someone can't find a reason not to do it.

This complements the *where you sit is where you stand* theory, the difference being that this is more of a personality trait than an organizational thing. I also refer to this as the *Goal Line Stand* theory. People who advocate this principle are not concerned if they are preventing some other organization or component, or even their own organization, from completing a job. There will always be a problem or a reason not to do something. Lawyers are the primary culprit under the guise that taking no initiatives is the ultimate protection against litigation.

I've had cases where at the eleventh hour government agencies such as Small Business Administration, my favorite whipping agency, would recommend not awarding a major contract that had been the result of an extensive competition, because of a minor flaw in the projected small business subcontracting plan, which was the fault of the law and not the bidders. The mere thought of the time and expense of a new procurement under their plan would be mind boggling.

Probably the worst goal line stand offender I had dealt with is the Advisory Council on Historic Preservation. The law gives ACHP the *right* to the goal line stand. In fairness, with ACHP, I have found that following procedure is far more important than the actual results or consequences of your action. As long as they have the *opportunity* to perform a goal line stand, they're happy.

As far as individuals, there are always people not content with other people's success, and will be ready for a goal line stand. "You can't do that." is a common call. When I hear this my first question was usually, "Is this law or policy?" If it's the latter, it changes the flow of the conversation.

There is no real rule for countering the goal line stand. Sometimes bullying or a power play works, but more often the solution is to play along, even if you have no real intention of succumbing. If the defensive line *thinks* it influenced the outcome, or was treated with proper respect, the problem will often dissipate.

Seven: When stuff hits the fan the first thing to do is to find a scapegoat.

I wish I can claim this as an original but somewhere along the way I heard it elsewhere. In government circles failed initiatives are generally credited to a retiree or someone else who has left the organization.

As a manager I would never advocate this approach to resolving a problem, but I can't deny that this mentality exists and it usually manifests itself in the form of preventative measures. The term "cover yourself" or "paper trail" permeates bureaucracies, and with good reason. There are those who perceive their jobs as finding a *gotcha* at someone else's expense. One *gotcha* can negate many *Ah Ha!* moments.

Six: Nothing succeeds like failure.

This is one of my personal favorites. It covers those folks who do well in the bureaucracy by distancing themselves from any form of responsibility which involves a degree of risk. It also covers political programs and initiatives which are total busts but because nobody would dare admit it the solution becomes to throw good money after bad, twist any factual data into something which creates the illusion of being positive (like almost anything coming from the White House) and reward the initiators. It also covers kicking people upstairs to get them away from hands-on involvement.

Every organization has people who bounce from task to task because they succeed at none. These are the first to be volunteered to be put in charge of those new initiatives which any responsible career person knows are doomed to failure, or they go to nebulous conferences, training programs or industry exchange programs because they are expendable and a warm body is needed from whom nothing is asked other than to not embarrass the agency.

My pet peeve when it comes to initiatives doomed to failure is the dreaded reorganization. I hate reorganizations and I resisted them. In my mind most reorganizations are just a rationale for a new administration to think they have done something productive towards their legacy. It provides a time for the administrative types to shine or impress, and gain some Brownie points. Those whose mission it is to produce a product will continue to do so regardless of how the organization plays out. I have no objection to a minor organization tweak to accommodate a mission change or to improve the fit of an individual to a job, but wholesale reorganizations are disruptive and over time will eventually reorganize back to their original state. Reorganizations, however, are great for the furniture industry.

Those responsible for initiating a reorganization will generally walk away from living with it, actually believing that it was a success.

Five: *You only have the right to f* me once.*

This is self explanatory. Shame on me if you finesse me once. Pity you if you try it a second time. Business is business but if you work for me or do business with me I'll expect you to be forthright and honest. I'm not one to hold a grudge but there are some people who managed to get on my banned list, meaning I would not meet with them or talk to them because they screwed me. The list included a customer representative, a "confidential assistant," a reporter and a union delegate. My administrative assistant was under instructions to call Security and have any of them detained for trespassing if they passed the reception area.

The female reporter was looking for a negative story. What reached print was a misquote of me and a complete distortion of the facts. She knew nothing about construction and probably couldn't tell the difference between a change order and a pizza order. When I was directed by my political boss to submit to another interview, which I insisted would be held in my conference room, I had a negative attitude to start and gave little more than yes or no answers. In our office she was referred to as *The Princess of Darkness*. After she became too pushy and obnoxious while trying to put words in my mouth I slowly got up and announced that this meeting is over. I was not going to be embarrassed by *Newsday* again. Upon exiting the conference room and encountering my administrative assistant, Christina, who looked at me with facial movements that said, "How did it go?" I muttered just loud enough for all to hear, "The only thing worse than being interviewed by that bitch would be to be married to her."

The next article was less than flattering.

Four: *If something is due in 3 days and it doesn't come in 3 days, it won't come in 4, 5, 6 or 100 days.*

This is a general lesson applicable to all business environments. One of my secrets of success was my dogged perseverance, a recurring theme, and my insistence that others be attentive to schedules and deadlines. In the construction field, the expression that *time is money* was never more prevalent. The carrying costs of even the smallest delays in a construction project can be the difference between profit and bankruptcy.

More often that not, especially in a bureaucracy, if something is overdue the likelihood is that it will never come. The intended respondent may hope the situation goes away, may not consider it a priority, or is just plain oblivious to deadlines. There is nothing mystical about this. Follow-up is key to every business situation, and even non-business situations.

I had a real life opportunity to apply this principle. If you are squeamish, proceed directly to the next rule.

A few years back I went through a right of passage in the form of my first kidney stone. I have been told, and I have no reason to doubt it, that the pain of a kidney stone is worse than childbirth. Childbirth is painful, but at least it is finite. Stones are a different story.

The condition was diagnosed at my first emergency room visit, and I was assured by the ER doc, and my own specialist the next morning, that "it will pass in 24-48 hours." Well, five days and three ER visits later, while in excruciating pain, I cited the aforementioned principle, almost verbatim, to my doc. He agreed that if it didn't happen yet it wasn't going to happen without follow-up. I'll spare the details of how these things are removed but when it was all over the doc told me I was indeed correct. The stone was lodged in scar tissue and would never have passed without intervention.

The next time you have to badger someone for an overdue response think of my kidney stone.

Three: A good bureaucrat can say nothing and mean every word of it.

This tidbit was scribbled in a thirty year old notebook with the annotation; "Professor Meyer." I don't recall the professor but I like to give credit where it is due. He might have originated this rule but many have practiced it to the ultimate. It is definitely worthy of discussion because I encountered every magnitude of windbag at every level of government.

When sentences are punctuated with words and expressions like *viability, functionality, fungible, administratively acceptable* or *strategically interactive* you can bet what you're hearing isn't worth the paper it's not printed on. I personally *take umbrage* at such *obfuscation* of reality. Anything in such vague context should be *expunged* from the record.

Two: There is no correlation between the size of a project and its potential for disaster.

Professor Parkinson would have fully understood how the United States Congress appropriated one billion dollars for our signature Foley Square project, consisting of a high rise courthouse and a federal office building in lower Manhattan, with no debate. It was done strictly on the strength of Senator Daniel Patrick Moynihan inserting a few sentences into an unrelated piece of legislation after some slick give and take. Yet, after the project was completed, Senators Howard Metzenbaum and John McCain were looking for headlines and a reason for court bashing, so each held hearings and ordered a full inspector general report and separate Senate task force investigation from which a major conclusion was that the government should have purchased cheaper carpeting for the courtrooms and the judges' chambers. This conclusion was based on a year long study. It cost more to bring people to the hearings than the amount of the investigated expenses. Those investigations came at the heels of another self-serving "investigative" report, this time by the office of Senator Max Baucus, which was so misleading and inaccurate that if it did not come from a government entity, would have bordered on fraud.

I wasted a day at a Senate hearing down the street from the Capitol, answering questions about carpeting while the C-Span cameras rolled.

After much political posturing the issue went away when a retired GSA employee wrote a letter to Senator Baucus with appropriate distribution of copies. The letter contained the detailed response that the GSA administrator refused to allow. If the letter went public, it would have knocked the entire credibility from the IG and Senate reports. It was actually beneficial to the project team and the agency that so much debate centered on such a small issue, because it diverted attention from other avoidable cost excesses which went unnoticed.

As a postscript to the story, and a lesson in life cycle costing, the original carpeting is still in place. Had the cheaper carpet been purchased, it would likely have been replaced at least twice, or worse, would still be in the courtroom in dilapidated condition.

One: There is no adversity so great that someone can't make a buck out of it.

I learned this from a crusty and wise old college professor. This needs little explanation because we see examples of it every day.

War profiteering is legendary. When a hurricane or flood hits, contractors come out of the woodwork. FEMA swarms over the area with contracts, financial guarantees and overtime for their employees.

Within hours after the first plane hit on 9/11 we were getting calls from vendors offering services ranging from cleanup to catering. I will not make light of the tragedy of 9/11 but I can say from experience that the sudden need to replace a few million feet of prime New York City office space created an incredible bonanza for property owners, especially those with property which previously would have been considered less than desirable.

One thing is certain: After any disaster politicos rush to the scene for the photo op and to be certain that they don't get accused of neglect. Most important, they're there to assure that the party in power takes full credit for the recovery efforts.

*   *   *

In the trade they are known as *poverty pimps*. These are people employed by a government entity or in a business allegedly operated by the oppressed who are purportedly helping the disadvantaged but whose main objective is to perpetuate their own livelihood.

A prime example would be one Mr. Cleveland "King" Cole, president and chief executive officer of the Corporation for Economic Development of a heavily minority suburban New York community. Cleveland knew every angle better than any government administrator. He was advised by a pinstriped attorney and slick accountant who always seemed to be in Florida when Cleveland was ordered to produce documents.

The King made a living out of failing. For him, the adage that *nothing succeeds like failure* was most appropriate. He formed corporations which then qualified him for special contracting consideration for minorities and small businesses. He obtained a grant to purchase a building which he was to make available to minority businesses at reduced rentals. Unfortunately he filled it up with bogus corporations controlled by his umbrella corporation which had no assets. When he tried to use his rent roll as collateral for another government contract GSA auditors found that he hadn't collected a cent in rent from any of his corporations, each of which was in a business which depended upon the suffering of others and each of which eventually failed, leaving a stack of unpaid bills. Salaries to its officers were always paid on time.

What amazed us most about Cleveland was that he was able to keep a straight face when negotiating. When he was trying to lease space to the government in the very building which he controlled through a government grant he boasted that his building was nearly full even though we already knew his rent roll was, as he would have said, *all flash and no cash.*

The plot went deeper. The architect he was paying generously with taxpayer dollars to file his building plans and to prepare a proposal turned out to be an unlicensed Great Imposter hopeful who was one step ahead of the sheriff, the Department of Justice and every consumer protection agency in New York State.

Cleveland, who was actually a very personable and charismatic individual (part of the reason he was able to sell people their own clothes), was a perfect example of how a buck can always be made from other peoples' suffering. To our knowledge, nobody other than Cleveland and his immediate band of henchman ever benefited from all his poverty pimping.

CHAPTER 5

We're Not Happy Until You're Not Happy

The average person has never heard of General Services Administration. When I told people I worked for GSA they would say, "Oh, Girl Scouts of America." If I would correct them and say GSA is a government agency they would say something like, "Oh, you work for the city? My brother-in-law works for Sanitation."

It was not hard to understand this unfamiliarity. Unless you worked or did business with the government, you would have no reason to be aware of the agency's existence.

The GSA I left in 2004 bore no resemblance to the GSA I joined in 1965. We went from a regulatory function dreaded by clients and people with whom we did business, to a high performing service agency recognized as one of the best places to work in government, in the opinion of Partnership for Public Service, a respected non-partisan, non-profit group that rates federal entities.

GSA was created by Congress in 1949 as a result of a recommendation by the Hoover Commission to consolidate service functions of the federal government. There was a need to properly manage the acquisition of real and personal property. Government agencies were actually competing with each other and were not getting favorable pricing. There was also a need to dispose of a vast inventory of surplus real property after World War II.

From its start until the mid-eighties, GSA had an annoying oversight function. Other government agencies had no option but to come to GSA for services. In so doing they had to comply with a myriad of administrative requirements which often seemed more significant than the end result. I grew in the real estate area of GSA. A customer, then called *the agency* but thought of as *the enemy*, had to submit proper paperwork for any request to GSA. If the paperwork was incomplete or incorrect it was returned with no action. The agency had to comply with standards on space usage, office furnishings, lighting intensity, temperature, etc. If it was freezing in the office but the thermostat read 70 degrees GSA took no action. It reminded me of my army basic training. It was March 22nd. The calendar said it was spring. We turned in our winter gear. It was twenty five degrees outside with a Yukon type wind but our drill sergeant reminded us that, according to the army, it was springtime "and you have been issued *etiquette* clothing."

Among our performance measures had been the speed in which we completed requests from customer agencies. This statistic was easily gamed by canceling lingering actions for a technicality and reestablishing it as a new request when it was close to completion. Even in those prehistoric times the government had deceptive reporting practices.

It was a frustrating relationship for everyone. Little wonder that the agency struggled for survival. Were it not for the fact that it was a convenient dumping ground for party friends who needed work and a great agency to execute pork projects, we probably would have been long gone.

Things began to slowly change in the mid-eighties when the Reagan administration appointed Terrence J. Golden as GSA Administrator. Terry had been a successful real estate executive who was involved in major development projects with The Trammel Crow Company.

He questioned some basic premises of our business, such as why it was so complicated and procedure driven to deal with GSA; why federal buildings were so non-descript and why federal office space had to be as Spartan as something you would see in a forties movie. He planted the seed with GSA, the Congress, and our customer agencies. He looked at GSA policy, which is easier to control than legislation, in order to reduce procedural burdens. The culture change began.

What Terry initiated made a lot of sense but it took another 10 to 15 years for GSA to stop the inertia of the past and change the way of thinking. Contracting specialists were so ingrained with regulations and had the fear of the inspector general looking for a *gotcha* that it was tough to adjust. Realty people were used to by-the-book standards and human resources people still thought it was their job to regulate the people who performed the mission of the agency.

In 1996 David J. Barram, a seasoned computer industry executive, became administrator. Shortly thereafter, Robert A. Peck was appointed commissioner of Public Buildings Service. The agency began to change rapidly. David concentrated on information technology and turned most PBS issues over to Peck, a former major in the Army Special Forces, who had a law degree and a great interest in architecture, as well as a lot of political savvy gained as chief of staff to Senator Daniel Patrick Moynihan. It was Bob Peck who actually drafted Moynihan's *Guiding Principles for Federal Architecture.*

Barram was determined that GSA would set the government standard for information technology, and that it would be available to every employee whose job would benefit by it. He wanted people to learn so he broke with bureaucratic thinking by declaring that GSA employees could use their government computers for personal use on their own time. (In the past, people could get fired for playing a computer game or making an online purchase using government equipment.) There were limits. Employees could still get fired for downloading porn or placing bets on the computer.

Concurrently, Peck established the Office of the Chief Architect to further advance a concept called "Design Excellence," which originated in the Terry Golden years. He appointed a career person, Edward A. Feiner, as the agency's first chief architect. Things began to change rapidly.

The government now hires architects under what is known as the "Brooks Bill," which allows GSA to select professionals based on qualifications and a technical proposal rather than low bid. It made a huge difference. Instead of getting the cookie cutter buildings common to the sixties and seventies, world class architects began to bid GSA jobs, something they would never have done in the past. Due to the initiatives of Peck and Feiner, names like I.M. Pei, Richard Meier, Marcel Breuer and Cesar Pelli are now seen on cornerstones of federal buildings and courthouses.

Peck also determined that PBS business practices lacked accountability. As an example, the common remedy for exceeding a budget was simply to increase the budget. This practice ended and all components of PBS, from major construction to operation of buildings to travel and purchase of paper had to operate with a finite amount of funds generated by the Federal Buildings Fund (FBF was the revenue received by GSA as "rent" from occupants of GSA operated space). He instituted a performance measurement system which demanded accountability to both the GSA and our customer agencies (heretofore referred to solely as "customers"). When Bob left at the end of the Clinton years I told him that if he did nothing else he could consider his years a success because when GSA is mentioned in the press it is no longer followed by the tag line, "the government's housekeeping agency." The Barram-Peck team also took the dramatic initiative of liberalizing delegation policies, making GSA a provider of choice rather than a mandatory supplier.

---

[1] In 2009, Robert A. Peck was reappointed commissioner of Public Buildings by the Obama administration.

The work of the Democratic appointed Barram-Peck[1] team was actually perpetuated when they were replaced by the George W. Bush Republican team of Stephen A. Perry as administrator and F. Joseph Moravec as commissioner of Public Buildings Service. It was almost seamless. Perry, a former human resources executive, instituted a GSA-wide performance measurement system and Moravec, a successful real estate executive, continued and expanded Peck's initiatives. During many of his talks within and outside of the agency, Joe would say "There is no value with greater import than customer service." Joe was also the one who, after researching some of GSA's colorful history, said; "Our motto is no longer 'We're not happy until you're not happy.'"

Joe tightened budget accountability, especially in the construction arena, because cost overruns were killing the agency and awakening the interests of too many members of Congress. He demanded a review of all federally owned property in the agency and initiated disposal of functionally obsolete and other non-productive property as well as directing funding for repairs to those properties which would most benefit by the investment. As a final legacy he violated the standard "It can't be done" and "We've always done it that way" attitudes by instituting a program to utilize real estate brokers on a nationwide basis to do most of GSA's legwork and negotiating, thereby leveraging its resources and allowing more time and effort to customer relationship building.

In my government years I saw GSA go from an elephantine bureaucracy to a highly businesslike organization and a leader in the real estate industry.

*   *   *

I served under eight presidents, eleven GSA administrators and nine regional administrators. It was generally the regional administrator ("RA") who had the most influence on me and most shaped my career. They were of diverse personalities and varying abilities, but the one common thread they all had was a godfather somewhere. Either it was their personal political connections or that of their family. Few actually worked their way up through the system and reached the pinnacle via merit, certainly not in the New York region.

They all had their own personality quirks, favorite programs and sore spots. The first RA under whom I served and had very little contact with because of my lowly position was a gentleman named Arthur Miller (not the playwright). He was the force behind the federal government's being an original major tenant in the World Trade Center and the government acquiring a strategic downtown site on which the flagship 26 Federal Plaza was ultimately built. Arthur had a thing for the number 26, hence the street address. His office was situated on the 26th floor and his telephone number ended in the digits 2600. I never did know the origin of this quirk. He was definitely not a marathon runner.

There was an RA who could talk the couplings off of a freight train without saying or committing to a thing.

Then we had Stormin' Norman. Our original relationship was like oil and water but we later learned to get along. Right after he removed me as a division director, something it took him seven years to do, he put me in as project executive of the Foley Square project, which became my claim to fame in GSA. Things have a way of working out.

Lady Jeanne favored female and minority causes. It was common knowledge that if you were a white male in her administration you were going nowhere. This attitude cost the agency dearly in litigation before she left. Any woman with a trace of promise need only to threaten to quit and Lady J would see to it that she was promoted or a satisfactory job created for her. I had no complaints, though. She was good to me.

When Louisiana Clem came along we found out once and for all that we really didn't need a regional administrator.

He was followed by three appointees after the election of George Dubya. Mr. Arnold was quite effective and displayed minimal arrogance. Unfortunately he stayed but a few months before he received the call for the job he really wanted, with the Port Authority of New York and New Jersey.

After Arnold's departure Young Bruce came along out of nowhere. For most of his stay we got along very well. He just advanced a little too fast for his own good and that of the agency. Not to be cynical, but I've seen hotshot after hotshot go down in flames because they think they're exempt from the rules.

Young Tiffany followed him. Fortunately I was only weeks from retirement because from what I've heard of her tenure, there would not have been room for both of us. When she left I was told that she still hadn't learned the meaning of respect.

In a bit of irony, when our agency went through the 9/11 trauma and we were major players in the federal rebuilding process, we were between regional administrators, which was fortunate. Clem would have panicked and been ineffective to the point of probably causing a seizure of power by the careerists. A career person was running the show and we did just fine.

CHAPTER 6

My Legacy

My personal milestone career achievement was the completion of what was referred to as the "Foley Square Project."[2] This was a mammoth construction project, substantially completed in 1994 with much fanfare. At the time it was the most expensive project ever undertaken by GSA, with the total cost - including land, design, construction and financing - of close to a billion dollars.

It is not my intention to write a tell-all tale. If that was the case I could have written a volume as thick as the pre-internet Manhattan telephone directory, white and yellow pages, based upon my inside knowledge of the project. Then I would have a big problem controlling the traffic racing to my front door to grab a piece of me.

First there would be a United States marshal with a warrant for my arrest because a federal judge or two will want to hold me in contempt of court. Next would be the *Newsday* reporter who wrote volumes of trash about the project but missed all of the juicy stuff. There would be the producers of two network television programs wanting interviews because when they did their original stories they were so intent on creating a scandal about non-existent overspending and mob involvement that they missed the real issues.

Had we been permitted by GSA politicos to formally reply we would have completely discredited both televised episodes and the newspaper articles. As it happened, the careerists, through their underground network, took care of that and the issues never appeared on television again. To this day, the political public relations gurus probably think that they had something to do with it.

The line at my door wouldn't end there. A couple of congressional committees would resurface because a tell-all would reveal that their original investigative reports contained so much nonsense that they would need to save face. Finally, the Government Accountability Office ("GAO") and the GSA Inspector General would be there to see if I withheld information during their original investigations (a/k/a witch-hunts). The fact is that I withheld nothing, but I volunteered

---

[2] Foley Square, in the civic center of lower Manhattan, was named for "Big Tom" Foley (1852-1925), a saloon owner and local political leader.

nothing also, consistent with my business principle that you always have to tell the truth, but not necessarily *all* of the truth.

Sooner or later I would get a call from the regional public affairs officer. Knowing that I still consider her a friend, her superiors would likely dispatch her on a mission to see what I really know so that when the news releases with the usual spin were issued (called damage control) they could assure themselves that I would not be there to provide a rebuttal with the real facts.

What the muckrakers found and sought to write about amounted to little more than nonsense. What they missed was far juicier. Among little oversights which we managed to keep away from the press, the Congress and some of our *gotcha* minded superiors was the matter of a barge containing 24,000 tons of contaminated soil destined for a Texas landfill but which ended up on the bottom of the East River just yards from the Brooklyn shoreline; the accidental cutting off of the water supply to the federal prison in lower Manhattan during excavation, and; the costly redesign of elaborate lobby lighting three times to satisfy someone's ego, only to end up with the original design. To top everything off, at the eleventh hour the Office of the United States Attorney decided not to move to their brand new quarters, costing the government millions to redesign and rebuild the space for another tenant.

We dodged another bullet when our esteemed consultant, in conjunction with some architects turned judges, managed to design courtroom lighting which was quite elegant. Unfortunately it left many of the courtrooms with beautifully illuminated wall paneling, but with judges' benches that could not be seen without squinting. That oversight was corrected with a million dollars of project funds and was kept under the radar.

Then of course, there were the issues with Department of City Planning and the Municipal Art Society of New York. We submitted a plan for approval of replica vintage Bishop's Crook lampposts for the courthouse plaza. The building was completed in 1994. We are still awaiting approval a generation later. The last we heard, the examiner said, "I'm not sure if I like the color." The only positive feedback was that as part of the price of the approval, which was never received anyway, we had agreed to preserve the one remaining original Bishop's Crook lamppost on the site. Within days the artifact found its way to the scrapheap. Stuff happens.

That episode nearly overshadowed some other ridiculous dialog with another city agency. The specialist from the Parks Department demanded that we halt construction pending a proper removal and reinstallation of a small underdeveloped oak tree on the original site.

It was a pathetic specimen but the city demanded that it be preserved and we build around it. Our project manager, Charles, advised the developer to take care of the matter with the soothing words, "I don't want to see or hear anything about that tree again."

By sundown the tree was pulled from the ground and excavation continued. When the examiner returned, there was no evidence and all denied that a tree ever existed in that location. He must be thinking about a different tree on the site. This was confirmed when Charles pointed to a healthier oak, away from the excavation, swearing up and down that it was the subject tree and we're excavating around it. The only problem was midway through this conversation Charles observed that the base of the original tree was sticking out of a dumpster. He had to keep repositioning the examiner so he could not see it.

*   *   *

It was strange how I became in charge of the Foley Square project. I had just been removed as director of the Real Estate Division in the region. That job was considered one of the toughest in all of GSA and I was rather proud that I lasted for eight and a half years in that capacity. In the eleven GSA regions, thirty three real estate directors had come and gone during my tenure so it is understandable that I did not consider it a dishonor to be relieved of my duties.

There was only one problem. When our regional administrator, the impulsive Stormin' Norman Pearson removed me, he was certain he had a replacement in the form of a promising young manager in our Atlanta office. He promised him the world to come to New York including a variety of undeliverable perks.

The candidate backed out and Norman had to send his emissary to request that I stay on after he announced that I was being replaced. It was like a divorce lawyer telling you not to move out of the house until your spouse remarries. This was an embarrassment to the political side of the agency. The career side understands this and laughs it off as still another political blunder.

While this was happening I was a lame duck. I couldn't institute any initiatives because it would be left for someone else, who might have other ideas, to carry out. I couldn't rely on the regional administrator for personal or program support because he had already, in effect, fired me. If he agreed with me on anything it would be a sign of weakness on his end.

This little fiasco went on for six months until a replacement was found who had some semblance of qualifications and was willing to take the job. The new person came from an administrative background with no experience in real estate or the pressures of a position at that level.

During my lame duck period it was generally agreed by my superiors and the worried human resources staff that I would move to a nebulous staff position which served no purpose other than to warehouse a body until something else came along or the political boss left. Over the years I found that this was common in government so I didn't take it personally. On the positive side, at GSA you can be down but you're never out. I've known many people, not to mention myself, who went from purgatory to greater heights than ever.

While I was still on death row awaiting execution, my pardon came in the form of a new project funded by Congress in record time and which was to be assigned to the region for completion. The region was notified by central office that within twenty four hours, it must name a project manager for the mega "Foley Square Project." Translated, this meant find someone with an impressive resume who was available without a major reshuffling of management and who would be reasonably certain not to embarrass the agency.

Now Stormin' Norman sent the same emissary who delivered my execution message to plead with me to take this new responsibility. It was a proposed reconciliation. It was never my nature to take the easy route, so although I knew my decision, I mulled it overnight to not appear overanxious and to let the establishment have time to regret my original planned lethal injection. By eight the next morning I was back in the game with the grand announcement that I would become "Project Executive" for this billion dollar undertaking. I went from a bum to a savior overnight.

I bring this up now, because throughout this book I use "*Foley Square*" for an array of examples of my rules for survival in the bureaucracy and a multitude of anecdotes under the general theme of "What you see is not always what you get."

Unlike many government construction projects, this was designed so that it could not fail. I would love to give myself credit for the fact that it was ultimately completed on time and within budget but in this case we had the most generous funding imaginable and money was able to hide the many sins which in traditionally funded projects result in costly overruns. The project had strong political backing and the good fortune of timeliness. It was right in the midst of a depressed construction market, thus assuring very competitive bidding. Finally, as project executive I had the agency's backing to hand pick my staff, a rare luxury. Collectively, we would have had to make a real effort for this project to fail. Many tried along the way, presenting their own agendas or power plays, but as a group my staff remained focused on the job to be done rather than the distractions, most of which came from within GSA.

I had a group of excellent engineers, architects and administrators, all with one goal. When the project was over I was often asked to describe my role which I unabashedly said was that of a human bullshit screen. My task was to provide the hands-on people all they needed to do the job and to protect them from the distractions, conflicting agendas, ridiculous and self serving reports, and later on, the media vultures and headline seeking congressional people looking to take credit for saving the government from sure financial disaster.

We were blessed with a project which bypassed the normal arduous planning process because it was authorized by special legislation. Executive orders and legislation are the perfect avenues for avoiding the lengthy planning and funding process. The reality is that most major construction projects are authorized because of heavy political support of a champion in Congress who can push for funding, usually through a mutual exchange of support for pet bills of their peers. In this case it was Senator Daniel Patrick Moynihan who was the driving force. Years earlier it was Senator Moynihan who was responsible for the small treatise called *Guiding Principles for Federal Architecture*. The good senator, who was one of the most powerful people on Capitol Hill, was a proponent of good design and wanted to see the federal government as leaders rather than followers in the design of public spaces. One only has to compare federal construction of the fifties and sixties with that of the nineties and beyond. He was a friend of GSA and through his continued support he made it possible for the feds to go from the low-bid mentality to the best qualified, even if it meant not the lowest price.

Senator Moynihan was the broker in the complicated transaction which made Foley Square possible. It involved the City of New York relinquishing two parcels of land to the federal government for fair market value. The city would be a 50 percent tenant in one of the new buildings at a rental equal to the amortized cost of their proportionate share of the building, less a credit for the appraised value of the land. On the surface nobody lost on this deal. The feds in turn were to privately finance the project so that no cash appropriation from Congress would be needed. He sold this deal to his compatriots in both houses of Congress and as a result, a single paragraph was inserted into an unrelated budget bill (Public Law 100-202) which authorized it all to happen. This whole charade went through the approval process in about 90 days, about four years less than it takes the average small town project to be funded. Professor Parkinson would have been proud.

The original pressing need was for courthouse expansion. One afternoon Senator Moynihan, the GSA regional administrator, the chief judge and a deputy mayor looked out of a window in the old courthouse and decided that the parcel across the street was just what was needed.

GSA originally only needed that one parcel, a city-owned parking lot opposite the old Federal Courthouse, to build a courthouse annex. The city had no immediate plans for that site, but wanted to see development of a major site on Broadway, between Duane and Reade Streets and right opposite the Jacob K. Javits Federal Building at 26 Federal Plaza. At the time, it was a parking lot and filling station for city-owned vehicles and far from the highest and best use of this prime property. The late eighties and early nineties were tough times in the real estate industry so any further city attempts at development would likely be fruitless. The value of any rentals would not even cover debt service for the construction costs.

Enter the federal government, the only organization able to construct an expensive building that did not command commensurate market-rate rentals. The government has a socioeconomic mission also so it doesn't think of short term. It creates a market by stimulating job growth and ancillary development around its projects. In this case it worked out well. The 31 story building known as 290 Broadway was a throw-in to the deal.

Negotiating the land purchase from the City of New York became such a difficult task that the senator had to step in again. Although the parties agreed to the price after much wrangling, the process whereby the city could actually accept the money and transfer the land was so convoluted that at the behest of all parties, he introduced legislation authorizing "friendly" condemnation and permitting private financing of the land purchase. Public Law 101-156, approved in November, 1989 got everyone off the hook.

If negotiating the land purchase was problematic, then negotiating a lease with the city for occupancy in the office building became a near impossible task, even given the parameters of the earlier agreement. The lead negotiator for the city was a female drill sergeant who we called Frosty because of her warm personality. She brought a huge cast to every meeting and each time we thought we had a problem solved someone else brought another equation to the mix. People would constantly walk in and out of meetings and we found ourselves negotiating with a dysfunctional band of wind up toys. After six months of meetings we thought everything was ready to be signed and sealed, only to be told by Frosty, "OK. Now it goes to the Comptroller's Office for review."

The fact that we had a schedule and construction interest was piling up was of no consequence. We had paid the City of New York $104 million for the land up front and now we were paying interest on the Treasury instruments used to finance that amount. In the real business world, title and money would not have changed hands until the day before the demolition crew arrived. This was another little tidbit that the media never quite picked up. Negotiating the lease all over with the Comptroller's Office proved to be a real trip. A new assortment of extraneous issues kept popping up. Improving the subway entrance, participation in the federal day care program, free lunches in the cafeteria, etc., were all put on the table. The management lesson here is to make sure the people you negotiate with have the authority to make the deal.

The whole negotiating scenario came to a head when our general counsel came from Washington to participate in one of the meetings. The city team of attorneys was there along with the financial gurus and the political eyes and ears. The usual began to unfold. City people kept entering and leaving to take calls, make calls, go to other meetings or just plain take a stretch. At one point there were no city people left in the room, leaving the feds to negotiate with each other. General counsel could take no more. He ordered us all to leave and directed our regional counsel to call the lead attorney from the Department of General Services with the ultimatum to take or leave the lease as it was written to that point. There will be no more negotiating.

This courageous act, uncharacteristic for a lawyer, broke the logjam. It gave the city the perfect excuse to back out of the deal, which was the best thing to ever happen to us. The feds used the space previously committed to the city, saving us the pain of more negotiating and what would have been constant disputes starting the first day of occupancy. The official announcement was that the city found it economically infeasible to undertake a financial obligation at the rental rates stipulated, given the condition of their finances and the depressed real estate market of the time. Goodbye Frosty.

From the start of the planning process to the end of construction took about seven years and close to $700 million in construction costs. Add land cost of $104 million, about $125 million in construction period interest and an immense amount of post-construction additions which conveniently came out of the original spending authority and we had a near-billion dollar project.

Construction was the easiest part. Dealing with the egos and protective turf issues in GSA was the most complicated. Combine this with some pompous judges, media and a few congressional representatives trying to score votes and we had a never ending circus. The discovery of the colonial era African Burial Ground during excavation of the site of the office building added a dimension which nobody ever expected and gave the project unneeded publicity. When all was said and done, and some fifteen years after the original discovery, in my estimate the African Burial Ground cost the government about $100 million in mitigation and memorialization expenses. You could never put a dollar value on the sensitivity issues.

*   *   *

I wouldn't want to minimize the impact of the African Burial Ground, or ABG, on the history and culture of America. However, it consumed GSA for years, taught us all a lesson in sensitivity and ultimately resulted in a major research project and first class memorial in New York. It brought out the best and worst in everybody, including activists, radicals, money grabbers and headline seekers.

During the course of the project I had the pleasure of meeting such celebrities as John Amos, Cicily Tyson, Phylicia Rashad and the late Noel Pointer, who lent their support to the community interests. I also dealt with radicals and power brokers like the late Sonny Carson, famous for leading a boycott against a Korean grocer in Brooklyn. Sonny and I actually got along rather well despite our radically different positions. It turned out that we grew up in the same neighborhood and as a high schooler I used to shoot pool a few floors above the boycotted grocer.

Then there were the scholars and educators, such as Dr. Michael Blakey, Dr. Christopher Moore and the late Dr. John Henrick Clarke, all of whom participated in the extensive research project which followed the unearthing of the remains. Along the way I also crossed paths with such powerful spiritual leaders as Reverends Herbert Daughtry, and Calvin Butts. I was told that Reverend Jesse Jackson made a quick visit to the site but I missed that event. Al Sharpton was conspicuous by his absence.

Among the more interesting individuals was a fellow we simply called *The Chief.* He was a man of the cloth so I would not disrespect the spiritual beliefs of his followers but he was unique. According to his business card, his real name was Reverend Finch, with the *Finch* preceded by a string of African sounding titles and names. He provided spiritual guidance as well as catering services and was based in Atlanta.

My first encounter with him was never to be forgotten. It was a day in which we were briefing a new Public Buildings Service commissioner who was serving out the final months of the Bush 41 administration. He was accompanied by his chief of staff, an African-American woman who was a careerist and very knowledgeable of PBS operations whom I had known and respected for years. We advanced through the ranks together.

The site was in the excavation stage. The foundation was being installed at the same time that archaeologists were still digging. Two opposite ends of the spectrum were cohabitating the same site, an amazing feat. To assure that the site tour went well I had our project engineer, Hiram "Hy" Lowe go down to the site and make sure the stairways we would descend remained accessible.

This was normal preparation for a VIP visit.

When the conference room briefing ended I told my secretary to call Hiram on his cell phone and tell him we were on the way down.

The entourage left the building through the Plaza exit and headed across Duane Street to the excavation site. Before we got there Hy came running towards me, obviously agitated. He wanted to convey vital information to me right away without others hearing.

"What should I do? There's some guy on the site who looks like Mr. T dancing all over place. He's got a whole bunch of people with him." Due to the sensitivity of the burial removals issue, we were very liberal in allowing site visits for people to learn, pray or pay respects.

I told Hy that we should hide nothing. Let the delegation see what really goes on.

Mr. T turned out to be the Chief, from Atlanta, who had a cult following and was there to bless the unearthed burials and assure that the remains which had already been removed were treated in a respectful manner at our Lehman College repository.

The Chief was dressed in what looked like a hospital robe. It was adorned with pins and buttons. He wore Nike sneakers and a baseball cap. I wasn't sure if the guy was really a preacher type, whether he was sent over by some theatrical agency or he was a crackpot. It turned out that he was not a bad guy after all.

The only issue we had with him was that he claimed he was brought in to remove a curse from the bones because of the way the government treated them. He advised that the curse also extended to the GSA staff. He said he detected "bad karma" and it was his role to "libate the site." All of this while a senior person whom he addressed as "King of the Village" stood by his side but never said a word. When we went to view the remains in the repository the Chief took out what looked like three beer coasters from his pocket, said they were holy, and forbade us to enter the room until he flipped them and all three came up the same side. If we disrespected the coasters the curse on us would remain. All-right, I could go along with that.

After the review he claimed now to be powerless to remove the curse and had to call his brother in Atlanta, who had greater powers, to come up. He expected the government to pay for this as we had frequently done for other community "advisors." He wanted a thousand bucks to travel north for a day. This was too much and I refused. I told him to check out his brother staying over a Saturday night so he would get a better fare. I was accused of being insensitive. As far as I know the curse was never removed.

As quickly as he came on the scene, the Chief disappeared, but not before conducting a series of Santeria ceremonies for his followers, leaving behind sacrificed pig heads, feathers, half spent cigars, pineapples, empty Dewar's bottles and assorted other vegetation and livestock for our cleanup crews to dispose after they attracted some New York sized rodents to the site.

All in all, it was a tough but enlightening experience with a few lessons in understanding and tolerance along the way.

It was also another example that there is nothing on earth that some people can't use to line their pockets with cash. Consultants, contractors, amateur photographers and hobbyists who saw an opportunity, local merchants and a host of others all made out on the deal. The real costs of this project far exceed that in any GSA news release. Take it from me. I signed a lot of the checks.

*   *   *

The project was not without its light moments. Both the discovery of the ABG and signs of the times in general dictated the need for increased awareness in what you say, do or write. This was problematic for my crew members, who were accustomed to operating like they were playing stickball in the Bronx.

Since a few people in the office took offense at our street language and our female references, I had to take action. There was also the more practical issue of the content of what we said or wrote, all of which was quotable and available under the Freedom of Information Act.

I gathered my troops around and conducted sensitivity training. Given my personal style the chance of success would be the same odds as extracting a diamond from a goat's ass. Nevertheless I had to try. I issued an edict that there will be no cursing or sexually suggestive remarks in the office or at any meetings. It was ditto for any ethnic comments, use of ethnic slang, or references to anyone's sexual preferences. I even went so far as to recite a list of words which will not be used, as George Carlin did on stage. This was not a punishment. It was intelligent business. One innuendo could generate an EEO complaint which would take hours of management time before resolution. Some of my staff had to relearn the English language.

To enforce this I placed a coffee tin on top of a file cabinet and ruled that there would be a fifty-cent fine for each offense after a one-offense grace period. It would be self-policing. The directive only applied within our own office. Elsewhere we could have a ball.

This innovation lasted about two weeks. There was $15.50 in the tin box, $15 of which came from me.

My staff pretty much set me up for this by inviting me to a meeting already scheduled with Maurice, an Internal Revenue Service official who was on my list of biggest pricks of all time for his egotistical and obstinate mannerisms, inattentive to the overall mission but cognizant of scoring points with his boss, the regional commissioner. I had a sign posted in my conference room, LEAVE YOUR EGO AT THE DOOR, expressly for him and a few like him but as expected, he was oblivious to the message.

At our previous meeting I went ballistic at his logic and my people knew that all it would take was little more than a "Hello, Alan" to ring my bell again. The source of my last outburst had been his casual mention of the need of a change of plans to the IRS office design, which was already in the construction phase. Anyone who has been involved in construction knows that time is money and if you decide to change your plan after your layout is designed and the material fabricated, it is extremely costly and time consuming.

When I pointed out that the IRS regional commissioner had already signed off on the original plans, his response was, "That was the previous commissioner. The new commissioner wants something different." This logic is like saying World War II hasn't ended because Emperor Hirohito is dead so the surrender agreement is invalid.

The fireworks and my $15 in fines began within about thirty seconds of Maurice walking into my office. I usually pride myself for my ability to let my adversary speak first and shoot his load. I join the conversation later. It's a better tactic. With some people I just can't wait. As soon as Maurice started with "My commissioner *wants*…" I thought of my first boss and his speech about the *general*.

I immediately piped up. "I don't give a fuck what *your commissioner* wants! Money talks and bullshit walks, especially yours." After a little dialog and 29 f-words later he stormed out of my office and went to tell *his* commissioner. My fine was up to $14.50 but when I turned to Henry Smith (a/k/a Motor City Smitty) of my staff and said, "He's still a prick" I reached an even $15.00.

I wish I could say the problem ended there, but like so many problems in a bureaucracy it seemed to never end until someone had the last word.

During this interlude our regional administrator was Lady Jeanne, a good person with a mainly political background. Her real estate experience had been primarily in the family business, which enabled her to make a claim on her resume. When the IRS change order came up, Lady Jeanne, in a typical Stormin' Norman type scenario, immediately assumed that her lowly careerists had screwed up. She said to me, "Well, Alan, if you knew there was going to be changes why didn't you stop the work?" Right. Stop a multimillion dollar interior fit out because an asshole who has no authority to commit his agency's funds said they want changes. The order of the day is put it in writing and certify funding, none of which I had. With a construction crew out there, as well as daily overhead and financing costs, you stop at nothing short of the plague.

When Maurice decided to go over my head to the regional administrator she overestimated his standing and ability, preferring to put her own people on the defensive for their incompetence.

It didn't take long to change her mind. The initial meeting was scheduled on behalf of the commissioner although Maurice then stated that the commissioner will not be attending. The commissioner probably never even knew of the meeting. Then there was the ego testing go-around as to whose office would host the meeting. After considerable wrangling, it was agreed that Maurice would meet with Lady Jeanne at the GSA office.

Her whole opinion of this situation changed when Maurice stiffed her by never showing up. She bought coffee and cookies as a welcoming offer.

We could have told her this would happen. In the case of Maurice, I point to my *once a prick, always a prick* rule of behavior. Now her tone went from putting us on the defensive to stating, "My loyalty is to GSA and my president. I can't allow them to piss away government funds like that. If they want to do this let *them* get the money from Congress and explain the reasons."

My relationship with Maurice never improved. The next time our paths crossed was when my project engineer and I were doing a walk-through and he and his commissioner were viewing the commissioner's suite, likely picking paint colors other than what was already specified. When he saw us he shut the door in our faces so we could not even greet the commissioner.

The matter of the changes was eventually resolved after intervention by IRS National Headquarters. The fiasco cost the government well over a million dollars. The whole thrust of the requested change had to do with the new commissioner's desire to alter the space so that a politically connected but marginally effective assistant he inherited would end up in an office as far away from him as possible.

Years later, long after the project was completed, our paths crossed again when I was in the top chair. I expected no respect to my position and received none.

I had been forced to intervene in a delayed project in another IRS location. Things were not going well, partly because of contractor performance and partly because of Maurice's meddling.

We were in DC at a meeting with a full cast, including Maurice's headquarters counterpart. We had a good relationship with the Washington crew but since the head of administration there had no line authority over Maurice he was a thorn to her also. Agency protocol and courtesy prevented her from taking any action.

The meeting started pleasantly enough but went downhill when I suggested that Maurice shouldn't be telling me who to assign to the project. Before long we were both accusing the other of being a liar (a fact which I was able to document to the delight of his Washington people). The inflections continued to rise until it was a shouting match. It reminded me of a hockey fight whereby the two combatants go at it and everyone else stands to the side. I kicked myself later for losing my cool but everyone enjoyed the show. My use of the f-word was limited this time because of the company. Maybe I still had the coffee tin on my mind.

I can't say who won the battle of words but after Maurice left the room, refusing to shake my hand, I received high fives from both sides. I had done what they would have liked to do.

Oh, yes, the project. Despite the obstacles it moved along and was completed. I heard later on that IRS gave Maurice an award for his excellent work.

* * *

Politicians love projects like Foley Square. A lot of local contracts are awarded for which they all try to take credit; the neighborhood is beautified; and, most of all, there are many ceremonies and photo ops.

We provided plenty of ceremonies. The pleasure was doubled in that Foley represented singular legislation and funding, but two separate and unrelated buildings. After the initial ceremony to announce the award of construction contracts for both buildings, attended by Senator Moynihan and a host of congressmen, assemblypersons, the mayor of New York City and every federal agency head this side of the Potomac, all other ceremonies were by building.

As time passed we had ceremonies for the official groundbreakings, the topping of the steel and the dedications. Long after completion there were more ceremonies. Design awards, Energy Star awards and renaming ceremonies. Years after completion the courthouse was named in honor of Senator Moynihan and the office building was named for Congressman Ted Weiss.

With all of the design and other awards received by the buildings I considered the project like a best selling book. Years after completion I kept getting residuals in the form of dinner invitations and plaques to add to my collection.

Ceremonies are the fodder by which politicians exist. It keeps their public relations staffs busy and it keeps our event coordinators in the spotlight. In the region, Theresa "Hedda" Patino was usually charged with putting these events together so the political appointees could backslap each other. Hedda was unflappable considering the egos she had to deal with. Seating arrangements became more important than the project itself. Foley was funded during a Republican administration but completed in a Democratic one, so the subtleties in the seating arrangements, the order of speeches and who stood where for the photos became critical.

Stormin' Norman had become so hyped over the original ceremony announcing the contract awards for Foley that all other business, including the project itself, was put on hold. Between seating arrangements, printing of programs, designation of speakers and even the military arm which would present the colors, Hedda was popping Valiums hourly.

When all was said and done, the event was completed near flawlessly. The right people got their pictures in the paper, the *New York Times* wrote a favorable review and the local politicians were happy about the jobs being created. Norman was so overjoyed that he directed me to give everyone who participated in the ceremony a little perk called a "fast track" award - a cash stipend ranging from $50 to a few thousand which a supervisor can give a staffer for good work with just the stroke of the pen.

Norm was thinking about the print shop staff, the administrative people and the special event folks. When I said to Norman, "What about the people who spent two years to bring the project to the point of award, such as the staff architects, the engineers and the procurement people?" he said rather matter-of-factly, "Oh, yes. You can give them something, too." It was like he told me to toss a $1 tip to the bellhop.

When you deal with so many ceremonies you reach the point of not taking them too seriously, or at least ignoring all the nonsense that goes with them.

One of the more absurd ceremonies was the "topping out" of the federal building ("290") part of the Foley project. In high rise construction it is typically held when the final steel beam is put in place. Its main purpose is to honor the construction workers. Typically, all of the workers sign the beam, after which the job superintendent signals the crane operator to hoist the beam to the top. An American flag is appended to the beam for all to see as it rises to the sky.

In the case of the government, the topping out is another opportunity for photos and sound bytes. Everyone gets in the act, taking credit and congratulating each other.

As I stood there listening to all of the oratory about 290, I almost choked when Assemblywoman Kathryn Freed spoke. She praised the project, praised the contractors, praised the community and even praised the government. I turned to my trusty colleague, Hy Lowe, the project engineer, and said, "Am I getting senile? Am I losing my mind? Isn't this the same Kathryn Freed who stood up at the environmental hearings and said that the government should cancel this project? Isn't it the same Kathryn Freed who stood up during the excavation of the remains from the burial ground and said we were evil and all construction should be halted? Just tell me if I'm nuts so I can retire now on a disability?"

Hy just turned to me and said, "You're not nuts."

At the 290 topping out ceremony we had another little embarrassment going on which we tried to camouflage.

This event was after the senior Bush left office but before GSA had a permanent chief under the Clinton administration. The acting administrator was a crusty old career guy who had no interest in Public Buildings Service events.

To represent the administrator, he sent a woman I had heretofore never met. Her name was Hilda Gould, a Carter administration retread who had been brought back to GSA for unknown reasons by a person who was mistakenly appointed interim administrator and had stayed in the job all of ten days. To this day I had no idea what Hilda did at GSA other than get paid every two weeks.

I first received a call from one of the regional administrator's lackeys directing me to be sure the region sent an emissary to greet Ms. Gould when she arrived at Penn Station. I then received a call from the region's senior personnel officer, a man named "No Action" Jackson but sometimes just called Mumbles (more endearing comments on him later) who said that "The administrator's office wants the project executive to greet her at the train."

That's just great. I'm prepping for a noon high visibility ceremony and I have to play chauffeur. Mumbles was not my boss and I didn't take orders from him. I called Matty D, my direct boss who knew just about everyone in Washington.

"What! Hilda Gould is coming? She's an embarrassment to this agency. Let her find her way down by herself. She'll probably get lost anyway."

Another call from Mumbles who was of equal grade level as myself but acted as if getting Ms. Gould to downtown was the most important project he ever handled. "The administrator's office wants this taken care of."

"Well, you seem to not have too much to do, why don't you put your cap on and drive up there?"

A few *hum ahums* later he said, "No, that would not be viable. It should be a senior project person."

I had more important things to do that morning than to argue with an idiot. Fortunately, one of my staffers, Mel Reed, a prince of a guy and the senior project manager, volunteered. According to Matty D, Hilda wouldn't know the difference between the project executive and the head chef. The only redeeming benefit was that we were assured she would not speak. This was good, but then again, why come if you're not saying a few gracious words on behalf of the administrator?

"Who am I looking for?" Mel had a right to know. He had no idea what she looked like but was assured that she would wait at the "main exit" from the trains. (Unlike Union Station in Washington, when you exit a train in Penn Station in New York, there are choices of exits.)

Matty said to look for a woman who looked like J. Edgar Hoover in drag. Another senior person in the region said, "Look for a sixtyish, overweight, slow moving woman." That narrowed it down a bit.

Mel decided that rather than risk using a government car, given the parking and traffic issues in midtown, he would take the subway to Penn and bring her back via taxi. Good choice.

Well, it would have been a good choice if he actually met her. At 10:30 Mel called. "I never saw so many fat grandmother types on one train. None answered to the name Hilda Gould."

Now everyone was in a tizzy. Mel came back without Hilda. The administrator's emissary was lost in transit on the mean streets of New York. Mumbles was frantic. He screwed up his major project in life and now was busy thinking of how this could be pinned on someone else.

All's well that ends well. As we were exiting 26 Federal Plaza a taxi pulled up on the Broadway side. Mumbles recognized Hilda and was able to escort her to her designated place near the speaker's platform and food table. Greenberg, Reed and Lowe, who were responsible for execution of this project, stood way in the back with the construction crew.

Before the ceremony began the proper introductions were made. Our distinguished central office representative wasn't upset at not being met at Penn Station; however, the taxi unnerved her. Mohammed the driver, when told to go to the Javits Building (26 Federal Plaza), drove her to the Javits Convention Center on the West Side. Then she remembered the little hint we give our out of town visitors. "Take me to the Immigration Building." That got her downtown in a hurry, followed by a fast exit by Mohammed.

Thankfully, Hilda was not called upon to speak. When she was politely introduced, along with the other dignitaries, she had a plate of food in her hand and a full mouth and was oblivious to the courtesy she was accorded.

As a memento, the developer had distributed souvenir baseball caps to the attendees. Hilda's mission then became to accumulate as many caps as possible, ostensibly for the people back in Washington but more likely for her grandchildren. She stuffed them into her tote bag. As a result, some of the construction crew did not get their hats until a new supply was ordered (which of course was charged back to the government).

When it was time for her to go, Stormin' Norman asked me if I could escort her to Penn Station to make sure she gets there without incident and in the company of a sufficiently high staff member. He made it clear that he wouldn't do it. Matty D suggested I give her a subway token and point her to the A train.

On our trip back to midtown she got a real dose of New York culture. Taking the subway to Penn Station would have been logical, but this would have been a total violation of protocol. Instead, I used a New York maneuver to ace out a tourist for a cab on lower Broadway.

This driver was also named Mohammed. I knew we were in for some fun when I gave the destination, and he said, "Penn Station? That in New York?"

I said "Thirty-first and Eighth" and we were on the way. We cut off cars narrowly missing a few sideswipes, toured some run down sections of town, viewed a few hookers looking for business and listened to the steady sound of Mohammed's and all other cabby's horns before eventually pulling up at the Eighth Avenue side of Penn Station.

We were greeted by a regular Penn panhandling hustler anxious to needlessly open the cab door so we might toss a dollar bill. I shooed him away while trying to politely guide my overweight guest out of the cab. A bit upset at the loss of business, the greeter looked back at Hilda and said, "Be careful Mama. I just wanted to get you home safely." Meanwhile, a taxi and a postal truck collided across the street, symbolically, right in front of the historic Main Post Office.

Hilda was oblivious to all of this. She just wanted to be sure she still had the tote filled with caps and was anxious to get on the train. I didn't want to let her out of my sight until she was safely deposited on the Metroliner. Any slipup could have been a career altering move (although I'm not sure in which direction). She would have had to make an effort to get on the wrong train but I took no chances. I negotiated her through a change of ticket and I escorted her all the way to the PASSENGERS ONLY BEYOND THIS POINT sign adjacent to Track Five.

I saw no EMS personnel in the next few minutes and heard no sirens so I assumed she descended without incident. I grabbed a can of beer at the convenience stand and caught my train home on the Long Island Railroad level. That day was the first and last time in my career that I ever saw Hilda Gould.

*   *   *

During my years as the head of Public Buildings Service for the region a lot of projects were initiated and completed. The process often spanned several administrations. I will be the first to agree that some of the initiatives of my predecessor were completed during my tenure and likewise, some of my initiatives were completed after my departure.

We built office buildings, courthouses, free standing child care centers, border stations and jails. If I had to point to some of the more satisfying accomplishments, I would look towards the less glamorous and more practical.

Every year many projects compete for a limited capital budget. Repairs have less glitter than new buildings so Congress is never too quick to appropriate money for infrastructure improvements. Too often we use Band-aids and rubber bands to keep buildings together. Repairs produce varying returns on investment so it is often a matter of bang for the buck.

The GSA regions traditionally submit a capital budget years in advance of the fiscal year in which the money is actually spent. The submission must first make a cut within our central office in order that the complete GSA submission to the Office of Management and Budget comes in within a reasonable semblance of the anticipated appropriation. If it passes OMB it then has to be approved by Congress after the staffers again review all of the proposed projects and weigh the request against the money to be appropriated as well as the merits of the competing projects nationwide. Value for the dollar, need and politics all figure into the decision.

For this reason large appropriations for mundane things like upgrades to bathrooms seldom make it to the final budget. Congressmen like to get their pictures taken at groundbreakings for new office buildings, not bathroom repair projects. At groundbreakings, politicians get to shovel the dirt, both literally and figuratively, and discuss what a wonderful job they did and to seize credit for an initiative which started before they were in office.

Our regional headquarters building, and the flagship building in our inventory, 26 Federal Plaza, was a cash cow, even though it was over thirty years old and deteriorating. During the economic boom starting in the mid-nineties, rentals paid by our tenant agencies were commensurate with the New York market. There was no financing to repay; capital expenditures were kept to a minimum and limited to those which would support the tenants and generate an immediate return on investment.

The building is 41 stories high and every year we would request money to repair 82 bathrooms. Every year the request would be rejected. We needed a million dollars for this effort and that would only cover cosmetic improvements, not replacement of the aging fix-tures.

When Commissioner F. Joseph Moravec made his first visit to the region after assuming office in the spring of 2001 I decided to do something drastic and unorthodox. When dignitaries visit we usually created a love-in by scrubbing down the place, bringing out our best dressed and most articulate managers and then touring our more attractive space and visiting satisfied customers. We would show nice courtrooms, recently renovated office space, hit a historic building or two and then head to Chinatown for lunch.

I wanted to tell it like it is. Before the visit I recruited two of my managers, Kathleen Flaherty and Dan Garfield, and had them tour the ladies and men's rooms respectively on every floor. "Bring me back the worst," was the marching order.

Kathleen came back with the clear winner. The ladies room on the twelfth floor serviced employees as well as a large public contin-gent. That was the floor that applicants for citizenship visited. After talking to people on the floor I found out that most female employees go to the thirteenth floor to use the facilities, preferring not to set foot in the rest room on the twelfth floor. The word most often used to describe it was "disgusting."

I conducted a pre-commissioner reconnaissance inspection. Our maintenance crew kept it relatively clean, considering its heavy use, but the wear and tear was evident. Stalls were chipped and loose; faucets out of service; drains clogged; dispensers hanging off the walls; floor and wall tiles discolored; lighting poor and the toilets sounded like Hoover Dam. If all else failed we could appeal for an energy saving investment.

Dan found a few men's rooms worthy of touring but the horrific twelfth floor ladies room was going to be our showpiece.

The commissioner generally traveled solo, unlike many political appointees who preferred an entourage. I and the division directors did our obligatory briefing of the commissioner in our conference room. We gave him a fancy book with a lot of nice pictures and impressive statistics. In government, more than anywhere, you can always lie with the right statistics.

Then it was time for the tour. We didn't want to create an impression of pulling a slick maneuver nor did we want to sugar coat anything. "We thought we would take you to some of the problem areas first." He actually appreciated that we were giving him a reality tour rather than an orchestrated one.

The first stop was the twelfth floor ladies room. On the way I explained to him that we would really like to upgrade all of the restrooms in this, our largest building (and in fact, the second largest federal building in the country, behind the Pentagon) but the cost was prohibitive and given the low profile of such a project it would be unlikely to get funding in the near future. We all knew that the commissioner was very much attuned to customer satisfaction and what it meant to the value of property.

Kathleen cleared the place out and the team of serious looking suits entered the room, looking like they were going into a surgical consultation. The commissioner and I were in front of the line and everyone who followed carried a clip board. While we were checking out the stalls and personal care product dispensers the baby changing stand came crashing down. This was convenient timing and contrary to belief, unplanned. Everyone scribbled on their notepads.

The group weaved through the ladies room like a conga line. In the minute and a half that it took us to enter the west door and exit the east door we were assured of a $1 million line item in our next budget for this project. *Then* we went to Chinatown for lunch.

The project has since been completed. I consider this one of my major achievements and, along with the high profile Foley Square project, part of my legacy. Kathleen recently told me that every time she visits a ladies room in the building she thinks of me.

PART TWO

The Formative Years

CHAPTER 7

Victoria's Secret Agent

Of all of the customer agencies I have dealt with over the years, the elite law enforcement agencies provided the most intrigue. FBI, CIA and other agencies that are cloaked in some aura of secrecy or top security always provided their share of adventure, mystique and laughs.

My first introduction to this unique segment of government came early in my career. GSA was responsible for securing offices for elements of the Central Intelligence Agency throughout our region. What was actually done in these offices was anybody's guess because I rarely saw people in them save for a secretary or clerical person (named Mary). In those days talking about the CIA was like talking about colon cancer. It was done in whispers or code names. Rarely was the term CIA ever mentioned by name or reduced to writing. Just as you wouldn't have said, "My dear aunt has cancer," you would also never say, "This request is for the CIA."

For reasons known to somebody, somewhere in early GSA, the CIA acquired the code name "Agency 25." In the offices that we set up for them, the front door would be labeled something like "Ramani Import-Export Company." More often than not there would be no entry on the building directory.

One thing that was for sure: They fooled absolutely nobody.

In my training years, before I had such a thing as a top secret clearance, I was sent by Alex to visit "Agency 25" in their coded office in an upstate city, while I was there to inspect and report whether the less influential government agencies were operating within their approved space guidelines. All I was to do was enter the office by appointment and present a sealed envelope to the secretary (Mary) who would then get it to the agent in charge for review and signature on a floor plan and I would return two hours later to retrieve it. The agent must have been hidden in a closet, out of view of anyone without a top secret clearance.

I entered the Victoria Building but I had a dilemma. I knew that this particular "Agency 25" office was coded "Shamrock Personnel Services," which was a strange camouflage business for an office in which few people ever entered or left. I looked on the directory and there was no Shamrock. I looked at my papers and there was no room number.

The elevator starter called over from his perch, "Can I help you."

Now my inexperience was getting the best of me. I was stymied. What would James Bond have done? "Well, I'm looking for, uh, an, uh, employment office. Sham, or something like th...."

The starter's face lit up with pleasure out of the satisfaction that he was able to help a visitor. In a voice which was many octaves above soft-spoken he announced to the entire lobby, "Oh! You want the CIA! Sure, they're in Room 525."

So much for my days as a secret agent. It must have been my polyester sport jacket or the fake leather government-issued attaché case that blew my cover.

I found my way to Shamrock and performed my messenger duties. Mary was very polite and said "The agent will review it and get it back to you." I agreed to come back that afternoon to pick up the bundle. I told Mary that if the agent had any questions I would be glad to answer them. She thanked me and opened the door. I was in the lobby staring back at the Shamrock on the door thinking that if this is a personnel service they treat their job applicants rather shabbily.

Looking back to that first trip into a CIA inner sanctum in upstate New York, when I finally passed through the doors to Shamrock Personnel Services I knew I was in a government office regardless of all of the cover attempts. The accoutrements stood out like a virgin in a logging camp. Mary sat at a standard gray metal desk. On the desk was the standard issue government message pad and on the wall the standard issue government calendar.

On Mary's desk was the ever present GEICO brochure, found in most government offices in those days. These were little charts designed to help employees keep track of their use of annual and sick leave. These public information documents have been passed out by the insurance company for more than forty years. Originally GEICO misled the public by calling themselves *Government Employees Insurance Company*. Their colorful brochure had superfine print in the rear disclaiming any association with the United States Government but they had most government employees at the time lulled into thinking that they were offering special deals to the career bureaucrats.

In all of my years with the government I don't recall a face-to-face meeting with a CIA operative. I met clerical employees who guarded the doors to the offices and I guess gave you a pat down if you had to go beyond the reception area and I a met a few administrative types who were liaison people for their facility planning function. Even their administrative people referred to the agency in a detached third-party manner. "I'm Mr. Farnsworth (Yeah, right.) from *that one agency*," or "*The company* prefers to be located on a higher floor."

For all of its secrecy "Agency 25" could have posted notice of its presence in the middle of the town square.

* * *

As secretive as the CIA had been, the FBI was the opposite. Their presence was always conspicuous and their key personnel were right out there with us. Their attention to detail was meticulous. Any major decision involving an FBI office required input and approval from the local special agent in charge and headquarters. Their administrative people who provided support for their space and facilities functions were generally very capable.

Working with the FBI was always fun. When you were in their conference room you had the feeling that this was a television police drama setting, given the photos of the "Most Wanted" all over the place.

Although FBI agents try to keep a low profile they often do a poor job. They are the best dressed of the law enforcement people.

Take the time I was riding up in the elevator at 26 after a Chinatown lunch with two of my colleagues. Somebody made a vague comment related to building security and I looked at the best-dressed person in the elevator and said, "Well, we can feel secure. We have the FBI with us."

The gentleman looked at me and said, "How do you know I'm with the FBI?"

"You're in uniform," I told him while observing his standard gray suit, white shirt and paisley tie. The only thing missing were the sunglasses.

"A lot of people wear gray suits." Now we were in a debate.

I looked at him, ready to again demonstrate my forensic skills. "The fact that you pressed the button for the twenty-fourth floor might have been another hint."

"Oh." The elevator stopped at sixteen and I got off, ending this intellectual exchange.

The FBI maintained a garage on the upper east side of Manhattan for vehicle storage and maintenance. The garage was as secure as their offices and just as difficult to enter without a complete security review and background check. This is where they kept surveillance vehicles with delicate equipment and vehicles seized as evidence.

I was in charge of the Real Estate Division when the FBI came to GSA and asked us to find a new garage for them, or I should say, demanded that we lease a particular garage. Had this been a less influential agency we would have gone into our goal-line stand routine and found every reason not to acquire this for them without at least some token harassment: "We can't do a sole source lease; the place doesn't meet our safety requirements because the never-used rear exit door is a hundredth of an inch narrower than code; the landlord is on our debarred list because he once had lunch with an alleged mobster, etc. You get the point.

But this was the FBI, the epitome of law enforcement so we were going to put our top people on the case.

The ball started to role when Liz, my secretary, walked into my office and announced, "There are two gentlemen here to see you. They claim they are from the FBI and they showed me their *prudentials.*" Privileged agencies often arrived unannounced, like in the movies, as if they were about to make an arrest.

This was not a time for humor, because as I learned throughout my career, law enforcement people have their own brand of humor. They take to outsiders poking fun at them like members of the bar association take to lawyer jokes.

After being informed of the gravity of this situation and how this garage was essential for national security, in the name of GSA I agreed to give it expeditious handling and put our top people on the case. I also agreed to personally oversee the project.

I had Liz fetch "Queen" Roseanne Romano and "Brooklyn" Tony Cavello.

Rosanne was a senior leasing specialist. She was right out of Bensonhurst and had an attitude to match. She was somewhere between middle age and maturity and strutted like an aging movie star. She was what you would call full-figured so she reminded me a bit of Jane Russell in those fifties Hollywood extravaganzas. She wore flashy jewelry, conspicuous makeup and carried herself with an aura of royalty. When she showed up at a meeting with her six-foot frame and her big boobs protruding from her fur coat she commanded immediate respect. In the office she was known alternately as "The Old Gray Mare" (when she slackened up with the red coloring), or more often, "The Queen of Kings."[3]

---

[3] For those unfamiliar with the geography of New York City, Bensonhurst is a section of Brooklyn. Brooklyn is officially known as Kings County.

On the other hand, Tony, a former auto mechanic, was a perpetual womanizer and an absolute slob. Give him a twelve-ounce can of Pepsi and he could burp the alphabet on command. However, he knew everything there was to know about garages and auto maintenance equipment. The one thing Rosanne and Tony had in common was a foul mouth. The FBI was going to love these two.

On the very first trip to visit this dilapidated garage that the FBI had pre-selected, I accompanied Rosanne and Tony in our government vehicle. Tony drove.

We got off the FDR Drive and proceeded west on East 71st Street, a street filled with nannies, uniformed doormen, chauffeurs and dog walkers. When Tony spotted an attractive woman walking her poodle he rolled down the window, gave a whistle and said something like, "Hey, Chickie, can I ride you home?" For all I knew this might have been some diplomat's daughter that he was trying to hit on. What I did know was that we were in a car with government plates that could easily be traceable back to us. I beckoned Tony to concentrate on his driving while I was sinking down in the seat.

We reached the garage where we met the FBI and owner's representatives as scheduled. Unknown to us the FBI had already seized a part of the garage and had moved some vehicles inside. This, of course, compromised our bargaining position.

During our discussions Tony had excused himself to go to the men's room and then inspect some of the car lifts, since his role was more technical than financial.

We spoke about occupancy dates and a general cleanup before the effective date of the lease. The lessor's representatives were doing exactly what I would have expected. They began taking away everything they promised to the FBI before we began to negotiate in earnest, a standard tactic. "Oh, we never promised to provide more power to the lift area," or, "Of course we'll put up a security fence at one end. We'll get you a price."

While this was going on at an improvised work table at one end of this warm and as yet unventilated garage my eyes focused on the other end where I could not quite believe what I was seeing. It was Brooklyn Tony urinating against the rear wall. With the moisture still seeping down from the masonry he zipped his fly and walked back to rejoin the meeting. When he sat down he leaned over to me and whispered in my ear, "The lifts work fine. Men's room needs repair."

As if he had to put an exclamation point on the thought, he rolled his eyes in the direction of one of the FBI representatives, an attractive business attired woman, leaned over once again and whispered his latest thought. "I'd like to give her a jiffy lube."

The negotiations for this lease were contentious. The lessor made the usual mistake of thinking the government would be a pushover and an instant meal ticket. He continued to offend Rosanne by treating her as if women were second class citizens in his world (which they were in the real estate business for longer than many other industries). He referred to her at *that woman* or *the girl* which in any other situation Rosanne might have considered flattery.

The meeting ended with all parties committing to some followup work.

Rosanne had a way of turning the heat on and off instantly, a product of her Brooklyn street smarts. It was never personal, strictly business.

There was a particular midday lull back in the office which was broken by aggressive dialogue coming out of the bullpen. It was loud enough to get my attention.

The roar was coming from Rosanne's cubicle. The phone was to her right ear. The prospective landlord for the garage was on the other end. Her normal voice was audible a city block away but this was exceptional. "Look you thief. I'm tired of all of your bullshit. You can make the Indian on a penny cry with your crap. I'll give you seventeen bucks a foot for that shithouse of yours and twenty grand more for powering up the lifts." Her inflection was rising, the sweat was pouring from her forehead and her jewelry was jingling. The staff was cheering her on with a few *Roe-zann – Roe-zanns.*

She wasn't done. "If you don't like it we'll condemn the fucking place at ten bucks and if you want more your shyster accountant will have to open one of your sets of books to the court. If the judge doesn't put your ass in jail maybe you'll get some more money in a year."

There was a brief pause for some obvious squirming and posturing at the other end which we all knew was fruitless.

"Call me back in an hour and give me your decision." The one way conversation got a little louder. "And when you call back you don't address me as *Roe, Missy or Sweetie.* You call me *Ms. Romano!*"

With that last admonition she slammed the receiver down and plopped back into her chair. As if she had just turned a switch, she calmly turned around to her friend in the adjoining cubicle and in a near whisper said, "I'm hungry, Terri. Let's go to Chinatown."

When she returned an hour and five minutes later there was a yellow phone message sheet on her desk indicating a call from the owner. Liz had scribbled the message, "He said to tell Ms. Romano he will take the deal."

She looked at it, smiled and said to nobody in particular. "I could have gone to twenty but the asshole pissed me off."

*   *   *

In reality all federal agencies are technically law enforcement, since all get their authority from a combination of the Constitution, enabling legislation and the United States Code. Those law enforcement personnel who apprehend real criminals have privileges consistent with the hazards of their profession. Early retirement, hazardous duty pay, a lot of overtime and often preferred parking for their cars or the official vehicles they use due to the erratic hours they work and the potential dangers of them parking in public places.

Then there are the pseudo law enforcers who try to horn in on all of the fun. Parking spaces are sacred, especially if they are free and for personal use, so you can understand why over my career I have heard every justification in the book for a government-provided parking space in a federal building. The pecking order, by law, is law enforcement first, then other official vehicles, then high officials, handicapped and so on down the line. The last priority is personal parking, which according to an IRS gyration is considered a benefit and is taxable at the estimated fair market value.

You can just imagine the skullduggery which goes on to justify the parking and claim it is official rather than personal. It used to hurt me when I would see some fat-ass political appointee who was too good to take the subway, claim a space while a hard-working disabled person who was not physically able to use public transportation was denied a spot in the building and had to use a private lot.

"We're law enforcement" is what I would hear from everyone who chases bad guys to those who issue OSHA violations or review payrolls in a comfortable office to assure wage rate compliance.

People would go to great lengths to prove their case. They bring in everything from arrest or violation logs, their operating manuals which may loosely refer to them upholding the law when they find paperwork out of order or a minimum wage violation, or even some seized fruits and vegetables. The best came in our Buffalo office when an inspector from the U.S. Fish and Wildlife Service whose job it was to apprehend sportsmen hunting without a

proper permit produced a couple of dead Canadian geese he con-
fiscated when he ticketed a hunter for poaching fowl on a federal
preserve.

Imaginative, but as I often heard my prior bosses say, "You can't
put ten pounds of shit in a five pound bag." There was still no room
for his car or his geese in the building.

CHAPTER 8

All The President's Advance Men

Working for the government, at a young age and with minimal experience, you can find yourself making critical decisions, affecting the lives and livelihoods of many people.

I was with GSA for about two years and as a trainee I was learning the business of planning and managing space the government way. It required learning the laws under which we operated and the often cumbersome procedures and policies. After that it was common business sense and the ability to write well and stay organized. We had architects and engineers on staff and under contract to take care of the technical end.

My first real assignment involved finding space for tenants in federal buildings in upstate New York on an as-needed basis. I worked under the guidance of a senior technician and we both reported to the same supervisor. We were involved in the planning for new federal buildings in Buffalo, Rochester, Syracuse and Albany. The scenario was that each proposed project had to survive a preliminary planning process and if there is congressional support they went through a funding ritual which normally involved appropriating money for site and design first. Once the building was designed and after the obligatory political haggling, construction funds were appropriated.

One quiet summer afternoon I was sitting at my desk shuffling a few papers and observing the cruise ships, when the phone rang for Alex.

I heard only his side of the conversation.

"Hello, commissioner."

"Yes."

"Yes"

"Let me find out."

The receiver clunked to the top of the steel gray desk and Alex emerged from behind his partition. He looked around, not happy that I was the only person in sight.

"Where's Charlie [my immediate supervisor]?"

"He's in Newark at a meeting," I replied.

"Where's Milt [senior technician]?"

"He's with Charlie."

"What about Pat?" This would be Pittsburgh Pat who he would only ask for out of desperation.

"Off today."

Now he looked at me realizing he reached the bottom of the barrel and had to provide critical information to the commissioner. Displeased that his career was in the hands of a 23 year-old trainee he said, "You've been working on upstate, haven't you?"

"Yes."

He phumphered a few times, knowing he was entrusting me with some political flimflammery. "The White House wants to announce a project for upstate New York." This was during the Lyndon Johnson administration, when I first became aware that White House news releases were well orchestrated con jobs.

Alex went on. "Which project do we need more, Buffalo or Rochester?"

I knew that both projects were designed and awaiting construction funding. Now, with thirty seconds allocated to think about it, I was an advisor to the Congress. I looked up at the ceiling, winced a few times and silently contemplated that whatever the choice was I would likely spend a lot of time in one of those frozen upstate tundras.

Both cities had a minor league hockey team, which was a passion of mine. Buffalo, however, was closer to several Canadian hockey-mad cities, expanding the personal fulfillment possibilities.

"Buffalo. Most of the current space is obsolete and....." That's as far as I got. It was an early lesson in getting to the point immediately without extraneous bullshit.

"Thanks," was Alex's only comment as he reentered his bunker and retrieved the receiver. "Buffalo, Mr. Commissioner."

Within days Congress had signed off on the funding and there were massive press releases on how the Johnson administration was helping upstate New York so vote Democratic this year. That is how the Buffalo Federal Building happened to be completed in 1969 (Nixon presidency but it was started during the Johnson administration) and the Rochester Building not until 1972, under Nixon administration funding.

*   *   *

Almost half of my career was spent assuring that government agencies which came to GSA for space in which to operate (as if they had anywhere else to go) faced every obstacle imaginable before actually acquiring said space. Our work unit was called Space Management Division at the time and we became known as the government's space cadets because we were preoccupied with what we referred to as a "utilization rate." In simple terms this meant the amount of space used divided by the number of people in the space. The standard was 135 square feet per person and we were charged with going to great lengths to maintain that standard. Only office space mattered. Warehouses or specialized space such as laboratories didn't count so we did everything imaginable, in consort with the customers we served, to put everyone in office space for statistical purposes. We went over our monthly reports diligently and part of our employee evaluations were based on utilization. It really was a matter of gaming the numbers rather than saving the taxpayer any money. Politics are no different today.

This was one of the first lessons I had in which the goal of one business organization is in direct opposition with that of another. It was a perfect example of a conflicting agenda. In order for us to do our job well we may have prevented someone else from doing a good job. It made perfect sense in those days.

Eventually Congress changed the appropriations laws and government agencies became directly responsible for their space and facilities budgets. This resulted in self policing to an extent. It also developed a whole new cottage industry within the government. GSA instituted user charges for space, similar to a rental charge, based upon the fair market value of the space. Therefore we had to develop standards and procedures for things like measuring and classifying space, appraising space and handling appeals from tenant agencies who thought they were being overcharged. In theory the appeals could have gone all the way the Office of Management and Budget ("OMB"). This whole process would have made Professor Parkinson wince, because more time and effort was spent on administration than on the actual completion of the assigned task. Internal staff increased, people were promoted to head up new offices or task forces and contractors had a field day.

When things started to change in the late eighties it was because political leaders at GSA at the time, such as GSA Administrator Terry Golden, questioned how we were serving our constituency. They recognized that the taxpayers would be served better if we paid some attention to customer service rather than customer non-service. It took a long while to change the mindset. It was not necessary to jam everyone into cheap, low quality space anymore and despite policy, it wasn't essential to locate everyone in urban areas which had little hope of redevelopment, especially if the mission of the agency involved servicing a large geographic area. The term "utilization rate" slowly left our vocabulary. The space cadets now became customer account reps or project managers.

During those formative years I received a lot of mentoring and I learned a lot from my bosses, Sid, Alex and Charlie. It was not all good but nevertheless influenced my development as a manager and my analytical (meaning "cynical") approach to a lot of situations.

My early trio of bosses had me convinced that everyone was the enemy, be it a customer, vendor or a GSA employee. Since at the time government agencies were not directly accountable for their space and facilities expenditures there was often an all-you-can-get attitude or some self-promoting among our clientele.

Although my bosses were cynical and bureaucratic they did have a sense of humor, especially Charlie, who probably had a Napoleon complex and took pride in exercising his power to obstruct.

One of the first "management" lessons I learned from Charlie was to establish who had control of a relationship with some subtle little hints which translated into, "I know your game so let's cut the bullshit up front." Some of the lessons could have come right out of Parkinson's work. For instance, he instructed me to never set up a Friday meeting with customers based in Washington, and never set up a meeting the day before or after a holiday. "They just want a weekend in New York," he would explain. "They'll come up with a contrived reason to meet, ask if you're available Friday and then they'll go back and tell their boss they scheduled a meeting with GSA for the only time GSA was available. That gave them a free trip to New York for the weekend."

He was right at least some of the time because there were people who developed the pattern of only meeting on Fridays, often for frivolous reasons. It took me about twenty years to get over the concept that I had to be a policeman for someone else's travel habits.

Then there was the universal sign that we were being handed a line of crap. If we sat at a meeting and someone was giving us a spiel as to why they had to have a particular amenity not in the handbook, which we by nature would automatically reject, one of us would touch our ear. This became the sign throughout the division and depending upon the level of absurdity, it would range from a mere touching of the ear to a downright yanking of the earlobe.

Since we were regulators at the time and did everything by the book in the least costly manner, people would come to us to justify things like why they had to be in the suburbs instead of an urban area; why they needed special parking privileges at government expense; why they had to be on an upper floor with a water view; or why they had to be in the most prestigious building in town. When I got into management, but before GSA changed its operating position, I developed a policy that we do everything by the book except that I would accommodate an absurd request if someone could give me reason that I hadn't heard before.

It took years for this phenomenon to happen. It was a fellow who we affectionately called "Nelson" Eady who said he had to have a corner office on a high floor on the Hudson River side of 26 Federal Plaza because he has an asthmatic condition and needs the afternoon sun. When I heard this I practically pulled my ear out of its socket before I said, "You win." What I didn't know when I was handed this nonsense was that he was an amateur photographer and loved taking pictures of classic cruise ships which just happened to pass our building on the Hudson River side, enroute to and from their midtown berths. I was taken but I couldn't get upset because I was beaten under my own rules.

Another gem that Charlie and Alex taught me was to schedule important meetings, those which required a decision or commitment, for late morning or late afternoon. The rationale was that the closer we came to mealtime or quitting time, the more restless our adversary would be and the more likely it was that they would come around to our thinking just to be able to get out.

As a corollary to this, I made sure that meeting rooms were not too comfortable. The more comfortable the room, the more time would be wasted on background information and self-indulging garbage. Make the room a bit crowded, a bit cold (or warm) and without fancy amenities or refreshments and you would be surprised at how quickly you get to the business at hand.

As a branch chief I had a very small office. I would customarily hold meetings there, especially those which I wanted to end quickly. There was one with the military which was requested by my old friend and Alex's old nemesis, Sylvester. The military meetings in those days traditionally included civilian people from the Army Corps of Engineers ("COE") and uniformed people from the services. This particular meeting involved a consolidated recruiting center so there were COE people, led by the always dapper Sylvester with his fedora and silk scarf and uniformed officers and enlisted people from each service. In all there were about fifteen people crowded into my ten by ten cubby hole. A few were seated and the rest were standing elbow to elbow, like they were jammed into the Bronx bound number 6 subway train. Sylvester knew what we were doing and actually cooperated with the scenario, hoping to minimize the trash talk and get to the business at hand.

After ten minutes of discomfort, all decisions were made. Meeting over.

Alex also taught me to read your adversary - that's what our customers were in my early years - and *his* needs. There were no his or hers in those days. Alex firmly believed that females should only be pounding a typewriter. He would tell us not to offer agencies any more than necessary even if we had the capability of doing better. Some agencies definitely carried less prestige with us. Department of Agriculture, any branch of the military, or the many smaller bureaus of the Department of Labor or Department of Commerce were treated like second class citizens and given third rate space. Prestigious agencies like the State Department or FBI had far more political clout and were awarded more civilized quarters.

*   *   *

In the spring of 1967 Symphony Sid bestowed an honor upon me, even though I was still in my training years.

Puerto Rico was part of our region but was regarded as a distant outpost and because it was a resort, it was considered a perk to go there for business. Consequently, trips to the island were closely scrutinized.

We were in the preliminary planning stages of what was to be a new federal building and courthouse in San Juan. Sid decided that I should be the one to visit the island and do the space programming because he knew I wouldn't treat it as a boondoggle and I would get the job done. It was to be an unprecedented two week trip, and since it was out of the Continental United States approval from Washington was required. This was done by a series of snail mail memoranda back and forth to explain and justify the purpose of the trip. The approval eventually came, signed by the assistant commissioner but authored by one of his many staffers. It approved the trip with the condition that a full trip report be submitted to Washington and contained a vague insinuation that if additional assistance is needed the author would be willing to participate in the journey. Sid didn't bite. He merely said, "That prick (whom we called) Lighthead approved your trip."

At the time the region had a San Juan field office headed by an area manager who was hired because of his political connections.

There were several issues of which I was aware but was too naïve to fully appreciate. First, he and Sid mistrusted and totally disliked each other. They were at constant odds with conflicting agendas. The area manager did not report to Sid, hence felt no obligation to comply with his directives.

A second key issue, which I was to come to appreciate over the span of my career and many future visits to the island, is that the area manager, Mr. O'Hare, was American with no Latino blood whatsoever. He and others like him would never be fully accepted or trusted by the staff in Puerto Rico. Anyone who was not a native Puerto Rican was at a clear disadvantage. New York born people of Puerto Rican ancestry or non-Puerto Rican Hispanics were considered gringos.

Unknown to me, when Sid sent a memo to the area manager advising that I was coming to Puerto Rico for this task, Mr. O'Hare, whom I had never met, replied that I shouldn't come because the job would be done locally. This is why, when I showed up in his office on a Monday morning I was treated as if I had a case of Montezuma's revenge. O'Hare barely looked up, never shook my hand, and muttered, "I told Sid not to send you."

Welcome to Puerto Rico.

He eventually warmed up to the point where he assigned me a car and told me that the senior buildings manager, Mr. Burwell, would set up appointments and escort me as needed. I was not thrilled about driving in San Juan so I welcomed any chauffeuring that I could get.

As was typical when doing business on the island, things always took longer than expected. Later in my career it was easier to deal with these types of issues because I learned more about the culture and attitudes and accepted it. Not that I had a choice. During the ensuing years I made many trips to Puerto Rico and I enjoyed the warmth and sincerity of our staffers there.

I learned that the first matter of protocol when you came to the island as a representative of a government agency is that you had to call on the governor or his representative; the chief judge; the United States attorney and several other dignitaries as a courtesy and to explain your mission.

By day three I was finally ready to start the job. Mr. Burwell had set up appointments over the next week with all of the prospective occupants of the new building, who were located in a variety of military and commercially leased locations. I did what were called "space requirements surveys," essentially nothing more than a laborious inventory of people and equipment placed on worksheets. These documents eventually became the planning tool for a 400,000 square-foot federal building and courthouse, constructed in Hato Rey in the San Juan metropolitan area.

One afternoon Burwell set me up with an appointment with Department of Agriculture representatives who were situated in an old building in the Santurce section called the Stubbe-Segarra Building, named for the ownership of the building. Santurce is a busy area, filled with older buildings that would never have met the most lenient of today's building codes.

"I have to talk to Stubbe," Burwell told me, "so I can drive you over. Then you can grab the bus back to the hotel when you're done and I'll pick you up in the morning." That was fine with me.

We pulled up to the building and proceeded to a small parking lot behind it, which was reserved for building occupants. It was guarded by a frail, elderly and somewhat disheveled gentleman who manually moved the sawhorse for authorized vehicles.

Burwell, unlike many of the other Americans assigned to Puerto Rico, spoke fluent Spanish. The conversation began with a slow courteous dialogue which I didn't understand, except for the fact that it wasn't going too well because the elderly man didn't move the sawhorse. The conversation slowly became louder, more animated and very aggressive, as if one of the parties was being shaken down. Eventually they began shouting at each other full blast and the old man got up, made more hand gestures and kicked the sawhorse to the side.

Mr. Burwell shook his head, muttered something in Spanish which I assumed meant "asshole" and pulled up alongside the back door to the building. He motioned for me to go in through the door and said, "I'll see you tomorrow."

I looked back quizzically and said, "I thought you had to meet with Mr. Stubbe?"

He glanced in the direction of the old guy who was now arguing with a UPS driver while judiciously guarding the parking lot. "That *was* Stubbe."

Prior to departing for Puerto Rico Sid offered to get me a good deal at a hotel. I was reluctant given his penchant for frugality, but per diem was limited and I couldn't afford to do this trip at a deficit.

When I left the airport I told the cab driver to take me to the Royal Palms in the Condado section. The place turned out to be a rather nice looking apartment hotel, located between two resort hotels. "Welcome to *P-w-e-r-r-t-o R-r-r-i-c-o*," said the friendly desk clerk.

When I gave him my name he scanned the reservation register, looked up at me with a warm smile and acted like some ambassador had just arrived. "Ah, Señor Greenberg. Welcome. I hope you *wheel* be comfortable here." Since this was not a true hotel, the desk clerk himself grabbed my bags and personally escorted me to a top floor penthouse suite. He left a slip of paper on the table which indicated a room rate of seven dollars per night. This was 1967 but seven bucks for a luxury room at a beachfront place was still cheap. I couldn't quite believe it but I didn't want to beg the issue by questioning it. Instead I went to settle my bill every few days to pay for the days I already stayed so I didn't get a big surprise at the end. The money I saved on my per diem was used for weekend entertainment which I otherwise might not have indulged.

I also managed to save a few bucks on meals by taking Sid's advice on the manager's cocktail parties. For two weeks I ate mainly finger food at night. The heartburn was worth it economically.

When I eventually checked out I again got the royal treatment and the manager insisted upon hiring a car to take me to the airport. They clearly were not making any money on my visit.

I couldn't help but inquire of Sid when I returned as to how he was able to get me such a deal. Even the frugal Sidney could not have fleshed out a bargain like this.

Turns out Sid had called a buddy of his in San Juan for the favor. The friend happened to be the special agent-in-charge of the local FBI office who passed on the request for the favor to one of his deputies, just like Don Corleone would assign work to his lieutenants. As best I could figure, the bargain hotel where I stayed doubled as a safe house for witnesses and also was involved in things law enforcement agencies considered "of interest," so these little courtesies were kind of a payback for past business and a quid pro quo for the FBI and others to occasionally overlook some minor infractions.

The desk clerk at the hotel must have thought I was right from FBI headquarters, even without a paisley tie. I never did find out what the FBI had on them.

Mr. O'Hare and Sid eventually retired and the relationship between the Puerto Rico office and the mainland improved. By the time I was a senior manager, communications had become so technologically advanced that the employees at our field offices were as close to the region as if they were sitting in our building.

Over the years I returned to the island many times. I followed the San Juan project from pre-planning through design, construction, occupancy and its life as a heavily trafficked public building. When I left GSA, the building, like me, was aging. I took personal satisfaction that my contributions to the project thirty seven years earlier were still visible.

When I visited I was treated like family. Of all of the trips I made to the islands, my spouse only accompanied me once. Towards the end she finally came down just to get some beach time while I was working. On Monday morning I was to be picked up by our local representatives. While I was waiting in front of the hotel (this time it was the Ritz-Carlton, not the Royal Palms) my wife was asked by the service manager if we needed a cab, to which she replied negatively, stating that I was being picked up by business associates. "OK, muy bien."

By this time in my career I looked more like a professor of economics than a hot shot government manager. When the big, black Crown Victoria arrived out came our local director to greet me, accompanied by the head of the federal police in full uniform and with guns on both hips. We shook hands and I got in the car. When I looked back the jaws on both my wife and the service manager were open so wide that they could have attracted gnats.

To all of my friends in Puerto Rico, it was a marvelous ride and I thank you for the hospitality.

*   *   *

For every trip to tropical San Juan there were ten trips to upstate New York, which, during the winter months, was like going to the Yukon.

The little escapade involving the sequence of scheduling construction for the Buffalo and Rochester federal buildings was long behind me when, out of the clear, the issue resurfaced years later. Thankfully, I had no direct involvement in this adventure.

It was towards the end of Richard M. Nixon's first term in office, when the White House again wanted to horn in on upstate politics and get some publicity. Remember, the planning for the Buffalo and Rochester buildings came during the Johnson years but this was not going to stop the Nixon White House from reaping the benefits.

It was déjà vu all over again. The White House (It's always *The White House*, never a named individual.) called the GSA administrator; the administrator called the commissioner; the commissioner called the regional administrator; the regional administrator called the regional commissioner (before that title was changed to assistant regional administrator) who in turn called the director of real estate; the director called his branch chief. The branch chief was out as was the senior technician so the question eventually went to an advanced trainee. Not me this time. I was already a journeyperson and handling New York City projects.

The trainee panicked a bit when told that information was needed for the White House.

"Which White House?"

"*Our* White House." That sure clarified things.

The question from the White House was whether we had an event in upstate New York for the president to attend. The subtlety behind this was the president or his political advisors' recommendation that he show some attention to the area. Our commissioner in Washington knew we had some completed and near completed buildings which would be ideal for a politically motivated presidential visit. These events always provide a friendly audience and an opportunity to flaunt the administration's commitment to an area by it's spending for a new building, even though it was originated during the previous administration.

When the trainee was asked by the ever-intimidating Alex which project would be better for a dedication to be attended by the president, Buffalo or Rochester, between his nervousness and the lack of clarity of the question he completely misread the issue. His guess was Rochester because it was a smaller and less troublesome project, oblivious to the fact that it was well behind Buffalo in construction. It was nowhere near completion whereas the Buffalo building was completed and occupied.

Rochester was passed up the line faster than a Domino pizza delivery and by the end of the day we were planning for a spring dedication in Rochester, which by now was on the president's calendar. The whole plan fell apart when Charlie returned and offered that Rochester was a year from completion. It was Buffalo that was ready for a formal dedication.

Now the agency felt a collective embarrassment and was ready to institute its policy of finding some poor slob to pin blame on when disaster strikes. Unfortunately there was no time for that. When the administrator heard of this faux pas he was determined that we were not going back to the White House to admit an error. White House appointees, like him, never make errors. He was determined that there would be a dedication in Rochester, completed building or not.

With that command the region planned for what amounted to a bogus dedication. I was not part of management at the time so my recollection is from a non-participant's viewpoint and from stories which were told to me later on, mainly at cocktail hours.

The first thought was to take the president to Buffalo but tell him it was Rochester. This was dismissed quickly. So it was decided that the Rochester dedication would go on as planned, even if there was nothing to dedicate. People would be coming to see the President, not the building, so as long as it didn't rain, we could keep people out of the building and hold the festivities on the plaza.

It was like preparing for an opening night on Broadway. We had a few months to get the show rehearsed and the sets built. Since the exterior was complete the task was not as bad as it could have been. All we had to do was complete the lobby and hope nobody wanted to tour the upper floors. Morton Berkowitz (a/k/a Sporty Morty in deference to his thrift), the project engineer and a tough negotiator, began to negotiate change orders to accelerate completion of the lobby. It's tough to negotiate with sharks when you have no leverage. Morty did the best he could although this one cost the taxpayers dearly.

Then all the president's advance men got into the act.

Advance Man One came and directed that the bleacher seating go on the east side of the outside walkway. Morty objected, citing that the afternoon sun would be in the eyes of the spectators. Advance Man One insisted on placement in his designated location. Then Advance Man Two came and didn't like the angle of the sun in the afternoon and demanded that the seats be removed and reinstalled on the opposite side of the walkway, just as Sporty Morty had recommended. A few days later Advance Man Three came. I guess he was the executive advance man. He checked out the sun, the moon, the wind velocity and the view and then ordered that the bleacher seating be returned to its original position.

The other contribution of the three advance men was that at the last minute they collectively decided that they didn't like the color of the rope on the flagpole. The Coast Guard color guard was dispatched to find a more suitable rope. After scouring the downtown area they eventually found what they needed at an Army-Navy surplus store. They rigged up a new gaudy gold rope only minutes before the arrival of the president.

The GSA people and all the president's advance men were so caught up with the action that they failed to notice that directly across the street stood the offices of the *Rochester Democrat and Chronicle*. In front of the building their reporters were taking copious notes of these strange maneuvers while their photographers took pictures of the entire nonsense unfolding on the plaza. As indicated by its name, the paper had not supported Nixon.

The dedication miraculously went off without a hitch. Nobody got past the lobby to observe the unfinished condition of the building and fortunately nobody asked when the building would actually be occupied. It was no surprise that the day after the "dedication" the paper said little about Nixon's speech. They did, however, run a series of photos showing the bleachers, first here and then there and then here again. They also had a photo of a bunch of guys in suits watching a solitary uniformed coast guardsman scaling the flagpole to change ropes.

The building was completed and ready for occupancy close to a year later. The president did not attend the grand opening.

CHAPTER 9

A Man for All Reasons

One mysterious character I encountered early in my career was the legal scholar Herman "Top Dollar" Lerner. Herman was in his sixties when I first met him. He never remembered my name (or anyone else's for that matter) and despite the fact that I sat twenty feet from his cubicle, each time he saw me was like we never previously met. Like Symphony Sid, Herman had trouble remembering names, but at least Sid remembered faces and knew the people who spent their working hours in the same office.

Word was that Herman originally got his government job when he appeared with a letter of recommendation from the local party boss. Herman's most successful attribute was the ability to maximize pension income. He previously had a career with the City of New York for which he received a pension. He legally collected Social Security at age sixty five, while still working for the federal government. When he eventually retired from the Feds he collected still another pension. While with GSA, he had a side law practice which he worked out of a mail drop in a fleabag Broadway office building. Finally, after retiring, Sid brought him back as a part-time "consultant" to provide him even more income, although the real benefit was that he continued to use his cubicle and the government phones and stationery to operate his legal practice. While this was going on, his wife, a retired New York City teacher, was also collecting a city pension and Social Security. They had five pensions between them and Herman was still collecting "consulting" fees and the few bucks he could scrounge from those who dared to have him represent them on legal issues.

His legal practice was less than lucrative. The clientele consisted mainly of relatives involved in minor issues. The only time a co-worker used his services was for a petty landlord-tenant dispute for which Herman blew the statute of limitations for filing. It was thrown out of court about two minutes after his client paid the filing fee and Herman's retainer.

Herman's specialty in the government was site acquisition. At the time we coexisted his major preoccupation was to acquire small tracts of land in New York and New Jersey for GSA to build prototype buildings for Social Security Administration offices. What the government pays for these properties is a product of the amount authorized by Congress and the appraised fair market value of the land. There is always a little latitude in appraisals because the process is very subjective. Congressional appropriations, on the other hand, are rigid. You cannot spend more than Congress authorizes. That would be a career-ending move.

Herman acquired his nickname, Top Dollar, because of his habit of entering into a negotiation by offering somewhere between 90 percent and 125 percent of the appraised fair market value, leaving it to his much more capable subordinates to negotiate out of these predicaments in time for him to get his picture taken with the local mayor or congressman when the deal is finally made.

Herman came and went from the office unobtrusively and on his own schedule. Other than those who had some interaction with him, nobody really knew him or understood what he did, if anything. He had a secretary named Mary and two subordinate technicians who did the real work and regularly kept him from embarrassing the government.

All was under control with Herman until the day he was literally caught with his pants down.

It was a rainy summer day when Herman arrived in the office fashionably late, as usual. He was wearing a light poncho over his suit so he was not prepared for the driving rain which drenched him and the three newspapers he carried. Since the lower part of his body was unprotected from this act of nature, he was water soaked from his johnson to his toes.

When Alex saw this dilemma, and Herman feebly attempting to wring the excess from his trousers, he couldn't resist taking advantage of a man when he was down. Alex had a zero tolerance for anyone who didn't do an honest day's work or didn't act like he was saving the government from fiscal irresponsibility. Seeing Herman in distress made Alex pounce like a buzzard.

He approached Herm at the entrance to his cubicle and said as many words to him as he had in the prior year. "What happened, Mr. Lerner?"

"Caught in the rain."

Still with a straight face, "You're soaking wet, you could catch a cold."

"Huh? Yeah. I've got to dry off."

Incredulously, Alex looked at him and without blinking an eye said, "Well, why don't you just put your trousers on a hanger and let them dry on your coat rack?"

Herman looked back somewhat in disbelief, but Alex's unflinching demeanor was very convincing. Everyone around him knew perfectly well that he was pulling Herman's chain.

Top Dollar was duped again. Since he rarely left his office he figured it was fine to sit in his skivvies for a while. He actually took off his pants and hung them on the wall of the cubicle and then proceeded behind his desk. When he needed something he traditionally just shouted over the partition (he hadn't mastered the telephone intercom) for Mary, his secretary, or Burt, his assistant. Burt was much more solicitous so he tended to call for Burt far more than Harry, his other technical person who was highly qualified but less tolerant of Herman's inadequacies.

It took Herman all of five minutes to forget that he was sans trousers. He was helped by Ricardo Ricco who had observed these shenanigans from his bullpen seat at the back end of the office.

When he saw Burt leave for the men's room he dialed Herman's extension. "Hullo," was Herman's businesslike way of answering the phone.

"May I speak to Burt Goldschein please?" Ricco worked in the same office as Herman for six years so you would think he just might recognize the voice but Herman was again unmindful.

"Burrrt!" Herman bellowed from the cubicle in his deep gravelly voice.

No response.

"Burrrt!" again.

With the second no response Herman barked backed into the phone. "He's not here. Call back la………."

Ricco interrupted. "Tell him to call Mr. Duncan of Senator Williams' office." Now he had Herman's ear. Dropping the name of a politician always commanded attention. "Be sure to leave the note on his desk. It's very important."

"OK, give me the number."

After meticulously writing down the name and number he hung up and proceeded to leave the note for Burt on his desk, as directed. As expected, when he left his cubicle he was oblivious to where Burt sat and that he was without his pants. There he stood on the office floor, red and white boxer shorts down to his knees, gartered argyle socks and winged tipped shoes. That truly was a sight to behold.

Chaos ensued. Three different Marys let out a collective scream. The other technicians in the columns of desks looked up and recognizing the eccentricities of the character involved, shook their heads, laughed or muttered a few "What the fu….".s. Alex's comment was something like, "I guess your pants didn't dry yet."

When Herman finally realized what was going on he calmly returned to his cubicle, sat behind his desk as if nothing had happened, and called over the partition. "Maaary! Don't forget to tell Burrrt he has a message. It's important."

It was Burt who supplied an endless array of stories about Herman's misadventures. Burt was conscientious but a bit of a windbag himself so he and Herman got along well. As Burt became more proficient under Herman's tutelage, no easy feat, he assumed that one of his ancillary duties was to keep Herman from embarrassing himself or the government and to apologize for him when he did. Restaurants were particularly problematic. Herman would walk into an establishment in his usual stupor, bypass any waiting customers and the sign which said "Please wait to be seated" and just plop himself where he chose. Then he would shout orders to the nearest wait staff member as if the person were his exclusive servant. Herman had a slight hearing loss and Burt often said "I would love to be able to blame his aloof behavior on the hearing loss, but in reality he is just a pompous asshole."

Burt recalled the time the two of them were driving to Binghamton in western New York State. They stopped in Elmira for a meal break. Herman went through a stop sign right in the middle of town and was promptly apprehended by a local badge. Herman thought that the trooper considered himself at Herman's service and when he approached the vehicle the conversation went something like this.

OFFICER: Good afternoon, sir.

HERMAN: We're from the government. Where can we eat around here?

OFFICER: May I see your license and registration, please?

HERMAN: A nice corned beef sandwich would be good.

OFFICER: Are you aware that you passed a stop sign?

HERMAN: Huh?

OFFICER: On the previous block.

HERMAN: A nice restaurant?

OFFICER: No, the stop sign.

This one-on-one went back and forth for a while. The officer, having seen the government plates and GSA insignia on the car, figured he was dealing with two bureaucratic clowns and the city would never collect the fine anyway. He gave up and merely said. "You gentlemen please watch the traffic signs. Have a nice day."

HERMAN (To Burt): We'll go to the restaurant near the stop sign.

There were restaurant stories galore. When Herman handled the check Burt generally would go back to their table and supplement the meager tip Herman left, if any, although Burt also said that no amount for the tip would be worth the aggravation and humiliation that Herman would put the server through.

When the two finally arrived in Binghamton, there was a courtesy meeting with the mayor and city planners prior to the negotiations for a privately owned site. Politicians love when the government has a project in their town. Property values increase if the government is buying, jobs are created and contractors make money. It's a classic win-win situation.

When the meeting ended and the goodbyes were exchanged, Herman was still thinking of the events earlier in the day and perhaps his meal in the restaurant by the stop sign. He shook the mayor's hand, eyed the city planners and said, "It's always a pleasure to meet with the fine people of Elmira." He had completely forgotten that he was in Binghamton.

Another restaurant incident occurred when Herman, Burt and two other staffers went to lunch with the town attorney of an upstate New York community. Herman magnanimously picked up the check for all. After they said their farewells Herman turned and said, "Burrrt, your share is...." By the time he collected from Burt and the other staffers, who didn't even work for him, he had enough to cover the town attorney's meal as well as his own. It was widely circulated around the office that going to lunch with him could be both embarrassing and costly.

A claim to fame was his boardinghouse reach, which enabled him to stuff his suit pockets with cookies at any official function. He outdid himself the day he put a corned beef sandwich in his pocket with mustard dripping from the sides.

What do you expect from a guy also known as Paper Hawk, for his propensity to pick up used newspapers on the subway in the morning? He was the kind of guy who would go into a beanery for breakfast, take a newspaper from the stand, read it with breakfast, slobber coffee and crumbs all over it, tear out a few discount coupons and then put the paper back on the stand. Why pay for a used newspaper?

Herm also used the government cafeteria in our building to entertain his business clients. He would enjoy his subsidized lunch and then leave his tray right on the table and walk out. I guess he thought the government provided busboys to clean up after him.

Herman was so oblivious to the people around him that when a group of former employees visited the office and walked in to say hello to him out of courtesy, he at first didn't remember where he knew them but from the conversation realized that they were former associates. He began to warm up and say things like, "How's the new job?" or "How long has it been that you're gone?" At that point I took my clue and got up from my desk got in line, shook hands with him and said, "Nice to see you, Herman."

I received the same response. "How's the new job?" He had no clue that I was still employed there and sat a few feet from his cubby hole.

There is a final word of wisdom from a mentor. Burt would tell the story of their car ride to the Rockaway section of Queens County in New York City to eyeball a potential site. On the ride out during which Burt insisted on driving this time, Herman said, "Now Burrrt, when we get there don't call attention to yourself."

This would have been excellent advice had Herman not alighted from the clearly marked government car and opened up a huge site plan in front of him. Despite the precise dimensions indicated on the plan and certified by the engineer who prepared the drawings, Herman held the open plans in his arms in front of him and paced the site. It only took a few minutes for a crowd to gather. The little gesture touched off local real estate speculation which jacked up the price the government would have eventually paid, had Congress ever appropriated money for the project.

At least he had his pants on.

* * *

During my transition from the technician years to the management years I made the acquaintance of several additional people who would be with me for a good part of my working life.

In the typing pool sat Bronx-born and bred Elizabeth Colleen "Liz" O'Hanlon. Elizabeth was a lovely lady with no hidden agenda. Going from typist to secretary was the extent of her career goal. She put in her eight hours conscientiously and then went home with no worries.

Liz slowly graduated from the typing pool to the branch chief's secretary. When I later became chief of that very branch I inherited Liz. As was customary when one came into a position like that, you rarely changed support personnel unless there was a major calamity or personality conflict. Liz stayed on as my secretary and moved with me for a good part of my middle management career.

For all of her virtues as a person she had a few flaws in the work place. First, she was non-assertive so as branch secretary she had trouble delegating or even requesting others to do work on my behalf. Her second flaw was her absolute desecration of the English language. Much of this might have had to do with her limited education or that she simply heard things differently than the rest of us. For these little quirks she ultimate received the nickname Dizzy Lizzy which stayed with her most of her career.

Nobody ever wanted to hurt her, but she would drive us crazy with incorrect messages or using words with a completely different meaning than what she meant. When I first became branch chief she reminded me that she would need some odd days off for follow-up medical appointments from her recent *evasive* surgery.

Since the two of us worked closely for a long time I was generally able to translate what she said into what she meant. When she left a message from "Juan the Gardener" I knew she meant Warren Gardner; I knew Caponello meant Capolino; Stan Horace was Stan Harris, etc. Every now and then she would slip up, causing embarrassment. One such instance was when she left me a message to return the call of Mr. Golden who at the time was the Administrator of General Services. After calling Washington and getting an annoyed reply from a staffer that the administrator had never called me, I found out the message was actually from Mr. Goldner who worked for me and sat thirty feet away. She also caused me grief when she left a message from a Dr. Harper who was an oncologist in a hospital where my wife had a minor surgical procedure. It turned out that the call was actually from a Dr. Halper, a radiologist who told me all was fine.

I grew to know exactly what Liz meant when she used terms like "preach what you practice," "pound wise and penny foolish," or "Price Westinghouse." My favorite was when she described a restaurant incident during which a customer possibly saved the life of another diner by applying the "Heineken maneuver."

Another interesting personality who grew on me over the years was one Giuseppe Verdi DiGiacomo, who acquired the natural nickname of "Joe D." Joe was a loyal and hard worker with a heart of gold. He was a family man who went to church regularly. As a productive employee, however, he was a liability. When Joe was brought up past his "level of incompetence" he could do next to nothing right. In addition, like his associate Alfred Neuman, he had that unique ability to be in the wrong place at the wrong time.

Joe's command of the written word was something to behold. When inspecting a parcel of property for which he was given by-the-numbers instructions, he started his narrative with those now famous in GSA words, "I exposed myself to another building. It was an elevated building with the front door on the side."

Joe came to GSA as a draftsman, a skill he learned in a two week course at the Apex Institute under a GI Bill grant. The art of manual drafting disappeared from GSA, given the development of computer programs to do the task and the economics of outsourcing the work on an as needed basis. Joe eventually ceased his drafting function and the agency attempted to train him in the realty field. It was as a realty specialist that Joe had the opportunity to demonstrate his lack of ability with great frequency. He was generally tasked with support roles rather than taking the lead in any type of negotiation or space acquisition.

When his boss at the time, Large Lewis, sent him to Freeport, Long Island to do an inspection of the Grace Building as a possible new acquisition, he produced a meticulously detailed report of the Grace Building, but unfortunately it was of the building with the same title in Massapequa, New York.

Then there was a final measurement to precede acceptance of a major block of renovated leased space in the Statler Hotel in Buffalo, which had been converted to general office space. Notwithstanding the architect's certified measurement of the space, Joe, using a tape measure throughout every crevice of the two floors of occupancy, insisted that the space was less than one percent below the architect's certification and the stated leased amount. He demanded a credit even though the space was leased on a lump sum and the square foot rate was backed into only because it was required in our documents. This nonsense went on for weeks, delaying occupancy and generating a claim which we ultimately had to settle at great expense.

Perhaps Joe's finest achievement as a leasing specialist came when Large Lewis entrusted him to rent parking and garage space for the GSA motor pool in Trenton, New Jersey. What could go wrong?

Left unsupervised, Joe awarded a lease to a garage owner who was equally inept. Joe stuck the boilerplate clauses in the lease which were applicable to an office rental. When our inspector general looked at this lease because of a complaint from an unsuccessful bidder, they determined that the description of the leased premises was so vague that they couldn't determine what space the government was actually renting. However, they insisted that GSA enforce the terms of the lease, thereby requiring this owner to provide a garage with daily cleaning and controlled temperatures as if it was an office.

Joe wouldn't bend. Large Lewis who was a reasonable person would have overruled Joe and succumbed but the IG insisted that the terms of the lease be enforced and there be no "waste, fraud and abuse."

Within six months the lessor was so strangled by the lease that he lost his property to the bank. Saddled with this impossible lease the property had no investment value. The bank's house counsel was a slick New Jersey attorney who challenged the terms of the lease. The GSA Board of Contract Appeals ruled that the lease was invalid and ordered us to amend it with terms as originally intended before the two characters got involved. The bank later resold the property, which now had value with a solid government lease, to an even slicker New Jersey developer who ultimately assembled a parcel for subsidized residential development.

Giuseppe Verdi DiGiacomo went back to laying out desks at a drawing table using a template, as he had originally learned at the Apex Institute.

CHAPTER 10

Opinion of Counsel

As I became more skilled on the job and was thrust into new situations, usually under close supervision, I met more of the people who would influence my career and life.

When I began having interaction with our legal staff, or Regional Counsel, as that office was known, I learned why lawyers are regarded one step ahead of car dealers. I used to hear Symphony Sid screaming at our legal advisors, even though he had a law degree himself. I knew early that there was a natural conflict between productivity and legal representation.

The first time I stepped into the office of Associate Counsel Hartwyck M. Wilford III, I was flabbergasted. He was on the phone, buried behind a desk full of papers but he gave me a nod to wait at the door. He did not shoo me out of the office or request privacy. By the tone of his conversation my impression of government service was about to change, at least for the moment.

He was in a serious conversation with Sid. "Don't get caught," were the first decipherable words. I was concerned that I was witnessing something which could later get me fired as an accessory. "Just don't get caught," the wise counselor repeated. I was worried.

My nervousness peaked when the tone rose and he said in a final bit of animated counseling. "Look, Sid, it's fifty bucks. Just don't get caught. Nothing else."

For weeks I walked around with this apparent indiscretion on my mind. My opinion of both Symphony Sid and Hartwyck M. Wilford III, Esq. had diminished. My faith in humanity returned weeks later when I found out that the fifty bucks represented a pool of cash from the Regional Counsel staff and that "Don't Get Caught" was not an admonition, but a thoroughbred horse owned by Wilford's uncle and racing at Belmont Park. Sid was merely taking the wad of cash to the local Off Track Betting parlor to place the wager which was shared by some ten people, including Sid.

I quickly learned that "Legal," in addition to their learned counsel, was a source for sports debate or trivia and access to the turf accounting trade when the OTB office was not handy. Over the years we got along rather well, save for those incidents when their insistence on the perfect contract and one hundred percent protection for the government (and the legal staff) overrode the need to get the job done. I have seen many perfect contracts in my day. Unfortunately no contractor would dare sign them.

*   *   *

Along the way, counsel's office was headed by a series of appointees. One, "Sweet" Caroline Taylor, Esq. was regional counsel for a few years. During her tenure she was primarily pre-occupied with matters concerning government ethics, committee reports, budgeting, petty cash accountability, labor disputes, office equipment and compliance with historic preservation statutes. Fortunately she was rarely involved with real estate or construction contracting matters. Her deputy, Mr. Wilford, handled all of that and did a miraculous job of keeping her out of the loop.

I had a roller coaster relationship with legal. While I appreciated their ability and diligence I had difficulty with what seemed to be an attitude to protect the government from suits and claims rather than complete a project. On labor-management matters I had major issues with "The Knights Who Say No" and their lack of aggressiveness and pre-emptive action, a matter that haunted me during most of my management career and beyond.

Several of my conflicts with Sweet Caroline were over donuts. Yes, donuts.

Caroline devoted much of her career to assuring that no government employee ever violated any ethical standards, no matter how much this policy cost or embarrassed the government. There are always a few bad apples but I doubt if any would sell the government out for coffee and donuts. Caroline kept vigilance.

Government policy allows acceptance of token food and even a full meal under certain circumstances. There are restrictions, most of which are tied to common business sense and the premise that perception could mean more than reality. If you were seen in a fine restaurant with a contractor, even if you paid your own way, it could be interpreted by an observer as a compromising situation. You avoid those possibilities.

My first conflict over the sinkers came during my tenure as director of real estate. We had some surplus street level space that we were trying to lease out. Prior to issuing a formal solicitation we placed a newspaper ad seeking interest. Among the inquirers was a corporation holding a few Dunkin' Donuts franchises. They sent a letter requesting a copy of the solicitation. Clipped to the top of the page was a coupon advising that the bearer was entitled to two free donuts at "any participating location." Before passing the letter on to Kevin X. Reilly, Esq., our surplus property guru, I hand wrote a tongue in cheek comment on the letter, "Better check with the ethics counselor on the donuts," with an arrow pointing to the coupon. Anyone who knew me well would have known that I was just joking, but not Kevin X. He also had a compassion for all others to be squeaky clean.

Despite his love of donuts he took it upon himself to refer the issue to the ethics counselor. I knew nothing about the referral, the three hours of meetings and the citations from the various sections of the United States Code on the subject. My first hint of this was when a letter to the Dunkin' Donuts franchisee was presented to me for signature, written by Reilly, but reviewed and edited multiple times by counsel. The original coupon for the two donuts was attached to the letter, which essentially advised that in accordance with the code, we were not permitted to accept gifts (not so in the case of donuts but I had neither the time or patience to challenge it). The fact that we were returning the gift would be no reflection on them and they were still welcome to bid on the surplus space.

I signed the letter, put the carbon copies in my out box for distribution and ripped up the original. The next morning I had two delicious cinnamon donuts with my coffee.

That was not the final donut episode.

Years later, while working on the Foley Square Project, history repeated itself.

Each short-listed bidder, as part of the process, had to make a formal presentation of their proposed design and project management plan for the new courthouse. One of the bidders was a consortium of a major developer, a major architectural firm, and a large builder. For the purpose of this book I will refer to the presenter as "Bidder 502."

The Bidder 502 designation came about because a design jury of prominent architects evaluated initial proposals and in accordance with accepted procedure, they were not to know the identity of the bidders. We hadn't thought about how we were going to code the submissions so when I received an inquiry from a developer I looked behind me at the plastic bag under my credenza with a pair of Levi 501 jeans I bought at lunchtime. "Mark your drawings '501'" I told the bidder. When the submissions from all the bidders came in they were coded 501 through 505.

For the morning of their scheduled presentation Bidder 502 asked that we set up a speakers' podium, a screen, a table in the front to display the models and a table in the back for an undisclosed purpose. No problem.

It turns out that the rear table was for coffee and donuts, delivered by a local caterer. They had actually asked me if this was OK a few days before. I saw no problem with a modest spread limited to just the coffee and the donuts. There is nothing improper about this, even in rigid government circles.

The fireworks started soon enough. When Frank Bennett, the Managing Partner of 502's New York office got up to introduce the team members and begin the presentation, a shriek came from the rear. "Excuse me! Excuse me! Before we start I have an announcement," said our learned counsel as she bolted to the podium as if she was about to tell Bennett that his fly was open.

Caroline seized the microphone. Some of the development and government team members looked in my direction. Knowing that whatever was about to happen would not be good, I slowly slithered downward.

"Our developers have generously provided coffee and donuts for us," she told us, as if we didn't notice. "As you know there are restrictions on government employees accepting gifts (A donut is now a gift?). If you plan to have coffee or a donut you should leave payment in the cup on the table. A fair price would be fifty cents for coffee and fifty cents for a donut."

The development team looked at me. I was only able to shrug my shoulders and roll my eyes. The damage was done. Their momentum was halted. My own people looked at me but they witnessed similar drills in the past so it wasn't as startling.

Frank and his team were dumbfounded by this turn of events. He lost his whole train of thought on this presentation of a $300 million project because of a coffee and donuts issue. The presentation continued although most were already distracted.

Caroline, as things would have it, had no change with her and borrowed the fifty cents from Hartwyck for her coffee. At the end of the day there was fifty cents in the cup and a whole lot of leftover coffee and donuts. Nobody wanted to be seen approaching the table because they knew Caroline would come up to them to assure they made payment.

We ended up spilling out the cold coffee and inviting all (except the legal staff) to come to our office for donuts that afternoon.

As things turned out, the 502 team, for all of its efforts, never got the contract. They maintained that they lost out because of a poor presentation.

* * *

Caroline's pursuit of justice and integrity was relentless, except for herself.

She was the regional ethics officer, which meant that each year she and her staff would spend endless hours reviewing the financial disclosure statements submitted by any employee who was remotely involved in contracting. The senior managers had to provide far more detail, disclosing the names of all institutions in which they or their family members held bank accounts, stock holdings, real estate, etc. or had a financial or employment interest. It was her job, or so she thought, to be sure there were no conflicts of interest; hence if one owned ten shares of AT&T she would want a statement which certified that you would recuse yourself of any participation in decisions affecting telephone service. It got worse. If you owned a mutual fund which had AT&T shares she would expect the same certification. This applied to yourself and immediate members of your household. When my daughter was purveying hamburgers at McDonald's I had to certify that she had no influence in their pursuit of government catering contracts.

Some of us managed to keep Caroline very busy, which was a service to the organization; the more time spent on nonsense meant the less time she would spend on real issues which would then be delegated to her capable staff.

One of our Asian associates, Wing Hom, excitedly came in one day claiming good information on a Chinese penny stock dealing in electronics. This was going to make us all rich and at least twenty of us bought shares. When Carolyn saw these shares of Tianjin Industrial listed on so many financial disclosure statements she practically launched an attorney general investigation. She thought there was some kind of conspiracy and we had to be dealing with privileged information (of which she would have liked to have been a part).

The investigation quietly went away, as did any value to the stock. We had been led to believe that this information came from Wing's brother in Hong Kong but it came from his barber in Flushing.

My problems with worthless stock were nothing compared to what one of my senior bosses had to endure.

His wife was a principal in a major department store chain, thereby a stockholder who would presumably benefit when the government bought a few pencils from the store. My boss had to step aside from participation in any decisions involving a purchase from the store. But that was not the most severe conflict of interest. His wife also had a side fashion consulting business to the rich and influential. Caroline demanded a list of the clients, although none had anything to do with the government or its contractors. She issued a letter of counseling to my boss stating that his wife was to be very careful about future clients who might have a relationship with GSA. She wanted to know what advice my boss's wife gave her clients. His wife responded in writing, stating that she helped people pick the right gown for a social event based upon the person's height, coloring, body shape and current styles. My boss thought that the real reason for all of this probing was that Caroline wanted some free fashion advice.

To be assured that Caroline stayed out of important issues, Hartwyck, an early daily arrival, would personally pick up Counsel's mail from the mailroom and remove any correspondence which he didn't want her to see or involve herself. He would divert administrative or personnel stuff to her and insulate her from almost anything of real substance, thus keeping her occupied and allowing her to eventually take credit for the real work when a project was completed or a major contract executed.

Things got so bad that Hartwyck and I met in staircases, the cafeteria or the men's room to avoid her interference. On more than one occasion I submitted a bogus request to legal which I knew would keep her busy. Legal had to approve requests for permission to serve alcoholic beverages at parties in the building so one of those requests was usually good to keep her busy composing a reply and list of conditions for a day or two. There was always a risk, however, that she would want to meet on the subject and that would wipe out the better part of a day.

*　*　*

I always felt a bit of personal satisfaction when a pompous attorney becomes humbled.

The incident started out as an ordinary spring day but it didn't take long before all hell broke loose, once again triggered by the uninvolved.

The structure of the new courthouse at Foley Square was nearing completion. The builder was in the process of constructing a tunnel (for prisoner movement) between the new building and the Metropolitan Correction Center ("MCC") across the street.

The process for the city to convey an underground easement to the federal government to allow this construction was so convoluted that once again we reverted to the court for a friendly condemnation. Aside from the expected engineering complications involving utilities under the street, maintaining traffic flow and allowing access to the MCC during construction for the secure transport of prisoners, we had to deal with the usual gang of attorneys and other obstructionists who thought we might disturb a buried 200 year old cistern (This was the site of the notorious Five Points neighborhood, depicted in the movie *The Gangs of New York*.) or we might deprive someone of their First Amendment rights by moving their protest across the street.

The scene was set for a large gathering of suits on the driveway which accesses the MCC.

One of our archeology scholars who had been observing the construction under a contract which the government was funding in order to keep the historians and preservationists at bay noticed what to her appeared to be a segment of a human bone in the excavated earth, which she sifted with a strainer. This is just what an archeologist lives for. Stop the project!

Instead of notifying the project director whom she knew would be unsympathetic towards this historic discovery, she chose instead to first call her boss who then called the GSA head archaeology guru in the region, Bart "Bigfoot" Lofton, who took it upon himself to walk to the site and direct the job superintendent to cease all excavation.

I became aware of this expensive calamity in the making when I received an urgent call from the developer's project manager, Mike Anderson who skipped the usual salutations. "Who the fuck is this Lofton character – the new job supe!"

At this point, Cardinal Hayes Place had already been blocked by the contractor, preventing the U.S. Marshal from securely moving prisoners into the MCC where some were incarcerated and others were held awaiting trial at the adjoining courthouse. The marshal and the warden were already bonkers over this because that very afternoon an alleged hit man for South American drug lord Pablo Escobar was being delivered for trial.

The lineup of suits included the developer's project director, the government project team, and representatives of the contractor, the U.S. Marshals Service and the Metropolitan Correction Center. Rounding out this group was a team of crack government attorneys to make sure the government's rights were protected at all costs.

Ms. Caroline, our chief attorney was there. She supplied a lot of words about the National Historic Preservation Act that nobody wanted to hear. Hartwyck was a voice of reason. The legal team was rounded out with Gabriel Sacks, an idealistic liberal who didn't believe in prisons anyway. His claim to fame was to make rambling speeches and to prepare contracts and agreements which were so lengthy and incomprehensible that nobody would ever sign them, thereby protecting the government by doing nothing which presented a risk even if it meant not completing its mission.

There were about fifteen people all jabbering at once at the vehicle entrance to the MCC, blocking access. Anderson and Lofton almost came to blows; the attorneys were citing the United States Code; the marshal claimed we were obstructing justice and the warden said if we didn't open Cardinal Hayes Place for vehicles soon he was going to have to move prisoners in shackles through the street.

Meanwhile, the archeologist, the only non-suit there, said if we didn't stop the construction we would be in violation of New York City Landmarks Commission regulations (as if these construction and law enforcement people could really care). For every minute of delay on the job the cash registers were ka-chinging.

I've always had the utmost respect for the U.S. Marshals Service. They have a tough job which they do with utmost professionalism. All of us at GSA normally tried to accommodate their needs. The last thing anyone needed would be to have a prisoner escape or a judge shot because the marshal had a lapse.

Our attorneys huddled in a corner of the pack, discussing strategy. Just then we got the word that the caravan escorting Escobar's man was approaching the area. A uniformed marshal politely asked the group to move to the side, away from the approach to the underground entrance to the MCC. Everyone complied except the three attorneys who continued to stay immobile on the site like discarded trash. When the uniformed marshal approached and again suggested they move away, Mr. Sacks said something like, "We are government attorneys. You can't tell a group of lawyers where to stand. It's a free country."

There was no further discussion. A dozen armed marshals exited the vehicles with M-16 and 9mm rifles, wearing bullet proof vests, shouting "Hut-hut!" and assumed their positions for the prisoner movement. A construction worker was ordered at gunpoint to get his head away from the fence and the attorneys were prodded with the business end of semi-automatic rifles to change their opinion about where they chose to stand. Sacks forgot about the U.S. Code and his

First Amendment rights and headed for the sanctity of his office to write some more incomprehensible contracts. Caroline claimed the entire episode was staged. The day was shot as far as any further tunnel excavation.

By the time the day ended, Charley Fraser, the GSA project manager, Hartwyck the sensible attorney and Howard Morton, the onsite affirmative action rep and neighborhood liaison for the developer had quietly contacted our preservation consultant who made the determination that the uncovered bone fragment was canine and of no historical significance. Caper over.

Howard told me that he was very nervous over what transpired. "The kids with the guns were tense. One wrong move by your lawyers and we could have had a shootout right on the site."

It was nice to see an opinion of counsel abruptly changed, even though it was at gunpoint.

The day was far from over. A newly appointed undersecretary of labor for contract compliance visited our regional administrator and toured the site. Her only interests were to assure that her office would be able to make newsworthy presentations to the contractors at the end of the job during which time they could emphasize that it was the Democratic Clinton administration responsible for the two buildings and all of the jobs provided during construction (the project was actually planned and funded during the Republican Reagan administration). She also wanted to stress that an upcoming project in Brooklyn should be awarded as part of "a Democratic gift" to the city.

To top off my day I fielded a barrage of inquiries from *Newsday* and the *New York Times* about some subcontractors on Long Island who were allegedly handling contaminated soil removed from the courthouse site. All they wanted was for me to grunt in such a way that I, a government representative, could be quoted as saying we are knowingly doing business with an indicted contractor. The facts of the case were that I had never heard of the subcontractor to which they referred. Of course there were others who *were* on the job which did not exactly, if you would pardon the pun, have clean hands. But then again, if we insisted that all of our subcontractors be squeaky clean, there would be nobody left to work on the project except lawyers. Fortunately nobody mentioned the sunken barge and I was not about to bring it up.

When I arrived home that evening I drank wine straight from the jug.

CHAPTER 11

More Rules of the Rogue

Although my ten original business principles should be remembered and respected at all times, they are not the only wisdom I have to offer. I spent enough time observing the idiosyncrasies of the bureaucracy to qualify as a civil service soothsayer.

It is a well-known criminology (and for our purposes, bureaucracy) principle that past performance is the best predictor of future behavior. A leopard doesn't change its spots. People don't change. If you didn't like someone in high school the chances are you won't like them at the thirty year reunion. Here are some random thoughts which everyone who has worked for, against or with a bureaucracy should commit to memory. They are guaranteed to happen.

The person receiving credit for resolving a problem is generally the one who caused the problem in the first place.

This is not my own. This was also with my "Professor Meyer" notes. It ties in to the well worn *credit to the uninvolved* theory. A perfect example would be the case of a former Administrator of General Services who, without consulting with any advisors, made an unexpected announcement tantamount to a recommendation to dismantle the agency. He "suggested" a plan wrought with politically unacceptable recommendations (fire everybody), illegal and impractical recommmendations (hire them back as independent contractors) and just plain incomprehensible political gibberish. It took the agency and the overseers in Congress by surprise. If the suggestion made any sense whatsoever the Congress would prefer to take credit.

After the initial turmoil GSA was directed to submit a plan for continuity, which was done by the careerists and actually resulted in GSA gaining more respect and more responsibility from Congress. This former administrator then pronounced to the world that he had saved the agency.

If you think I have a bug in my colon for this individual it is not without cause. When our successful Foley Square project was in the center of a media storm and congressional investigation, all of which found no improprieties, Mr. Administrator saw an opportunity to make himself a white knight at the expense of the careerists, once again before getting the facts.

In May 1994, Senator Howard Metzenbaum, who was chairing a task force on the Senate Committee on the Environment and Public Works, had read the *Newsday* article which insinuated but never substantiated improprieties in our contract. He promptly called the project a fiasco, referring to the GSA contracting personnel as criminals. Mr. Administrator got his name in the paper by announcing that he ordered a full inspector general investigation, concurrent with the congressionally ordered Department of Justice review. The IG report, issued September 27, 1995 (I still keep a copy with my career souvenirs) found nothing of an improper nature, yet the careerists who were in the center of this storm, including myself, still felt the stigma because he had refused to issue any type of statement exonerating anyone. All he did was show up in the New York office one day after a multiple martini lunch and talk about the "great things this administration was doing for us." During the course of the project there were fourteen separate investigations, none of which turned up one scintilla of evidence of any improprieties on the part of GSA staffers.

This same administration wanted to make a splash over how the Government saved money when the scope of the 290 Broadway construction project was modified to preserve the African Burial Ground. The politically appointed deputy administrator came to the site, spent three minutes getting briefed about this billion dollar project, told us everything we did wrong and then wanted to know how much money we saved by reducing the scope. No matter how many times I and my project engineer tried to explain that although we negotiated a $10 million credit, this was a project already fully designed and under construction so that the actual value in the original bid of the work to be deleted was in the vicinity of $20 million. The $10 million credit was actually a $10 million expense for which nothing was received. To top that off, there was more than $30 million in modifications to accommodate the redesign of the building, acceleration to preserve the original schedule, relocation of a major construction hoist, modifying mechanical equipment, steel and interior finishes, and more. When all was said and done, the $10 million "savings" was a $40 million expense. The administration still thinks it saved the government money. The forty million does not include any of the memorial and research costs which followed.

To add further insult to injury, this administrator was still in office when the buildings were completed, so his name appears on the cornerstones right below that of the president. Every time I walk down Broadway and see the cornerstone of the Federal Office Building I feel like barfing. It was my wish that on my last day on the job I would walk up to the cornerstone and urinate on it. It's just the right height.

Any memorandum that begins with words like "It has come to my attention…" means that someone screwed up and everyone is paying for it.

This happens all the time. It is generally an overreaction to something small. Take the case of another White House appointed GSA Administrator, back in the seventies, who proceeded to tick off the entire agency before he ever reported to work. About the time this pseudo southern gentleman was confirmed by the Senate there was some press about petty thievery within the agency involving construction and maintenance contracts. This was unfortunate but in terms of the volume of business that the agency did, and in comparison to private industry, the extent of this was negligible and could have easily been dealt with internally without fanfare.

But no, another politician wanted to make headlines. The Man from Tennessee magnanimously announced, "I am going to drag this agency into the twentieth century," assuring himself of just about no respect or cooperation out of the rank and file. Within months he created a subculture of people and organizations designed to oversee others and be sure we had perfectly foolproof contracts, even if it meant that nobody in his right mind in the private sector would ever sign them. He so spooked the agency with a *gotcha* mentality that for the next dozen years our contracting people were concerned more with protecting themselves than to execute the best deals for the government. During that time frame we became a stagnant organization, almost unable to function.

One of his claims to fame, or infamy, was that he had concluded that when we leased space and had the lessor perform the tenant fitouts we were not getting the best deal because we were in effect doing this without competition. The fact that we were competitively bidding the leases which included the scope of improvements was lost on him. He issued a declaration that from hereon in we were to lease space and contract separately for alterations. This was again contrary to the advice of his staff of knowledgeable careerists.

Any amateur who has ever leased space, occupied space or walked into an office building, especially in a big city, understands that when you lease finished space, your rent starts when the base fit-out is complete. Any additional specialized work comes later on your own nickel. With this in mind, if you bid all of your work out separately and you start alterations on the first day of occupancy, under a best case scenario you are talking about a few months of rent before actual use of the space. Compound that with the fact that most landlords want to either approve of your contractors or refuse to let contractors not of their own choosing touch their building systems and you have a dilemma. There is also the issue of those union or trade association fellows who might have something to say about who works in the territory which then limits the number of contractors who would even bid the job for you.

The Man from Tennessee also demanded that we have the perfect alteration contract, which at the risk of being redundant, nobody in his right mind would ever sign. During that wonderful era we constantly were faced with empty leased space for which we were paying rent, and our customers were not able to use. This gave our inspector general and the media a field day for "investigative reports" which revealed waste and mismanagement because of all this empty space. Once that happens the Congress pounces on it with its share of "Special Committees" to investigate further so a congressman can announce how he cleaned up the agency.

Oh, yes, the Man instituted one other strangling feature. He determined that everyone should have the right to bid government jobs so if a project lingered unawarded for more than 120 days it should be withdrawn from the market and issued for bidding all over again even though this was time consuming, wasteful and turned legitimate contractors off from bidding our jobs.

When he mercifully left GSA he actually believed that he brought the agency into the twentieth century, as he originally proclaimed he would do. In my mind, GSA was at its lowest point ever during that administration.

In the long run the agency and the taxpayers benefited because well after Mr. Tennessee passed from GSA and this earth, changes in the law and internal policy drastically modified the contracting procedures for the better. Somewhere along the way we became a service organization and not a band of obstructionists.

Mr. Tennessee visited our offices a few years later, as a consultant to a GSA landlord who felt he was not being treated properly on an escalation (yearly lease adjustment for increased taxes and maintenance costs) issue. He used his clout for entry via the then regional administrator who called me and the chief of leasing into the meeting to discuss the issue.

While the regional administrator, who reluctantly agreed to this meeting, chomped on a giant hero sandwich and had tomato sauce dripping on his desk, Tennessee did most of the talking.

To impress us he first reminded us that he is a former GSA administrator, as if we didn't know; and he was representing a high power client. In his southern drawl he pleaded his case. "What you're doing to my client is not *fay-er*."

He got no further. Umberto "Bert" Pisani, my chief of leasing was so annoyed that Tennessee used political clout to try for an advantage to his client that he abruptly stated, "Wasn't it *your* administration which instituted our letter of the law policy on lease escalations? You did say something about dragging us into the twentieth century?"

"But it just isn't......"

"And wasn't it *your* administration that was severely criticized by GAO (Government Accountability Office) for inconsistent enforcement of the regulations?"

By this time Tennessee was fading and realizing that he was not going to peddle any influence. "Well, please see if you can do anything (he never said *please* when he was with GSA)." What he didn't know was that since he left GSA the formula to calculate escalations was modified, which allowed the contracting officer to use more of the actual costs rather than Consumer Price Index percentages. The original settlement offered to the owner gave him the maximum possible.

When Bert and I returned to our office Bert told the contracting officer. "Give him the minimum. Not one cent more." We figured that the fifteen minutes this pompous consultant spent with us cost his client $100,000 plus whatever he was foolish enough to pay Mr. Tennessee in fees. Sweet revenge.

Don't gloat over your successes. The chances are you will go downhill from there.

This is another one from a wise old college professor. As someone who has always been close to sports, I can appreciate that you never gloat or rub mud in the faces of your opponent because it will come back to haunt you.

When I was project executive for the Foley Square project, I was a hero. This mega-project was built on time and within budget.

Thankfully I didn't allow the accolades go to my head. A few years later, when we built the Long Island Courthouse, which had the largest claim in GSA history, and the Brooklyn Courthouse, which was probably the largest cost overrun in GSA history, I was somewhere between a bum and a criminal, depending upon which judge you asked. The secret was that at Foley we had unlimited money and as a wise scholar once said, "Money can do anything but raise you from the grave." At Foley Square it even did that.

If there was ever a character who should have heeded the rule about not flaunting yourself, it was Cyrus "The Virus" Lantos, one of the more pretentious individuals the agency had the privilege of employing. Cyrus was an intelligent man who let a little success, luck and the right lineage, leave him with an inflated self-worth. He came to GSA as a management intern based upon an introduction from his uncle who was in a high level management position. Cyrus actually thought he *earned* the job.

Cy worked his way up the ladder through a series of administrative and support jobs without ever having to put himself at risk or be accountable for the results. With his intelligence and gift of bullshit he maneuvered his way into a position in charge of a new GSA initiative with the acronym BARPH. It stood for "Better Accounting of Real Property Holdings" and was doomed from day one. Just the name was enough to tell you it was going nowhere.

Cyrus assembled a staff, stealing good people from real jobs and acting as if he was in charge of the most important initiative in agency history. He called meetings nationwide to "roll out" the initiative and had workshops wherein he would demand the attendance of the highest regional officials. He would ask for statistics and then send them back demanding pie charts. He would ask for lease data and then demand extraneous backup such as what he referred to as *concentric circles* plotting each lease and its distance from the regional offices, even though it was irrelevant to BARPH. He had half the country drawing concentric circles for his data accumulation.

GSA threw good money after bad into this program so as not to admit failure.

What happened to the BARPH initiative is not really important other than to say that it was a complete failure, something that even someone as intelligent as Cyrus could have predicted. However, why mess up a good deal and an extended meal ticket? The Virus flaunted his presumed success and his power beyond reason. When his house of cards came tumbling down he received little sympathy from the co-workers he offended along the way.

The last time I saw Cyrus tells the whole story. At a meeting at central office I needed to copy some material. I was directed to a room "down the hall" where there was a high speed copier. I walked out of a well-appointed office into a large room with a linoleum floor, exposed ceiling and hanging incandescent fixtures. The room could best be described as a utility room.

After entering I passed several rows of filing cabinets before coming to an opening near a bare window. One side of the room housed the copy machine I sought. On the other side was a gray metal desk with Cyrus forlornly sitting behind it. On top of the desk was a single line telephone and a copy of the *Washington Post*, open to the want ads.

This is what life in GSA boiled down to for the infectious Virus. He went from a corner office and a big staff to a hiding place in a file room pending departure.

"Hi Cy, what's doing?"

"Not much. I'm just checking out the opportunities available to me." Even in his waning days at the agency he exuded an aura of self-assurance (more like grandeur).

I heard that he later surfaced in private industry with modest success. He no doubt included the BARPH program on his list of accomplishments for his resume.

This country has too many lawyers.

I don't think I'll get much opposition on this, except from attorneys.

If the ratio of lawyers to engineers was the same in this country as it is in Japan or China we wouldn't be losing manufacturing to Asia and South America and when you call for technical support for your computer you won't have to talk to a guy named "Chuck" in Mumbai.

I won't do any lawyer bashing because I have someone of greater credibility to do it for me.

Lee Iacocca's 1988 book *Talking Straight* contains twelve pages of non-stop lawyer trashing, highlighted by his summary. "I went home half sick. I couldn't eat or sleep. I came to the realization that our whole country was drowning in legal bullshit."

In Iacocca's 2007 book, *Where Have All the Leaders Gone?* he doesn't mellow on lawyers. Discussing the regulatory and environmental issues associated with developing a meaningful energy program, he states, "Here's a tip: Never turn the future of your country over to lawyers."

On a more serious note he also observes that it's a sad commentary when doing nothing for fear of legal ramifications, is a better solution than aggressiveness or taking reasonable risk.

Time after time I've heard our legal advisors inundate us with standard lines such as, "We can't do that, the bidders will protest," or "We can't do that, the contractor will file a claim," or "We can't do that, we can get sued."

This attitude quickly spreads to others, such as those engaged in human resources who often perceive themselves as regulators rather than support personnel. "We can't question the person's job application. We can be sued," or "We can't eliminate this applicant without an interview because he can file an EEO claim." The fact that the person had a felony conviction and a D+ college average was apparently not relevant.

As a manager with a production responsibility, it was no surprise that my relationship over the years with our legal and human resources staffs was a bit testy.

Always keep a supply of smart answers to stupid questions.

This is taken right out of that classic business textbook, *Mad Magazine*. In your career you are bound to field your share of dumb questions which are setups for smart answers. It's something I just can't resist, but I recommend that you use this advice judiciously. It's nice to humor people but don't humiliate them.

My attitude and aptitude for smart answers came while waiting on tables in the Catskill Mountains during my college days. Once, I was standing near the front entrance to the dining room just as it opened for breakfast, greeting guests as they made their way into the room. The entrance had to be at least 100 feet from my tables. When one of my elderly guests entered and spotted me at the door he smiled and said, "Goodmorningorangejuice." My reply was "Sure, would you like it here or at the table?"

Then there was the time when I was irritated; when I served a nice slice of chocolate cake for dessert to one of my ornery guests and he said, "I would like two pieces," I took a knife, cut the slice in half and said, "Now you have two pieces." That little move probably cut my tip in half. My irritability with petty nonsense was to continue throughout my career.

You can tell by my speech and my attitude that I am a New Yorker. I spent my entire GSA career in the New York office. I was one of the few GSA senior managers to have never moved during their careers. Often, when I traveled or met with groups I would get the anticipated question, "Have you lived in New York all your life?" My answer was always the same. "Not yet."

Finally, I refer to that great bureaucratic phrase, "level of comfort." After a meeting or presentation I have often been asked, "Are you comfortable?" to which I can't resist replying, "I make a nice living."

CHAPTER 12

Don't Kill the Golden Goose

The last time I saw Calvin Coolidge Coburn he was lying prone on a gurney, unconscious and covered with a blanket. I don't recall the exact year but the outspoken Calvin always would talk about "that Hillbilly peanut farmer in the White House" which narrows the time frame to the late seventies.

Calvin was one of those amazing characters about whom you sometimes wonder how he survived so long in business and life. Our career paths overlapped for about ten years and we worked together on a few projects, but I dare say that he never even knew my name.

He was small in stature and sported thinning grayish hair, worn in a crew cut. Word had been that he spent a lot of years with the US Army Corps of Engineers working on dredging projects in Panama and other tropical areas. This explained his propensity for seersucker suits, straw hats and to the extent that they were provided by others, Cuban cigars and Captain Morgan Rum. His favorite expression was "Don't kill the golden goose," and he used it often, generally when someone did something threatening to his routine, such as schedule a Friday meeting, or to endanger his appetite for anything which was free.

I had seen him stuff his pockets with sandwiches from a buffet, cheese Danish from a contractor-provided coffee break spread, and even reach into a box of cigars in a contractor's office to put a few in his inside jacket pocket. This must be what he meant by the golden goose.

Calvin was the ultimate master when it came to stretching the government travel dollar for his benefit. When traveling, he would sleep at the local Y, fill up on finger food at Happy Hours and, since the per diem was allocated based on the four six-hour quadrants in the day, he always managed to start his travel near the end of a quadrant, and end it shortly after a quadrant began. By doing this, if he managed to be away for just over twenty four hours, he would be paid per diem for six quadrants, or a day and a half. He also had this knack for imploring the motor pool dispatcher to assign him a station wagon, just in case he decided that the vehicle would also serve as a hotel room.

Calvin was an engineer. I was basically a customer agency liaison person early in my career. We worked in different offices, with different bosses who often had different agendas. I would work with our building occupants and our in-house or contracted architects to develop the project requirements. Calvin would execute the project with the contractor and often would serve the role of contracting officer's representative ("COR"). In the projects we worked together I was responsible to determine the space needs of the job, that they were in compliance with all federal regulations, real or promulgated, and that there was funding available. Calvin, as COR, was the onsite person to assure compliance with engineering specifications and certify that payments to contractors were in order. He would often negotiate pricing for change orders after the initial bid.

Despite a few idiosyncrasies, Cal was a capable and conscientious employee during the forty percent of the company time which he actually spent working. When we worked together during the construction of a new federal building in Buffalo, New York, Calvin spent his Mondays driving from New York to Buffalo in a GSA car. He claimed to have an aversion to flying but it was more an aversion to working on Mondays. Tuesday mornings would be spent organizing the work week and Fridays would be expended by the drive home. In between there was a generous amount of time dedicated to contractor-provided "working" lunches, and a few extended Happy Hours at some of the Chippewa Street bars.

It was on Chippewa Street before its regentrification that Calvin found himself in tight quarters. While sitting in one of the blue-collar bars he introduced himself as The Man. He claimed to be "in charge of the construction project," and was immediately assumed to be the general contractor. Times were tough in an industrialized Buffalo then (Remember *Full Monty?*) and with each free drink pushed his way Calvin promised a job to an unemployed tradesman.

I had long since departed for my room at the old Statler Hilton Hotel when Calvin instinctively found his way back to the Y without getting mugged by the downtown regulars of the era. Fortunately for him, he woke up with his head so jammed that he couldn't arrive at the job site until mid-morning or he would have received a major tune-up from the job seekers. It was not a pretty sight having to barricade ourselves in a construction trailer while the federal police held the job seekers at bay trying to convince them that this was a terrible misunderstanding. To assure that Calvin didn't arrive during this commotion, which then would have turned to possible homicide, we dispatched a junior member of the staff to keep him within the walls of the Y through the morning.

When Calvin finally arrived at the job site he had no remembrance of the evening before or the promises he made. He never knew how close he came to a disability retirement that day. All he did was to mutter "Don't kill the golden goose" about a dozen times.

Eventually time and alcohol took their toll. At the restaurant where his retirement luncheon was held a group of close friends and associates dutifully bade him a fond farewell with the appropriate certificate of appreciation from the regional administrator who, of course, was unable to attend. The choice of a venue for his sendoff was problematic. In the past he had been requested not to return to a number of the popular package luncheon places because of his complaints about portion sizes and accusations that the house was watering the drinks.

With Calvin at the dais, surrounded on one side by his boss (whom he despised) and a close co-worker on the other side who always covered for him during his indiscretions, he savored the moment. While he chomped on a Cubano, the young waitress offered his customary rum straight up.

"Is that Captain Morgan Rum?"

"Why yes, sir."

Calvin removed his seersucker jacket. "Leave the bottle."

His boss, feigning sincerity, said a few kind words and Calvin drank.

Friends said some kind words and Calvin drank.

A few contractors, who profited by Calvin's occasionally overlooking a less than workmanlike, but not quite fraudulent installation, spoke about what a dedicated servant of the public Calvin had been. Calvin drank.

The party ended and the folks strolled back to work, most a little groggy. Calvin and a few retired chums stayed longer. Calvin finished the original Captain Morgan fifth and then some. As I understood, he was escorted back to the office to say his final goodbyes and bring his personal possessions home.

I had my last glimpse of him as I left the building that evening. He was in the lobby, outside of the health unit, where he was unconscious on the gurney. The Captain Morgan had kicked in big time.

Calvin rarely mentioned his family although we knew he actually had some semblance of a traditional family relationship. His retirement was no exception. No family members were present or reachable. This left his co-workers with the dilemma of trying to get him home. The alternative was to have the health unit nurse send for EMS which would have deposited him in one of the city-operated hellhole hospitals until he regained sufficient consciousness to be sent home on his own.

Calvin had occasionally referred to a son who was "a big shot at NBC." One of his associates made an attempt to locate the son to get Calvin home. Calls to several NBC installations, including New York and California were fruitless. Finally through the use of a new device, a telephone directory sorted by address, a Ma Bell operator was persuaded to reveal the telephone number of a neighbor.

No real help. The neighbor didn't know the whereabouts of the wife or son and was not sufficiently endeared to Calvin or his family to offer any real assistance. What he did proffer, however, was that Calvin's "big shot at NBC" son did not work at NBC at all but was a grease monkey at a west side garage which serviced cars for the Channel Four news team. Another success story shot to hell.

His close buddy, Larson Peabody, took on the task of getting Calvin to a resting place. Public transportation was out, considering Calvin's prone condition. Putting him in a cab on his own was a major risk. The cab ride to Larson Peabody's home in Livingston, New Jersey was $75, a nice piece of change in the Jimmy Carter era. Larson paid the money, as if he had a choice. Calvin was led into the house where he stayed upright long enough to take a leak and flop into bed in the spare bedroom.

Legend has it by Larson's later tales that Calvin's cobwebs started to clear somewhere before dawn. He awakened, disoriented and unaware he was a houseguest of his friend. He wandered the house, opened the nearest door where he saw the outline of two heads in a double bed and then muttered something like, "Who's in bed with my wife?" while simultaneously taking a flying leap in the general direction of the bed but falling short and landing on the carpet with his head under the bed rail.

Still weakened by the events the day before, when Mrs. Peabody poked Calvin in the ribs with her foot he turned his head and focused on the strange surroundings. He had no recollection of how he got there. It wasn't until close to nine-thirty the night before that Larson had telephoned Calvin's home and finally reached his wife to tell her of his whereabouts. He was in no condition to be transported home at the time. She reclaimed him the following morning, a Saturday.

Larson never saw his close friend Calvin again. He never received a thank you for taking him home during his stupor, nor did he ever get reimbursed for the $75 cab ride. Calvin never went back to the office to claim his personal possessions nor did he return to attend subsequent retirement parties for his buddies, including Peabody.

*   *   *

Calvin might have been loose in his interpretation of compliance with specifications. He skirted the boundaries of ethical behavior but he was not an out-and-out crook. Most who fell into that category started as conscientious employees but let temptation and greed get to them.

Their careers abruptly end when their work station gets sealed by a United States marshal and they're carted off screaming "big mistake," usually never to be seen again.

Reference the case of Rick "The Quick" Bernstein.

Rick Bernstein was an engineer of average ability with an average work ethic. He was in charge of the project to renovate an old post office and courthouse in Trenton, New Jersey. In the seventies and eighties the U.S. Postal Service had been modernizing their mail handling procedures. This resulted in their reducing a lot of downtown facilities from major mail handling to little more than retail window service. In so doing, GSA had numerous projects to convert large postal work rooms into general office space for the use of other federal tenants. Trenton was such a project, along with some infrastructure repairs to this old but monumental building.

Just as Calvin had spent most of his working time in Buffalo, Rick spent his time in exciting downtown Trenton. It was not necessary to stay over quite as often in that he lived a reasonable driving distance away. He had the option at his own convenience to adjust his nightly domicile to the events in his life, a delicate balancing act considering his style. Rick owned a nice home; his children went to good schools, far above the norm for a public servant; and his wife wore expensive jewelry. The rumored lady friends also had nice jewelry. Rick frequented the best restaurants and enjoyed fine wine or a night at the track.

The job started out routinely enough. Rick dutifully inspected all work, assured adherence to schedules and processed no payment before its time. At first it was morning coffee in the contractor's construction trailer while reviewing daily progress reports. Then it was an occasional lunch. No real breach of ethics but some questionable judgment.

No cash changed hands until Rick overlooked a few building issues for expediency. There were plumbing risers which were not quite copper; sheetrock which was painted with one coat instead of two; and hidden electrical wiring which was never enclosed in the proper conduit. All of this work was not readily visible to the untrained eye. The first envelope found its way into Rick Bernstein's briefcase.

As time went on the breaches were greater and the envelopes thicker. As a COR, Rick had the authority to issue change orders in the field up to his authorized limit of $2,500, a fairly reasonable amount at the time. He started to arouse suspicion by the quantity of changes priced around $2,400. More significant was his authority to approve monthly progress payments in the five and six figures.

Rick's misfortunes began when the contractor and his girlfriend, who was also the company bookkeeper, parted ways. She went into the Internal Revenue Service office that Rick Bernstein was modernizing, and dropped the dime on her ex-boss and lover for whom she kept multiple sets of books. As happens every time, her boss had to save his own vulnerable ass, so with the aid of his slick lawyer, bought a deal to stay out of jail by giving up his friendly government project manager.

Since there was no physical evidence of cash ever changing hands, the sting was taken from the inspector general playbook after first building up some solid evidence with a string of tapped phone calls and marked bills.

When greed sets in people get careless. First they think they never can get caught. Then they get in so deep that it's impossible to get out. At a friendly lunch in one of Trenton's finest, at the contractor's expense, the discussion over the din of the surrounding conversations centered around the need to complete the job expeditiously and the cost to the contractor of extended time on site. Rick understood construction and he knew very well what this meant. Skimping on specifications and approving a few change orders for quantities a little more than would actually be provided.

When desserts came the envelope was slipped across the table to Rick who in one motion placed it in his inside jacket pocket. What happened next caused his pulse rate to go from 70 to 150 in about three seconds. From the surrounding booths came law enforcement, like a pack of hunting dogs after the fox. FBI, IRS and GSA Inspector General all grabbed wrists and pinched elbows. Which agent actually made the sack was a blur. He was whisked into the cloudy afternoon and to an unmarked FBI car where the GSA IG did the push-the-head-down-into-the-backseat maneuver.

While Rick was being arraigned in front of a magistrate in the very building he was in charge of improving, GSA IG, and the Office of the U.S. Attorney who would now be prosecuting the case made a crime scene of his desk at the home office. The contents were carted away and the familiar yellow ribbon was placed around the work station, adding a classy touch to the office decor. Rick "The Quick" Bernstein, like others before him and a few after him, was never seen or heard from again.

Rick made prosecution easy by the volume and clarity of his fatal lunchtime small talk, never realizing that he was talking directly into the microphone buried behind the tacky Venice street-scene painting on the wall at their booth. If there was an internet at the time he could have just posted the data on Facebook because with his phone tapped every incriminating conversation with the contractor was recorded as evidence. Also recorded were his lies to his wife, conversations with his girlfriend and arrangements with his bookie.

After he paid his fine, did his time and made restitution he went through a divorce since he disgraced and could no longer support his family. Rumor was that he was living in a one-room flat somewhere on the Jersey Shore and making a living driving a cab during the resort season.

CHAPTER 13

The Language of Government

The language of a bureaucracy can be the subject of a doctoral thesis. A good bureaucrat is like a good politician in that he can say nothing, yet mean every word of it. Where else but in a bureaucracy can things be "administratively viable," can a "level of comfort" be a substitute for a downright commitment, can something be "fungible," or can every tough decision put you "between a rock and a hard place?" The term "overview" can generally be construed to mean something between don't bother me with the details or don't give me enough information to make me responsible for this decision. Of course there is always a "strategic reassessment," a term which can come out of the White House, a failing corporation or the friendly office next door. Regardless of where it originates the meaning is the same. It's an admission that "we screwed up and we're finally going to stop throwing good money after bad."

In high management I learned that to "put a spin" on a news release or presentation meant to lie.

I made it a point of noting the colorful use of words and acronyms known only to government. Let's not confuse those who practice the language of government with those who merely fracture the English language.

There is a common thread of ambiguity in much of the government's everyday language even though different agencies use different words. At GSA, we always referred to our Washington leadership as "central office." Other agencies, such as Social Security Administration and Internal Revenue Service, use the term "national office". The military's central command is *The Pentagon* even though most of the components are not even in the functionally obsolete Pentagon Building. Many law enforcement agencies call the home office "headquarters." Some such as FBI or CIA talk about "the Company." Our federal protective officers refer to their office as "the house."

In my retirement speech I stated my thoughts about a lifetime of negotiating the unique language of the government and politics:

"I know a few buzzwords which I will now do without, or which will take on a new meaning.

"There will be no more 'regional rollouts,' no 'dog and pony shows,' no 'mandatory training,' no 'meat and potatoes,' except maybe at Outback. I won't 'drill down' and I won't go 'into the weeds.' Weed of course, meant something else to my genera-tion.....and yours. I won't 'protect anyone's turf' and 'equitable adjustment' (a well worn contracting term) will apply only to my golf handicap.

"There will be no 'strategic plans' or 'pilot programs.' I'll never again be encouraged to 'think out of the box.' The next time I have 'too much on my plate,' will be at the all you can eat buffet and if I say 'this gives me heartburn,' it's time to call the paramedics. Most of all, nobody will care if I don't 'sing from the same sheet of music' or if I 'fall asleep at the switch.' You can consider me 'dead in the water,' but I will still 'smell the roses.'"

This was the tip of the iceberg when it comes to the language of government. I don't know how many times we've had a "flavor of the week" new program for which "the train has left the station." This means that the government is about to not admit a mistake and pro-ceed to "stay the course," no matter how many "rocks in the road."

As a retiree I will not have to "wear two hats," except as a par-ent and grandparent. "Multi-tasking" will mean to walk and talk at the same time. Most assuredly I will not be told by a newly appointed arrogant offspring of a party contributor, with six months of prior work experience in daddy's business, that it "will no longer be busi-ness as usual," we must be "proactive, not reactive," or that we must "hit the ground running" on another ill-advised and doomed to fail-ure initiative. I will not be ordered to "reinvent" myself, to initiate a "culture change," to rid the organization of a "stovepipe mentality" or to pass anyone's "litmus test."

It is mandatory in a bureaucracy to use as many acronyms as possible. These are supposed to be memory joggers but more often than not the program derives its name from a suitable acronym.

How else would you get acronyms like TOAST (The Occupancy Agreement Service Tool), FAMIS (Federal Acquisition Management Information System), MARS (Management Analysis Review System), STAR (System for Tracking and Administering Real Property) or SOLAR (Storehouse of On-line Adaptive Reports)?

Certain words are all over a bureaucracy, thus we had IOS (Inte-grated Occupancy Services), IS (Integrated Solutions), CIFM (Com-puter Integrated Facility Management) and SDI (Spatial Data Integrity).

*   *   *

Communications ambiguities can lead to legal difficulties. One of our functions was to lease space for elements of the military that are not located on bases. This included the friendly recruiters who in my early career were trying to suck long-haired hippie types into the military to get shot up in Vietnam.

We would routinely send out a letter to the Army Corps of Engineers when each civilian lease was approaching expiration, requesting their advice as to whether they planned to remain. If they wished to stay, we would then exercise any renewal option if one existed, or we would negotiate a new lease.

In this particular instance which concerned a storefront recruiting location in growing Rockland County, New York, we received a letter from the chief engineer - (Everything came from the chief engineer in those days. Apparently he was the only one authorized to sign a letter, although we seldom had any face to face dealings.) - requesting that we "release the space." We therefore took no action towards exercising our renewal option. On the last day of the lease, when the Army Recruiting Office didn't move out, the lessor frantically called our office with a "What's happening?" inquiry.

We knew nothing of this impending business crisis. I called Sylvester, the diminutive, dapper, non-practicing attorney who was the author of most of the flamboyant letters signed by the chief. Syl wrote and spoke with an aristocratic flair. He said, "What's the problem? We sent you a communication on it. Our wishes are abundantly clear. We want you to *re-lease* the space."

That little play on words cost the government the benefit of the renewal option, as well as significant damages to the owner who already leased the space to another tenant.

*   *   *

Remember the earlier reference to my friend *Adderw* (Edward) who left messages with the letters of names arraigned in alphabetical order? Ed and I were friends and I was actually his boss early in my management career. As friends we got along well. As his boss, I learned why prior bosses always gave him good ratings – so someone else would hire him.

Among the games that Ed and I played as technicians, in addition to trying to baffle each other with alphabetized names, titles and government agency affiliations, was to come up with a "Word of the

Day." Once having determined our WOD we would each make every effort to get it into an outgoing letter to be signed by Alex or another boss. Thankfully, technicians were not allowed to sign their own correspondence because that would have put still another dimension to the English language as well as generate a fair amount of contract dispute litigation. Each of us would select a word on alternate days and register a point if Alex signed the letter with the word in it. You received an extra point if Alex signed the letter one of us wrote and the then the other one of us successfully got him to sign a second letter with the same WOD. Bonus points piled up if the recipient repeated the word in the response letter.

Alex was no dummy. After signing two letters to the same recipient with the word "expunge" in it he was taking note. Two more letters with "arbitrary and capricious" and then pairs with "flatulent," "fenestration" and "prestidigitate" became just too much.

The last straw for Alex was to see two letters for his signature on the same day with the word "*jardinière.*" We shot our last WOD. Edward and I walked in the following morning, sat down and were visited by Alex's secretary, Mary, who handed each of us a piece of paper. Mary explained that Alex would not be in that date but that he was so impressed with our writing skills that he thought we should enhance them by taking a few advanced training courses. The other part of the message had been that if we didn't pass our newfound educational opportunity with a B or better we can look forward to staying in the training program indefinitely. The good news was that the government would pay for the college courses.

These were the sixties. There were no government unions and no labor dispute procedures. Unless you wanted to relegate yourself to a career of menial duties you obeyed the boss. For the next three months Edward and I diligently sat at New York University Graduate School every Wednesday night, he enjoying "Creative Writing", and I in "Advanced Fiction Workshop." In class we thought about places like SFO, HON and SJU. In the essays we had as homework assignments we had ample opportunity to use our WODs.

In later years, when I was Ed's boss, our relationship strained because my ratings were impacted by his eccentricities and lack of production. What I got instead was plenty of philosophy and worldly advice. As he got older he developed a survivalist mentality. He preached that a man had a right to bear arms, animals are for hunting and women are for child bearing. His government family was protective of him in light of his longevity and loyalty to his associates. Just a few years before his full retirement eligibility, he wanted to withdraw his pension funds and sink the money into a military themed restaurant in Manhattan. His entire experience in that business was that he had eaten in restaurants in the past and his son was now waiting on tables. We knew that this hair-brained scheme would fail and would result in his family being added to the welfare roles.

Fortunately reason prevailed. We convinced him to wait. He quietly retired with his pension intact and was seldom heard from after that. The next time I saw him was years later when he attended a retirement party of another associate. It was an evening event held at Olivia's, a downtown restaurant with continental cuisine. Ed walked in wearing his favorite set of polyesters and carrying the same government issued attaché case he used while working.

When he put his case on the table, right next to the rolls, we were all shocked by its contents. He opened it up to reveal a finely tuned vintage Colt Peacemaker, fully loaded.

Now we were getting nervous. An unstable individual with a weapon in a New York restaurant was not what we needed at a retirement party. One of our guests said, "Ed, why don't we just check our weapons at the door?"

The attaché case went to the coat room and Ed received his claim check. Ed then proceeded to have a few too many Johnny Walkers to entrust him with a loaded weapon on the New York City subways. The issue was academic because after all of the reminiscing and telling the guest of honor how great he was, Ed departed without his piece.

This created a new dilemma. Ed was already on the number 2 train, heading to the Bronx. His weapon was in the checked attaché case. We couldn't leave it there. Bert Pisani was being picked up by his wife and suggested that he take the weapon home in the trunk of his car, if someone else would retrieve it from the coat check.

I volunteered because I could always deadpan it. "It seems my friend left without his briefcase. Why don't I just take it for him?" Since I was a frequent customer, given the number of GSA parties we had at Olivia's, the coat check person gave it to me and I left the customary dollar tip.

The weapon stayed in Bert's home, untouched for a month, until Ed eventually came to Queens with his son and a vehicle to reclaim it. For his efforts Bert received a lecture on a man's right to bear arms.

*   *   *

No person in GSA ever exemplified that a good bureaucrat could use a lot of words to say nothing better than one Mickey "Master of Disaster" O'Shea. A retired New York City fire inspector, Mick still believed that his role was to issue a summons rather than cure the problem.

Mick had gained a few pounds since his firehouse days. When he approached in a corridor he looked like a Ford Explorer with all of the doors open. In his current state he would have never passed a department physical. By the time he reached GSA he was unable to navigate a flight of upward stairs. Nevertheless he walked around our office space with his patented crew cut which was covered by a hard-hat with the NYFD logo; he wore his firefighter's boots but was unable to bend down to close them, and he carried a clipboard wherever he went to go with the pencil in his ear and 2" x 2" note sheets which were appended to him with a clasp intended to hold his tie in place in front of a massive belly.

He was hired as the safety officer to ensure that new leases and all existing government buildings comply with both local and GSA codes. When he found a minuscule deviation he would write a long-winded flamboyant memorandum addressed to the regional administrator, rather than his boss or the initiator of the inquiry. This would incite a near-panic because the first thing the regional administrator would think is, "What happens if this hits the press?" This was a valid concern because Mick's memos had a way of reaching the media before others even saw them.

Mick's reports were written in multi-syllabic English wherein he would report that the tenant "trumpeted" his suggestions (no matter how ridiculous or impractical) and stated there will be "vituperations" if his recommendations went unheeded. If he found (usually incorrectly) that there was a one tenth of an inch deviation from code in the height of a stair rail he would then headline his report that the property was unfit for occupancy.

His reports were filled with words like "ameliorate," "exuberate," "exurban," and "exoteric," although nobody had any idea what they meant in the context in which Mick used them.

His cubicle was decorated with photos from famous fires and laminated copies of the headlines. When you tried to speak to him about these events his conversation would be laced with "This is what a nickel's worth of fire can do," or "Be thankful that I didn't give you the whole nine yards." Finally he would say, "I only gave you half a ball of wax," as if more bullshit was coming. Our discussions usually ended with me telling him that for all of his reports' purported value they had the same consistency as toilet paper and he could use them for the same purpose.

The final straw with Mick came when he was sent to do a routine safety check for a large building on Long Island in which we intended to lease a small amount of space. The building, as we later found out, was in full compliance with all codes. However, Mick saw fit to recommend for this five-person office that the builder construct a new secondary exit staircase (through prime and rented office space) and voluntarily offer all current and past occupants medical testing because "contaminants conceivably can be present" from a military base two miles away which closed after World War II.

This caused another panic when a copy of the report found its way to *Newsday*, which prints nothing but the truth. When the damage control was over, and there were no code violations, no obstructed or non-existent fire exits and no evidence whatsoever of cancer-causing carcinogens, Mick was mercifully reassigned to duties taking hot water and rodent complaints in one of our more obscure buildings.

PART THREE

The Management Years

CHAPTER 14

Nobody Calls to Tell You That Everything is OK

Working for GSA was like working for the gas company. Nobody ever called to say everything was just fine and left it at that. There was always a "by the way" to follow, whether it was a favor, special treatment or to redeem a past marker.

One such greeting came from a rather gruff former high-level GSA official out of Washington, who later went to work for a contractor. He never had a direct supervisory relationship with me but had a program approval dotted line connection. That was sufficient to make my life miserable. I don't want to say I disliked this guy but I probably would not piss on him if he were on fire.

Among the memorable one-way conversations we had was a telephone call while I was overseeing a controversial court project in Puerto Rico. I had politely suggested that I did not think it advisable to obey a certain ill-thought-out directive of his because it was against good business judgment, not in the interest of good customer service and contrary to a direct order from my actual immediate boss. Herein is where we get in to those conflicting in-house agendas. Trying to hold any diplomatic conversation with this person would be like teaching table manners to a shark. I received a blustery threat that if I didn't comply with orders from "Washington" I might find myself managing construction projects in some lonely outpost in northern Alaska.

I think the real reason for the obstinacy was to create a crisis sufficient enough for "Washington" to intervene so he could justify a Monday or Friday trip to San Juan with his in-house sweetie which would extend to a weekend.

Years later we were face to face at one of those ceremonial events where people force themselves to act as if they like each other. This was only days after my moving into the big office. He glad-handed, backslapped and jumped all over me like a bull elephant in heat. Then came the inevitable "by the way," in the form of notice that his company was available to provide professional services on GSA construction projects in the region. I suggested that they would receive favorable consideration if they bid the northern

Alaska job because he would never work in New York. Sweet revenge.

*   *   *

I returned from lunch one afternoon to see a phone message on my desk from Liz from a "Mr. Wadeburger." This was easy to figure out. I knew immediately that she meant Mr. Wade Burger from our central office, who also happened to be the son of Chief Justice Warren Burger. After I took care of Wade, who was a nice guy and never was pompous about his lineage, I took a call from a fellow we referred to as Meyer the Buyer. The call started out something like, "Hey, buddy, how are you doing today?" With that friendly greeting I knew I was in for a problem. Meyer was with the Secret Service and our contact usually involved some sort of facilities planning for their offices within our region. Meyer was slicker than catshit on linoleum so I knew this friendly greeting was the forbearer of bad news.

I wasn't in the greatest of moods. That morning I had my annual physical examination which was a government-provided entitlement for managers. It was administered by the Public Health Service. The physician in charge was an elderly retired general practitioner, Dr. Laurence "Not So" Feinstein. Laurence had shaky hands and was a bit forgetful. One was always concerned that blood and specimens would get mixed up because his assistant wasn't much swifter.

I had passed a milestone in life, my fortieth birthday, so I was now entitled to an add-on: my very first sigmoidoscopy. When the shaky doc positioned me and was ready to do his thing which gave him a lot more pleasure than it gave me, he said, "Alright, stay still, I'm about to introduce the instrument."

Taking a line from Art Carney's Ed Norton character in *The Honeymooners*, I turned and said, "*Hello* instrument," just as the doc's trembling hands rammed it home. From then on, whenever I wanted to stick it to someone I referred to it as, "Let's introduce the instrument."

This particular conversation with Meyer involved another high-profile mission. GSA is tasked by Congress to establish office space for former presidents, to do it within an often unrealistic budget considering the demands of an ex-president, and to also set up space for the Secret Service security details to which an ex-president is entitled. The security is provided at both the office and the residence.

During my career two ex-presidents chose to reside in our region. Both Richard Nixon and Bill Clinton were actually pleasant and cordial customers. The aggravation came when we had to deal with Secret Service squads, presidential staffers, wives, secretaries, pets, pompous daughters, chauffeurs and the like. Similar to dealing with federal judges, staffers think they have the same empowerments as their bosses.

Meyer had been in charge of setting up the security detail in Manhattan when President Nixon contemplated buying a cooperative apartment in an Upper East Side brownstone. For about a month, while Nixon's lawyers were negotiating the purchase of the co-op, the Secret Service was running us ragged in an attempt to find a command center near the residence, which met all of their security requirements. The ideal situation would have been to be in the same structure, adjacent to the president's quarters but that would have meant buying or condemning another apartment in the building. The potential cost and public relations impact would have been devastating. Condemnation was out of the question. We were talking about million-dollar properties in the nineteen eighties, with ownership who could gather enough legal power to run the price up another million in a condemnation. In addition, if this were to go in front of an unsympathetic federal judge, such as a Jimmy Carter Democratic appointee, the entire process could unravel.

When Nixon zeroed in on his east side palace the search was on. At first the Secret Service wanted us to seize a McDonald's on Third Avenue because of its proximity and visual contact with the residence. Then it was one of a series of apartments in a luxury building across the street where daughter Tricia lived.

We made many trips from the Secret Service downtown office to the property during the negotiating stage and the co-op board's review process. We would often go with Nixon's private chauffeur. With all of the publicity about the dealings of the Nixon White House, he was very careful after his term of office, to not use people on his payroll or security detail, for personal services. His chauffeur, who somehow acquired a nickname from us of "Broadway Joe," was a dapper but crusty old gentleman who was independent and secure enough in his relationship that he took no crapola from anyone, including the Secret Service. When they would ask him to perform simple tasks such as to move his car so the Secret Service official vehicle could park in front of the residence, his body language was the "*fuck you*" that nobody else could utter.

During one of the rather tense waiting periods, across the street from the co-op and directly in front of the building that Tricia called home, the people from GSA, Secret Service and the president's chauffeur were passing the time with small talk while waiting for Nixon's chief of staff to arrive. Tricia appeared out of nowhere, having alighted from the building with her prissy French poodle in hand. She ignored the entire delegation, save for Broadway Joe, as if they were a band of day laborers in a shapeup hall. She asked Joe, "Do you know when my father will be here?" Joe shrugged in a matter that suggested that the arrival time is anybody's guess. She then acknowledged the delegation by turning to Meyer, handing him the poodle and announcing, "Hold him until I get back."

With Agent Meyer holding the ex-presidential pooch in his arms, things were getting testy. Judging by his pained expression, it was just a matter of time before the dog would piss on his crisp white shirt or paisley tie, all part of the law enforcement uniform of the eighties. He sheepishly looked at Broadway as if he was the president's serf but before he could hand over the dog, or even broach the subject, Joe said, "If you give him to me he's hamburger meat." Meyer made a quick mental calculation of his pension accrual and decided he has to work a few more years, so he chose to hold onto the dog.

While all of this intrigue was happening, the Secret Service technical team was inside the brownstone coming to the conclusion that the only way to provide the prescribed level of security was to set up in an adjoining unit within the building, a probability which would never happen. The other co-op owners were already mobilizing against what they perceived as a major intrusion on their privacy.

Because of the urgency of this case, I had assigned it to Lady Rambo. Her plain-Jane appearance lulled the Secret Service representatives for a while but it wasn't long before she out f-worded them and became the assertive one in this space chase, quickly eliminating pipe dreams, like taking over the corner McDonald's. When a nattily attired agent came late and confessed that he forgot about a meeting, she snapped back with "Did you forget to piss this morning?" All future meetings started promptly.

The outcome was that GSA located, at great taxpayer expense, a professional apartment on the ground level of a nearby luxury apartment building. The Secret Service and all the president's men checked it out and were pleased. Now we were pressed to make a deal by the president's team and the G-Men. The landlord, knowing this was the only acceptable location for the task force, was less than cooperative when it came to negotiating. We were not bargaining from strength, which brings to mind the wisdom of my boss at the time, "Stormin' Norman" Pearson. He once said to me, "You don't score points for negotiating, only for making the deal." This is the same Stormin' Norman who insisted on interceding in a sensitive negotiation and whose opening remarks to a potential lessor had been, "This place is just what we need. What will it take to make the deal?"

We eventually came to a meeting of the minds on the probable Secret Service new command post. In so doing we waived every rule, policy and law of procurement competition that we would have applied to a less influential client. By coincidence, this was the same East Side luxury co-op building which had once been an office building with the FBI as a major tenant. Notwithstanding the prestigious former tenant, its owners who made a fortune when the building was converted to a residential co-op, were implicated but never indicted for some nefarious associations with mob-connected families.

Every day Meyer would call to see if the lease was concluded and if his tiger team could set up shop. Every day there was another delay. The owner's lawyers were messengering papers all over the place and finding the usual problems which lawyers are so capable of doing.

Finally we were ready to sign the lease. It was the policy of the government to have the lessor sign first, which would put him in the position of having his property tied up until if and when the government decides to execute the lease. Pressure to close the deal was coming from the lessor and the Secret Service, while at the same time those ever truthful New York tabloids were reporting rumors that Nixon's potential new neighbors were not enthralled with the notoriety his presence would bring to their building. The buzz was that the co-op board would reject his application.

When I got my usual morning call from Meyer asking for the status, I gently approached the subject of the rumors. The silence told me that there was a lot of squirming at the other end of the line.

"Nooo problem, buddy." This is when you begin to worry. "The director wants to see this done."

"Is the president moving into the co-op or not?" I couldn't be more direct.

"Nooo problem. Everything is a go." Now I really started to worry.

"Then of course you will have no problem sending me the Service's acceptance of the space and agreement to pay the rent, right?"

"Yeah, yeah, we'll get it right out. I'll draft something for the director." This is something else I learned the hard way. When the spokesperson doesn't have final authority, either fiscally or politically, there is an instant out which leaves the risk taker sucking wind.

At this point I had the Secret Service, the president's staffers and my big boss, Stormin' Norman, all after me to make the deal. I was not the government's signatory to the lease, so I directed the contracting officer who negotiated the lease and who had the legal authority to bind the government to go ahead so Meyer could inform the director.

As I was to quickly find out, nothing in government is that urgent that it can't wait until all stakeholders sign off.

The lease was signed by the close of business that day with a note to the file, "Formal acceptance to follow." Snail mail was the official mode of written communication.

The next morning when I got on the rail for my commute I quickly came to the conclusion that I wasn't going to have a good day. The issue of Nixon's possible rejection by the co-op board had gone from rumor as reported by the marginally truthful *New York Post* to fact as reported in the reliable *New York Times*. The president withdrew his application, not wishing to have his presence create a distraction to the neighbors.

During the remaining part of my 46-minute train ride I had a lot to think about. I first thought of the old standby rule, "When stuff hits the fan the first thing to do is to find a scapegoat." I didn't think that would work because there were too many politically powerful people involved and the best a careerist could hope would be, to paraphrase Kenny Rogers' "The Gambler," is to break out even and die in your sleep.

I then calculated that I didn't have enough time or money in the system to retire before my disciplinary hearing. I reminded myself of the penalties to careerists who obligate the government to expenses beyond appropriations. I tried to think of what we will be telling the media when the *New York Post* called asking about the bogus lease in a luxury apartment house which we just signed, with no tenant. This was not going to be a good day.

I didn't even get a chance to break open my morning coffee, before my secretary put the call through. "It's Meyer of Secret Service." Somehow I wasn't surprised.

"Hey, buddy, how are you doing today?" I don't know if it was good or bad that I had already read the *Times* article. I stared at the AT&T speakerphone box and tried to determine if I should hit the "on" button so I could share the bullshit which was about to come.

"The East Side lease, did it go yet? The one for the proposed command center?" (Until I had the OK the night before the word "proposed" had never come up.) I couldn't see Meyer but I could just sense the positioning to cover both his ass and that of the Service for the embarrassment which was about to come.

I hit the issue dead on. "Meyer, why don't we just cut the bull-shit? Based on your word I put my balls on the table and we executed the lease. Now your guarantee isn't worth squat and I'm sitting here technically anti-deficient in a move that could get me fired, to say nothing of what happens when it reaches *The New York Post*, that great symbol of responsible reporting." Less than one day earlier, we had made a five-year commitment, worth over a million dollars. Our approach to the lessor for a rescission was greeted with something to suggest that the entire government team was smoking a strange substance to expect him to cooperate. The best we could do would be an expensive buyout. The press would be sure to highlight our stupidity.

As it turned out, good prevailed over evil. The problem was eventually resolved and neither the press nor the GSA Inspector General ever became aware of the situation. We figured that there must be a law enforcement or intelligence agency around which could use an inconspicuous luxury apartment on the East Side as a cover for something. We called our contacts at CIA, FBI, State Department, Defense Intelligence, etc. etc. until we worked a deal with one of the spy agencies to take over the lease. All of the paperwork was ultimately transferred, they took over direct payments to the property owner, and as far as GSA records were concerned, this event never happened. It was one of the great cover-ups of my career.

*   *   *

No project in my entire career was blown out of proportion as much as former President Bill Clinton's establishment of an office in New York City. There was so much media coverage, and so much late night TV fodder, that I would channel-surf between Jay Leno and David Letterman at night to see what kind of a day I was in for tomorrow. As with any negative or controversial news, the media and the politicians latch onto it, with different purposes. We then get flooded with calls and requests, followed by hearings and investigations, all of which eventually go away when they serve their purpose or when the initiator realizes that there is no political gain to be had. Like our customers, neither the media nor members of Congress call us to say everything is OK. They are always looking for something, not to inform the public but to sell papers or to embarrass members of the opposing party.

To put things in proper perspective, we ultimately leased 8,600 square feet of office space for Bill Clinton, at a rental of $346,000 per year. Our total leased inventory at the time was about eight million square feet in five hundred leases at an annual cost of more than $200 million. Judging by the scrutiny we (and the former president) received, one would have thought that this was the only project in the house.

I entered my final assignment, as the Big-Ass Boss of the New York region, in August, 2000. This was just when Clinton was winding down his final term and preparing for his and Hillary's post-presidential careers. Over the next few months the Clintons would be in the middle of multiple controversies. There was Monica Lewinsky, acceptance of personal gifts, questionable presidential pardons, and the allegations that the Clintons were ransacking the White House while their staffers were sabotaging documents required for an orderly transition. At the same time, Clinton's half-brother Roger was embarrassing the family and the Office of the President on a daily basis.

Congress provided for Clinton's transition budget to establish a post-presidential office, including money for the Secret Service for continued protection of the president and his family.

The reality is that an ex-president cannot spend indiscriminately for his office. There is a finite amount and no matter how much wheeling and dealing goes on, this amount cannot be exceeded or the person who overspends would get the treatment I would have received had the Nixon caper not been buried.

Because an ex-president is involved, the usual formal requests and budgeting certifications are generally waived. The money is in the GSA budget anyway. The procedure starts four to six months prior to the president leaving office, or the day after Election Day in the case of a sitting president who is not reelected.

At this point it would be appropriate to introduce Big Georgie as a cast member. Big Georgie was a gentleman in an office filled with sharks and opportunists. He was also the go-to guy in any difficult or sensitive situation. He had the authority and the diplomatic skills to resolve almost any issue, and keep politicians and careerists out of jail.

Big Georgie was the deputy commissioner of Public Buildings Service at the time. In that capacity he was the ranking career person. He was the advisor to the presidential appointee commissioner and the link to provide continuity between administrations. Georgie was "Mr. PBS" and had universal respect for his ability and integrity. He also had a sense of humor. He taught me the meaning of putting a little Vaseline on the pine comb.

One clear and crisp October day Georgie called to advise that he had heard from the president's staff and it was his desire to set up an office near the Clinton's new home in Chappaqua, New York. It was already widely rumored that the Clintons would establish a residence in New York so Hillary could embark on her own political career.

Chappaqua is an upscale rural community in Westchester County, with little office space available in the immediate area and a difficult commute for the staffers who would be the ones to actually work in the office. The Clinton camp agreed that White Plains, the county seat, would make more sense. This is a business and commercial center, served by a commuter rail and near an airport, with a large selection of available modern office space. When the word got out that we were looking in the area for the president, every con artist, third rate real estate practitioner, or politically connected entrepreneur in Westchester County saw fit to call us and magnanimously advise that they had just what the president needed.

We actually reached the point of recommending a White Plains location and with the president's acceptance my specialists would have begun serious negotiations.

Then Georgie called again. "Sorry, Al. No more White Plains. The president wants his office in Manhattan."

This made sense to me, given that Manhattan is in the center of commerce and the media. With Bill's reputation as a womanizer, I had another theory on this. "George, it sounds like there's more to this than meets the eye. My take is that they're going through the motions in Chappaqua for appearance purposes, but she's probably going to throw his ass out the day they leave office and he wants to be near the action in the Big City."

"Maybe so, but let's see what we can do."

Now that we were dealing with Manhattan real estate sharks I had to put my top person on the case. Elegant Edward was the man. Ed was the director of Realty Services Division, the former Space Management Division and the former Real Estate Division, of which I was at one time the learned director. Ed was in charge of our entire lease program. He was the best negotiator and most technically proficient at complicated and imaginative leases. Ed was also the best dressed.

The rest became a late night comic's delight. Clinton and his staff zeroed in on an 8,500 square foot unit on the 56th floor of a prestigious building on West 57th Street appropriately named Carnegie Towers. It was ideally suited to his purposes because it was a small footprint building so Clinton's office would have occupied an entire floor, making traffic flow and security easier. The deal we almost made was in the $80 per square foot range, which for the area and notwithstanding congressional and media opinions, was *below* market rate for comparable space. The owner was taking less money than he could have received from a less prestigious tenant.

When this news slowly made its way to congressional overseers the fun began in earnest. Congressman Ernest Istook, a Republican from Oklahoma and chairman of the Treasury, Postal, and General Government Appropriations Subcommittee, who had an absolute disdain for Bill Clinton, began to hold hearings, seeking again to embarrass the administration. Although the rate per square foot for the space was high based on a national average, it was not excessive for New York. More intrigue ensued when Clinton suggested that his "foundation" pay the difference between the budgeted amount and the actual rent, some $400,000. When people started to question this so-called foundation and its purposes and sources of funds, the bullshit meter went full tilt.

At the same time as Istook's investigation, the Government Accountability Office had initiated a study of spending by ex-presidents for staff and office facilities. Although this was not specifically directed at Clinton, one of the report's observations was that his office, even at the lower rate in Harlem where the office was eventually located, would be the most expensive office space of any ex-president.

Representative Istook was relentless with his "investigation" over the alleged overspending. More so, he was on a publicity campaign to continue to embarrass the president. He was using the media to threaten to pull the entire appropriation from Clinton and prevent him from establishing any post-presidential office at all. He had also taken umbrage over the fact that, before Clinton left office he signed an executive order which extended daughter Chelsea's Secret Service protection until the end of her college semester in June, 2001. Ordinarily it would have ended thirty days after the president left office.

Meanwhile, back in the presidential camp the brain trust was working overtime. Without any advanced notice whatsoever GSA was advised that the president already had a deal to lease space in a building in Harlem. Our first indication of this came from the dailies and the local TV news. Congressman Charles B. Rangel had purportedly brokered this deal. The only problem was that nobody told GSA, which had the task of making it happen. Since the congressman and the president had already announced that he was going to Harlem, and we had a political deadline to expedite the process, our negotiating posture was severely compromised. Every time Clinton walked along 125th Street glad-handing the local citizenry our job became more difficult. Then he made a ridiculous comment about how he loved to stop in at the clubs and restaurants of Harlem whenever he passed through New York in his college years. Yeah, right. Clinton's popularity in Harlem in fact had been enhanced by his administration's declaring a portion of Harlem an Economic Empowerment Zone. This had a far-ranging impact on the redevelopment of 125th Street, which he was now about to immortalize.

As if this mission didn't already have enough publicity, Clinton decided to hold a press conference in Harlem at 2:00 PM on a crisp winter day, in front of 55 West 125th Street, to announce his intention of taking space and establishing his office. By the publicity he was generating one would think he was still running for office. Elegant Edward was dispatched to Harlem to meet the building's management and at least try to work out a deal in principle and to be certain it could be done within the available budget. Then the fun began.

I had a television in my office which I rarely turned on. I didn't even have a remote for the cable box. On that day, however, the local Manhattan cable news station was covering Clinton as if he was barnstorming. All day I was hearing about the press conference which I was already starting to visualize and fear. Clinton was immensely popular in Harlem and even though he had left office, it would not be politically acceptable to do anything to embarrass the president.

About twenty minutes before press conference time my private telephone line lit up and Elegant Ed's cell phone number appeared on the caller ID indicator. With one eye on the TV and the other on the phone, hoping this was a friendly call (perhaps the president was inviting us all to join him for lunch at the famous Sylvia's the next day), I picked up the receiver.

"We have a bit of a problem," was all I heard from Ed prior to wishing that I would pass out. Somehow, "Houston, we have a problem," came to mind.

"The space that the president wants is already leased to the city."

This was just what I had to hear. The press conference was about to take place. A popular ex-president was about to surround himself with the locals, make an announcement which would impact the community and then head over to Sylvia's for lunch and maybe even a local club to play his sax. We would again be left holding the bag and become the bad guys. "Somebody better whisper in the president's ear that this is not a done deal," I told EE.

"I'll do what I can."

I watched the TV with close attention when the obliging president carefully told the TV cameras that "We hope to be able to lease this space," while extending handshakes and high fives to all comers. Then he went to Sylvia's.

Once again, we were called upon after the fact to do the impossible. We had a Democratic ex-president and a Republican administration in the city. Strike one. I had been involved in many transactions involving the City of New York over the years, and the one thing I knew was that their fiscal and decision making process was so convoluted that under the best of circumstances we would spend months negotiating frivolous issues with their Department of General Services. In the unlikely event that we came to a meeting of the minds, the entire case file would be passed to the City Comptroller for review and we would then start the negotiating all over again with a different cast. When it came to leasing transactions with the city, there were so many parties involved in the approval process, that even Professor Irwin Corey would have difficulty explaining it.

In almost any complicated real estate transaction, the city commissioners practically pleaded with us to exercise our power of eminent domain to acquire the property and establish a fair price. This takes decision making out of their hands. Conceivably, we could have condemned a leasehold interest of the occupied space for the government, but the political and media fallout of an ex-president seizing office space would be horrendous. In addition, the Department of Justice would have to file papers and go before a federal judge to justify why this was the only option. Not a good case.

After what felt like months of three-way negotiating, it seemed that there was no progress. Meanwhile the Clinton camp continued to press on for his Harlem office while the press kept beating on us and Clinton. The congressional and GAO watchdogs were just waiting for a "gotcha" situation. We all knew that this deal was going to be closely scrutinized and the lease, which would become a public document, had to be written tighter than a camel's ass in a sandstorm.

Clinton was out of office for months, yet he was in the papers and on the TV screens daily, getting far more media attention than George W. Bush in the White House.

Finally, the problem suddenly and miraculously resolved itself. The city DGS all of a sudden found no frivolous problems, needed no further approvals, and agreed to give up its lease. It seems that the Republican White House had enough of seeing Bill Clinton in the news. One call to Republican Mayor Rudolph Giuliani that basically demanded "Get this guy off the front page already," and the word went out to DGS to make the deal immediately.

When all was over but the shouting and picture taking, we issued a press release announcing that we had leased 8,300 square feet of space at a base cost of $31.50 per square foot if anyone cared to believe that. We immediately issued a correction to $40.21 to make up for the omission of electricity and amortization of improvements, a minor oversight by our Public Relations' office in Washington in an attempt to make GSA look good. The correction received nowhere near the coverage and distribution as the original. The first bit of skullduggery was to charge 308 square feet to the Secret Service for the cubbyhole they occupied. Since Secret Service space costs came from a different budget this was merely one element of the smoke and mirrors we used to make it appear as if we were within budget.

The improvements ended up being paid for in a partial lump sum of $400,000 from another fund and more than $500,000 was amortized as part of the rent. This was set up by the resourceful Elegant Edward in such a manner that the amortization was top heavy in the later years, as was the penalty if Clinton should walk out on the lease. The rent was also heavily escalated in the later years. This made the initial cost have the illusion of being lower. This was one of many instances in my career where perception was far more significant than reality.

I almost felt like we were part of the Clinton family. We also had to deal with freshman Senator Hillary Clinton and establishing her nine offices throughout New York State. The press releases that went out each time she opened a two or three person field office rivaled those for groundbreaking of a major federal building.

At the same time we had the issue of the Clinton residence in Chappaqua. We provided some technical services for the purchase but had no direct involvement. Not so, however, the omnipresent Secret Service, which had to set up the usual security details. This was *déjà vu* the Nixon project of a generation earlier.

It made sense for the Secret Service to be as close as possible to the residence. There was an old barn on the property which the Secret Service took over and the government funded its conversion to office space for the G-Men. GSA provided some engineering and contracting assistance but basically this was a Secret Service project.

Not without the usual controversy. The print media and the internet began circulating information that the Clinton's were renting the space to the Secret Service and collecting a huge rental. Although this would not have been illegal, since the landlord of the space for the

Secret Service security detail is entitled to compensation, and the Secret Service has a budget for this, the Clintons wanted no further controversy and they waived the rental. They did, however, have their property improved gratis by the conversion of the barn to office space. They would benefit by this enhancement when they chose to sell, unless the new buyer needed space for his horses or the Secret Service chose to restore the property to its original condition.

CHAPTER 15

From Boyz to Company Men

Thirty one years had elapsed from the day I entered my first managerial assignment to my retirement. To the day I packed it in I periodically received a mildly threatening memorandum advising that I had still not taken the mandatory basic supervision training seminar required of all new managers. My failure to complete this requirement would have "serious consequences." It sounded like a United Nations resolution. When prodded to complete this perfunctory task I would always ask, "Required by whom?" and never quite get a real answer, or the same answer twice. The main purpose of "mandatory training" is to keep the mandatory trainer working.

The first few management assignments gave me invaluable business and life experience. I learned what it was like to take responsibility for other people's successes and failures, whether or not you had anything to do with it. I also had lessons in dealing with every level of competency and every personality quirk known to mankind. If I had any real talent it was to push the right buttons by selecting the most qualified staff and letting them run with their strengths. To paraphrase what the very modest Reggie Jackson said when he played for the Yankees, "I'm the stirrer that mixes the drinks."

As a manager of a large organization, I often got involved, willingly or not, in the personal matters of subordinates. Over time I pushed people into rehab, helped get new identities, found jobs in other regions for people who had to leave town for their safety, helped people get restraining orders against abusive spouses or boyfriends, and even identified a deceased employee's partially decomposed body in the city morgue and arranged with a charity for a proper burial. I prodded people to counseling for anger management and schizophrenic behavior, pleaded for someone to be let out of jail and arranged credit counseling for someone one step ahead of homelessness. I can't count the number of funerals I and my associates attended for employees or their families, some of which involved violent deaths.

Inside the office walls, I dealt with a disgruntled wife confronting an employee having an affair with her husband; an estranged boyfriend coming back in search of his ex to do her harm; the arrest of several of my clerical staff for drug trafficking; a ladies room cat-fight involving the alleged informer on the drug bust and several in-office deaths from sudden and natural causes.

Sometimes there was even a little black humor to all of this. Max "The Knife" Langdon was an electrical engineer of limited ability and ambition. His nickname came from an incident involving his bringing a roasted duck into the office for lunch and pulling carving tools from his desk to do a precision slicing job. Max was putting on weight and getting up in years. His routine included a daily post meal nap at his desk. Nobody bothered him because he was no less productive asleep than while awake. The word on him was that he was a charter GSA employee. He would walk around with a cigarette dangling from his lower lip like it was stitched on. Ashes and tobacco juice decorated his yellowed white dress shirt. People got very nervous when he would prop the cigarette back into his mouth and start puffing while doing a close-up inspection of an electrical installation. Despite this quirk, he made it to old age.

One afternoon there was a fire drill and alarm test. When Max didn't arise to go to the designated shelter area nobody bothered to wake him, figuring the drill would be over quickly and why disturb him. The unsuspecting young fire warden, from another office, saw Max at his position and encouraged him to evacuate. No response. Max had passed away at his work station, a smile on his face and his belly full of roast duck.

Tallulah was a technician of marginal ability (which would be giving her the benefit of the doubt). Nevertheless she was part of the family and needed the warmth and comfort of the nest.

One day Tallulah came to work and advised that she had been knocked up by her "boyfriend." She said all will be well "because he loves me and as soon as he gets a job we will be married." She wanted to go through with the birth. The boyfriend disappeared and we had to make sure she had health care and some semblance of income dur-ing her maternity leave. When the boyfriend came back to stalk her after the baby was born it was one more case of getting someone out of town, a new job, a new home and a new name.

On the positive side, nothing pleased me more than someone succeeding, especially if the odds were initially stacked against them. Despite my often less than liberal values, I was pleased with the many affirmative action successes I witnessed. The government, more than any organization, has always taken the lead in providing opportuni-ties for those deserving of a break.

Notwithstanding the numerous traumatic and dramatic events, most of my time was spent on more mundane efforts, presumably related to the mission of the organization.

As I moved up the management chain, I noted recurring characteristics of people I encountered or supervised. I was fortunate to have either selected or inherited very qualified people along the way. However, I had my share of otherwise qualified people with certain little quirks which impacted the end result and drove managers crazy.

There are those who can work a project to death but never complete it. They create activity, make a lot of noise, but never put what they're doing to closure. Be it a fear of moving on to something else, a desire for perfection, or just a plain lack of confidence, things just do not get done.

Every now and then this characteristic would drive me up the wall, since I had ultimate responsibility for the successful completion of someone else's work. When I was director of real estate we had an emergency need for a law enforcement agency to be in functional space in a very tight time frame. I would get yessed to death about the progress of the job, but I didn't see the completion. I heard about meetings, inspections, architects and designers at work but I never heard about when the lease would be executed. When I probed a little closer I found that we were nowhere near a lease. First it was "waiting for acceptance of our offer" (which was never made), then it was "I need our safety people to inspect," then "I have to go out and take pictures for our appraiser," etc., etc. It never ended. I finally got so infuriated that I told our negotiator, Fred "The Furrier" Friedman to "get your ass out to New Jersey and don't come back until you have a signed lease in your hand."

"B-but I'll need legal review..."

"Out!" Lawyers block enough progress on their own without being blamed by others for failures.

Certain people can't make a decision or give a straight answer, no matter how simple the issue. One such fellow was an Asian engineer named Wing Lee who was so indecisive that he ultimately earned the contrary nickname of Absolute Lee.

"Do these plans meet code?"

"I don't know. The code was revised in 1992 and it may not be to the current code"

"How high is the building?"

"Feet or metrics?"

"Just tell me how many stories?"

"There are 13 stories but some are double height so the building has to be considered fewer stories."

"Well, how many?"

"The thirteenth floor was eliminated so whatever number I give you isn't entirely accurate."

I once got so frustrated with him that I said, "One last question. What time is it?"

"Well that's a battery clock on the wall but the wall clocks aren't calibrated so it may not be accurate. I can call the telephone company and get the exact time, by their standards, which may or may not be correct."

"Can you ever give anyone a straight answer without a qualification or another question? Just tell me what the fuck time it is?"

"Is there something wrong with your watch? I know a good watchmaker on Canal Street."

At this point I had enough. "Never mind the time. Just get me the code compliance review. Tell me if this design meets code."

"Do you want GSA code, ANSI or ASHRAE?"

He walked away muttering something like, "What is time anyway, in the overall scheme of life?"

Another type to drive a manager to drink is someone who has but one task or a single agenda.

With the development of e-mails, everyone got a license to communicate with anyone else, regardless of protocol or the chain of command. Countless times I received urgent calls, emails or visits from people who needed instant resolution of an obscure issue.

I was conducting a very important project meeting when my secretary, Lizzy, entered the room apologetically saying that Mr. Harris (she meant Harrison) was on the phone and he needed to speak to me on an urgent matter. Harrison, known as "The Shark," received that nickname for his incessant badgering over administrative minutia.

"Please take a message and I'll get back to him."

Liz dutifully went back to the office, only to return in two minutes. "Mr. Shark says it's urgent and he must speak to you immediately."

"See if Bert (a branch chief) can handle it. Otherwise I'll get back to him later."

Two minutes later. "No, he said he must speak to you. It's very important."

"OK, OK," I grunted, while getting up and heading back to my office.

I'm a little unclear as to what happened after that, because the details got lost amidst my cursing at the Shark, who wanted to know how many people took sensitivity training that month and he had to know it that second. "It's for the front wing," muttered the Shark.

"Tell the front wing that the surgeon has his hands in the patient's guts. Can this wait until the operation is over?"

"I need the information."

"Fuck sensitivity training! It ain't worth a crap anyway! I'll have someone call you."

The last thing I heard before my receiver slammed down was something like, "This is an important repor......."

I stormed back into the room, apologized for the rude interruption and told Liz who was leaving, "The next time the Shark calls me, don't even give me the message."

This incident was followed, as expected, by a memorandum authored by the Shark and signed by his superior, emphasizing the importance of sensitivity training and accurate reporting. As with most of these pet projects, the reports are far more important than the project itself. I trashed the memo.

* * *

In the course of the successful billion dollar Foley Square project various people threw a monkey wrench into the proceedings to cover their own agenda or special interest. Not enough Polish-Americans being hired; our monthly report on the use of administrative committees was late; not enough bicycle racks in the plan; what do we do about baby diapering stations; why we bought stone in Canada instead of from a particular representative's home state; etc.

Perhaps one of the most absurd contradictions of values came the very day of the public announcement of the award of the Foley Square project. I had just returned to my office from the ceremony which was attended by many dignitaries, including Senator Daniel Patrick Moynihan, New York Mayor David Dinkins and a host of members of Congress. I even had my picture taken with the senator. The autographed photo adorned my office for the duration of my career and continues to be prominently placed in my home office.

Having just been praised by many luminaries for my work as contracting officer on this project, I received a call from one of our in-house administrative titans. I may have had the authority to commit the government to a billion dollars in construction expenses, but my contracting warrant didn't extend to small purchases, so the purchase order I issued for a $20 subscription to *Engineering New-Record* was being returned for a counter signature.

*   *   *

As a division director I was just far enough from the day- to-day details to limit my hands-on activity to only selected and critical actions. On the other hand I was close enough to be involved in many of my employees' personal problems, idiosyncrasies and personality quirks.

When the regional financial operations were consolidated to the midwest many people in the New York office were faced with the dilemma of moving, leaving or accepting another job within the region. Due to the many regulations designed to protect career people from arbitrary actions, those who chose to remain were guaranteed another job in the organization. Specialized functions like our real estate activity were obliged to accept people with no experience whatsoever and retrain them for a new career.

One person our Human Resources Division thought would be an ideal candidate for a realty position was Timothy Joseph Pfister or TJ for short. TJ was doing a repetitive clerical function which kept him out of any real trouble in the Finance Division. When he came to us someone thought he would be well suited for our realty training program, assuring him that unless he failed, which would take an extreme effort, he would be guaranteed a progression from a training level to a journeyman's pay grade.

The word on TJ was that he was shell-shocked in Nam and never recovered. Nobody was quite sure if this was true but by the same token nobody wanted to hurt him, so he became a realty trainee, although he himself never initiated this action and didn't really know how he landed in this position. An enterprising HR person thought that this would be a good idea and HR would then be able to take credit for another success story, so long as TJ didn't work in HR.

Two things became immediately evident. One was that TJ spoke to no one. When spoken to he would either nod his head or utter a monosyllabic answer. He quickly acquired the nickname, the Silent Man.

The other was that he would never learn even the most rudimentary principles of real estate and could never function as a realty person. It is hard to be a crack negotiator if you don't talk to people. However he was in the program and HR was very interested in him succeeding for its own self-serving interests.

After six months and two quarterly reviews we came to the conclusion that TJ had to be taken out of the program. HR immediately resisted, citing his right to counseling and our obligation to provide him with a detailed training program and progress reports, the absence of which would negate any attempt at a negative personnel action. This would be like trying to make a diving catch of a ball which already bounced foul. No matter what we did, there was no possibility of ever making TJ a functional realty person.

TJ himself did not resist the action. He was willing to do as told. There were no grievances, EEO complaints or lawsuits. The only feedback we had was a call from his mother who wanted to know why TJ couldn't be successful like his brother who worked for the city's Department of Social Services.

We placed TJ in a clerical position, more suited to his lack of any noticeable skills. He performed marginally acceptably, assuring a lifetime meal ticket with the government and giving us the personal satisfaction that neither he nor the organization had been hurt.

In the twenty years that I worked under the same roof as TJ he said barely a word to me, or anyone else. When one of us would try to elicit a response from him by saying "good morning" he wouldn't even nod his head. If I would say, "How's it going, TJ?" he would shake his head negatively and mumble, "No good." This was the extent of our conversations over the years, with one notable exception.

Inside the head of anyone suffering from a social maladjustment or an emotional problem, there is often a catalyst which springs the brain to life. In TJ's case, we found out that he was an expert in early television. The manner in which we learned this could have been an embarrassment to the agency.

In 1993 when the office building component of the Foley Square Project was under construction, we were in what we called the art-in-architecture selection process. We conducted a competition to select suitable sculptures for the building. This required input from a panel of experts and in the case of New York City, the concurrence of the Municipal Art Society. The Society was chaired by Kitty Carlisle Hart, the former actress, cabaret singer and TV personality. An octogenarian at the time, Ms. Hart looked remarkably similar to the way she looked as a television game show panelist in the fifties and sixties.

This serious group of art critics was gathered on the corner of Broadway and Duane Street, observing the unfinished area for which an appropriate piece of art was to be selected. The society members were augmented by several GSA people. In addition to myself there was our project architect, our fine arts specialist, a small contingent of Washington hangers-on who always get into the act and a political appointee from the regional administrator's office to make sure anyone of influence knew that the Clinton administration wanted to cooperate.

The street corner was getting very crowded, to the extent that the hot dog vendor had to move his cart. Everyone was milling about, talking about what artsy types talk about and eyeballing the area in which the selected sculpture would be installed.

Enter TJ "Silent Man" Pfister. From the opposite side of Duane Street I observed TJ walking alone in a crowd heading in our direction. His usual head-down dour appearance suddenly turned to a bright smile as he approached the group. I was getting worried. As he got closer he raised his arm, pointing it directly at the impeccably tailored Ms. Hart. In a loud voice totally uncharacteristic of him, with more words than I heard from him in the prior ten years and with eyeballs bulging, he announced to Broadway, "I remember her. *I've Got a Secret.*"

He had already taken a pen from his sport jacket and was about to pick up some paper from a nearby trash can for an autograph. My response was to immediately step between him and his intended target and gently whisper in his ear, "TJ, first of all, it was *To Tell the Truth*, not *I've Got a Secret.* Now, get the fuck out of here."

TJ proceeded as directed, but in the twelve ensuing years until my retirement, I never got so much as a grunt out of him.

*　*　*

Gerhard Oskar Doernhoef, also known as GOD for his initials, or "Houdini" for what he did with my Real Estate Division budget, was one of the more difficult people to manage. Before my watch, Houdini, a hard worker, had ascended from technician to head of our administrative services unit during one of many reorganizations. Budgeting came under his purview. This was in the infancy of information technology and before anyone in government ever heard of cost accounting. Houdini would manually prepare and track budgets, including payroll, office expenses, and most important, tracking and projecting of our rental account. The one consistency of Houdini's budgets was that they would all be inaccurate. The trick was to find the error, which would usually be at the most inopportune time.

I would usually find a major mistake during our monthly budget meeting when he presented his update. This would be rectified by a reaming, the extent of which varied according to my mood at the moment. The routine would be that he would reappear in my office later in the day saying something like, "If it gives you comfort, I have revised the numbers." The major problems came when I didn't discover an error until it was too late, such as the time I went through a wonderful presentation of our budget request in Washington, receiving plaudits along the way, only to realize while I was talking that he had left the entire State of New Jersey out of his rental projections. I went from a slick presenter to a total moron in seconds.

While I was wiping the sweat from my brow I remembered what Symphony Sid said when the director before me took GOD out of a realty spot and made him our administrative person. Sid warned that you can't expect to make a CPA out of a longshoreman.

*   *   *

When one of my employees, Harvey Wood, left to accept a position with GSA in San Francisco he was accorded the usual Little Italy luncheon. He accepted his parting gift and then added his own twist to the event. "I thank you for everything. Now I would now like to leave a symbolic gift to GSA"

He reached into his Macy's shopping bag and pulled out what can best be described as the most hideous piece of art ever created. He said the misshaped wood carving was supposed to be some kind of a rhinoceros tusk. Harvey had a sense of humor and he knew that I, as division director, was not adverse to a good laugh. He lifted this creation and said, "I am leaving this piece of art, which I found in my basement, to GSA with the instructions that the director of the Real Estate Division shall present this as he sees fit to commemorate infamous achievements in the division."

This was an appropriate award because we had our share of well qualified recipients. Each time it was awarded the recipient's name was inscribed and the achievement summarized in a word or two. Names were added with each presentation, something like the Stanley Cup. When the first recipient, Frank Kane, was named because his careless mouth resulted in a front page *New York Times* article, the trophy bore the inscription FRANCIS KAIN – NEW YORK TIMES. People later received the award for such things as being bitten by one's own pet, injuring oneself at a company softball game while showing off, and in the case of our friend Giuseppe Verdi "Joe D" DiGiacomo, for coordinating a holiday party in which employees were charged with bringing in their special dishes. Unfortunately he requested that all volunteers bring a dessert, and he asked nobody to bring anything else. So we had a party with about sixty cakes and pastry platters but no other food or drink. Anyone who indulged at that party could have become a diabetic by morning. JOE DIGIACOMO – HOLIDAY PARTY.

Chuckie Romaine received the award for an oversight which caused the agency more embarrassment. Chuck was working with the State Department for a relocation of their midtown public affairs office. After holding their hands and showing them many, many leased properties Chuck was getting weary of the never-ending rejections and the reasons. It reached the point where the motivating force behind this property search was for the State Department's facilities manager to generate trips to New York. When Chuck found property he would set up an appointment and the State manager would come to New York to view them, usually on a Friday.

This ritual reached the point where Chuck now cut a few corners and would often simply give the man the addresses, let him go on his own, then sit back and wait for the rejection and the request for another round of properties and another trip to New York.

Chuck found a nice location on East 45th Street. He informed the State man, or so he thought. Unfortunately he gave the identical street number but for West 45th Street, not East. The State man visited, only to find an operating adult male peep show. Given his own sexual persuasion, the State man figured this was some sort of a joke by the macho Mr. Romaine and called me to demand an apology. Of course I knew nothing about this caper, nor was I familiar with his orientation, so I was dumbfounded. So was Chuck, who didn't realize his error.

When all of this was sorted out, a few dozen letters and office visits later, the State Department found a suitable location and Chuck received his infamous achievement award. The inscription simply read CHUCK ROMAINE – PEEP SHOW.

As director, I continued to present this award until it went to Ms. Gloria "Stretch" Carlson. She fully deserved it for generating the nastiest complaint letter that I had received in years. She was not amused by this honor at a hastily called afternoon ceremony and stated that she didn't care to be put in the same category as some of the past recipients. She then handed me back the award and told me I could stick it where the sun doesn't shine.

The award was finally retired and the trophy put back in the office formerly occupied by Mr. Wood.

One of the more deserving associates to get the trophy, and the recipient with the shortest pre-award service time, was Valjean "The Devil" Jones, a temporary employee in our typing pool. She was friendly and did her day's work without complaining. She also was a wee bit flighty, as I was to personally find out. I already knew that her command of English rivaled that of Liz because one day when she sat at the reception desk as a substitute she gave me a message from a Department of Defense official in *Rawhide*, New Jersey. It took a few moments before I realized she meant the military installation in *Rahway*.

Shortly after Val's arrival we had our annual holiday party in a downtown restaurant. The party itself went along without much of a hitch. The food and spirits had been plentiful and the dance floor was busy.

After downing my second Bud Light it was time for a men's room break. As I stood in front of the ice filled urinal taking a well earned squirt I heard some rustling in one of the stalls behind where I stood. When I casually looked over my shoulder I observed that under the door there was a pair of high heeled shoes pointed in my direction with pink panties around the ankles. I was either sharing the men's room with a drag queen or someone made a big mistake.

After a final flush and some more rustling behind the door the latch was opened. I didn't want to embarrass anyone but I also realized that whoever was behind that door might not have realized the error.

"Unless you're looking for a cheap thrill I suggest you stay in there a little longer."

Then I recognized Val's unmistakable voice. "What? Is this the men's room? Oh! My Goodness."

She left the stall, skipped the sink stop and slithered out the door, passing within inches. I found it amusing given that Val probably had a few too many Pinots but I wasn't about to do anything to humiliate her further by discussing it with anyone. In the true tradition of old friend Alfred Neuman, Val took the choice away from me by telling everyone first, with a lame excuse for her error, thereby exacerbating the problem. As time went by the story got bigger and better, rendering Valjean a well deserved winner of Harvey Wood's trophy. When I presented it to her at another impromptu Friday afternoon coffee klatch my words were, "Val, I would recognize your shoes anywhere." The inscription read VALJEAN JONES – MEN'S ROOM.

* * *

During my management years I had the pleasure of an acquaintance with the aforementioned Dr. Laurence "Not So" Feinstein of the United States Public Health Service.

Despite the fact that he stuck it to me in a very literal sense, Laurence was a friend when needed. One afternoon Branch Chief Arthur needed a word with me. Artie and I were quite friendly and respectful of each other so he needed no pressing reason to stop in to chat but this time he had a worried expression on his face. He also was not one to mince words.

"Geppetto thinks he has the clap." "Geppetto" was an endearing nickname for Julio Giampeti, half Puerto Rican, half Sicilian and 100 percent unpredictable, but a conscientious worker with the libido of a Brazilian soccer team. I didn't really need the full details but Artie was kind enough to pass them along anyway. "He said he's been fucking two of the best at some local whorehouse and going bareback. Now every time he pisses it feels like he's got a garden hose in his pecker."

There was more. "He's scared shitless that his girlfriend or his mother will find out about it if he goes to a doctor. He's also afraid of passing a dose on to Mariana (girlfriend and source of financial and moral support)."

Now came one of those silent managerial tasks akin to asking a favor of the Godfather. Artie and I had a word with a higher level manager who we knew would be discreet and was also friendly with the good Dr. Feinstein.

"Send him down," was the third party message from the doctor. I'm not sure of exactly what happened after that. What I do know is that after Julio visited the clinic we sent him on a quick "training" assignment for a week so he wouldn't have to make excuses for staying away from Mariana. Dr. Feinstein made sure he was tested and treated in the Public Health Service facility and the record of all of this never saw the light of day.

CHAPTER 16

Where You Sit is Where You Stand

One of my early bosses offered wise thoughts about how one's position determines his point of view. It's almost like an athlete looking at professional sports. Show loyalty to your team, but when the season ends and you go to your rival as a free agent because they will pay you more, loyalty changes quickly. One year Johnny Damon is a hero among Yankee-hating Boston Red Sox loyalists. A season later he is with the despised Yankees, quickly learning to dislike the Sox.

So it is in the bureaucracy. Loyalty to your organization is commendable, but when you get a better deal elsewhere, or you perceive yourself to have been dissed in your present capacity, allegiance changes in a hurry.

In those dark years GSA was considered a regulatory government agency, mainly because we tossed obstacles into the best of plans. The concept of regarding those we served as customers is relatively new from the perspective of an old-timer like myself. It was our job to save the American people from fiscal irresponsibility by passing judgment on how much space an agency can receive in which to operate and the various amenities to be contained therein. Our job was considered a success if we limited space allocation to a very restrictive and strictly interpreted guideline (developed by GSA as a self-serving tool) even if it prevented the agency from performing its mission.

Thankfully, over the years that image has changed drastically. Now federal agencies are charged by Congress with their own policing. GSA, at least in theory, is not in business to create obstacles, but to use its expertise to assist other parts of the government with administrative and logistical support. Silently, GSA has become a leader in advancing, among other things, federal architecture and the government's emergency response capabilities.

Nevertheless, there is a colorful past from the "We're not happy until you're not happy" days. Like any large institution, GSA still carries a bit of that stovepipe mentality.

* * *

Sometimes going by the book can be carried too far. There was the tale of the exuberant federal protective officer (known as an FPO, whose jurisdiction ends where the city street begins) who was guarding a federal building under construction. He heard the sounds of an infiltrator while patrolling the dark garage. He shouted "Halt," while staring the perpetrator eye to eye from a comfortable distance. The perp continued to slowly advance. Perceiving this as a threat to the government, his own person and humanity in general, the officer emptied his Smith & Wesson into the perp who died instantly from his wounds.

In the ensuing investigation it was revealed that the late perpetrator was a contractor's guard dog, on a leash, doing his own job of sniffing out infiltrators to the building. The officer claimed the canine did not identify himself when ordered to halt, and as per orders, he was authorized to shoot. The officer never was able to explain why, if the animal was attacking, the bullets were lodged in the dog's ass.

If there was any chance that this officer may have been given any slack prior to his hearing and the official firing, it all went down the tubes when, on routine duty in a government black and white, enroute from one federal building to another, he spotted a "suspicious" woman at a sidewalk fruit stand and exited his vehicle, cuffed her and patted her down. With bananas and plums flying all over the place he read this octogenarian her rights and steered her to the black and white with the usual hand to the top of the head pushing motion seen on police dramas. The "suspicion" had something to do with her displaying characteristics similar to someone he saw in a spy movie. The lawsuits began before the car ever reached a place of federal jurisdiction.

As embarrassing and frustrating as these instances were, sometimes we did catch a lucky break. Fortunately I was not involved in this one. One of our Tackleberry clones made an off-duty arrest of a respected professor while the officer was gawking at the women on a college campus. The officer suspected the professor was kidnapping an underage female. It didn't look good for the feds. The media attention and the likely litigation meant certain disaster. The threats began before the perpetrator reached the station house. The NYPD officers who took over were not happy. It forced them to assume jurisdiction of a nebulous case that violated all protocol. As it turned out, the young female was a student, not underage, but the good professor had been porking her since she was in high school and the last thing he wanted to do was to call attention to this relationship, which in fact did begin when she was underage. All charges were dropped. The FPO was told to stay out of that precinct.

FPOs always were a source of frustration in their exuberance to act by the book. One tale came from our Seattle office. The Seattle regional office is located on an expansive former military compound with numerous buildings and an interior road leading to the main gate. At this installation the regulations stated, and a sign at the front gate verified, that the compound closed at 6:30 PM. To an FPO, 6:30PM, or 1830 hours, means exactly that, not 1831 hours.

On this otherwise uneventful day, a visitor was approaching the exit just as the clock struck 1831 and the guard was closing the exit gate (the adjacent entry gate was to be closed next). The visitor innocently attempted to change lanes and exit the non-trafficked entry gate, to proceed home for a peaceful dinner with his family.

It was a blur as to what happened next because there were few clearheaded eye witnesses. Suffice to say that with sirens blasting and lights flashing this officer nailed his perp for penetrating a closed installation gate, a clear federal offense.

The next morning at 0800 hours, my colleague reported that he was sitting in his boss's office observing a very one-sided telephone conversation on the speakerphone between his boss, Jim Fahey; the officer in question; and the commander of the federal protective officers. Jim, the senior official in Seattle, had received a call at home the evening before about the disrespect shown to our visitor who, while being cuffed at the gate, tried to explain that he was a congressional staffer leaving a meeting on the base.

With his bald dome a beet red and blood vessels bursting from his nose and neck, Jim roared into the phone, "Just what the fuck do you think you were fucking doing out there, you fucking asshole?!"

I could only envision the squirming at the other end of the line. The speakerphone responded, "Well sir, um, um, the perpetrator proceeded to penetrate the security gate in his vehicle, a violation of Section Four of the Code of Federal Regulations and...."

"Stop, you asshole!" shot the voice from the ever reddening dome which was now being doused with a handkerchief dipped in ice water to remove the sweat pouring out profusely. "You're playing with me and I'm not getting any pleasure from it. Just where the fuck were you when you fucking observed this transgression?"

"I was [squirm] approximately 50 yards inside the perimeter gate, observing from my *vee*-hicle that the perpetrator was about to make an improper exit from federal proper...."

"And what the fuck is the purpose of the gate, you idiot?" Jimbo was now thinking of all of the reports to be done as result of this, to say nothing of the backlash from an influential Congressman who has the power to "recommend" his transfer to the Alaska-Yukon border.

"Sir, the gate is in position to allow securing this government installation after 1830 hours. The incident occurred at..."

Repeating his prior inquiry, as if the officer, his boss and the entire federal building didn't already hear it, "I said for you to tell me what the fuck the purpose of the gate is, you asshole! But you obviously don't fucking understand that the gate is there to keep people *out*, not to keep people *in*."

Jim eventually calmed down, until the next crisis. The FPO was scheduled to receive the appropriate "counseling" (not reprimand) for his error, without, of course, ever admitting fault. This would have included the stipulation that the letter of counseling would be removed from his personnel file if he did not get trigger-happy over the next year.

This never happened. Unfortunately, since Jim violated the terms of the bargaining agreement between GSA and the Fraternal Order of Federal Protection Officers by not offering the officer the opportunity to have a union official present during his discussion with management, all of Jim's efforts were for naught and inadmissible in any disciplinary action. The legal staff, unfortunately for Jim, in making their determination that GSA had no case, also recommended that Jim attend training in employee discipline procedures to avoid a repetition of *his* error.

Also regrettably for Jim, a female employee filed an EEO complaint about his abusive language. As a result, Jim was then on probation for a year after his drawn out settlement of the case, brokered by the regional human resources office. He had to issue a public apology, attend sensitivity training and discipline himself to only curse in front of male employees.

*   *   *

When I ascended to my final position in GSA, the local federal police were under my jurisdiction. Subsequent reorganizations later had them report to a director in Washington. In the post-9/11 government reorganization this function was again transferred, this time to the widening umbrella of the Department of Homeland Security, thus providing the illusion that security in federal buildings had improved.

I was never comfortable with Federal Protective Service under my purview. I was not a cop and did not want to make law enforcement decisions. I left almost all of the operating issues to our very capable regional director of Federal Protective Service. This setup lasted until the reorganization but along the way it provided me with my share of adventure. I stayed away from operating decisions but I was saddled with administrative issues, including disciplinary actions. In that capacity I had to deal with the federal police union and our own human resources experts. A federal union can't negotiate salaries so they negotiate a host of other issues including working conditions and penalty guides. This is something like a judge's sentencing guide but unlike the real court, when discipline is meted out, there is a never-ending route to appeal, which often forces the issue to be dropped or severely compromised out of frustration.

Every morning when I turned on my computer, I sipped my coffee purchased from the pushcart in front of the building, took a bite of my bagel if the Health Department hadn't seized them from the vendor first, and then crossed my fingers hoping that I don't have any e-mails about FPOs getting into trouble overnight.

At various times, besides shooting a guard dog and arresting an elderly woman, members of our sterling police force were accused of shooting up a bar, being drunk in public, domestic violence, abandoning their posts, refusing orders, stealing government property, selling parking spaces, unauthorized vehicle usage, improper use of their weapons, and so on. It never ended. I was delighted to have this function taken out of my jurisdiction.

* * *

On the subject of where you sit is where you stand, I was always able to depend on our human resources experts to find or initiate a problem.

A simple analogy would be to compare our disciplinary procedure with a police officer making an arrest. Without reading the alleged perpetrator his Miranda rights the entire arrest or conviction could be negated.

Likewise, when a manager tries to impose a disciplinary action, among the procedural obstacles thrown in the way are what are called the "Douglas Factors." These are ten considerations prior to proposing a penalty, including such things as the employee's past history, impact on the organization and punishment imposed in similar circumstances. Whenever I was involved in a disciplinary procedure, the first thing I ever received from the always popular HR people would be a personal memo on real paper (most inter office communication was via e-mail) reminding me to comply with all procedures or the proposed penalty could be appealed and negated. This was the case for minor transgressions like coming to work late or more serious ones like beating up your boss. If the manager didn't follow procedure then it became more important to counsel the manager than impose discipline on the employee. HR always loved to score *gotcha*s on managers.

After all of these reminders, the process starts. Disciplinary action must be proposed, the employee has a reasonable time to respond and then management must prove its case. HR is there to make sure all is done by the book. Then there is the appeal process ad infinitum. Eventually the manager becomes so exhausted that the proposed firing ends up as a one day suspension. A year later the employee gets his day's pay reinstated. Meanwhile, the manager ultimately is counseled by our HR experts for not dropping all operational issues and devoting 24/7 to properly prepare a case.

We constantly dealt with crisis situations, be they real, political or business disasters, but there was always someone preoccupied with procedural minutia. In the days immediately after 9/11, when we were operating a 24/7 command center, I still had people calling me because our training reports and other nonsense had been overdue.

Something was wrong with that picture. In my college and private industry training, I was always taught that all effort was to go towards the mission of the organization and the end result, not to the process by which you got there.

We had people whose job was to review contracts for compliance with rules and procedure. The head of this operation, Ira Carlino, who was known as "The Iratolla," always found an issue of non-compliance that could be reported back to the initiator along with a copy to the Iratolla's boss to show he was diligently doing his job. The Iratolla brought so much negativity with him that legend had it that he was banned from happy hour at some of the favorite watering holes.

This was the goal line stand again, where someone comes up with an inconsequential issue at the last moment in an attempt to prove they are part of the process.

It was particularly frustrating when years would be spent developing a contract only to have a review hold up execution because it was not tabbed properly, or it was not in a regulation binder. In many a meeting with Ira I abruptly got up and announced, "What the fuck are we doing here? Is it our purpose to have a pretty contract or to construct our building?"

Evil is punished. When GSA finally realized that this was a counterproductive function, the Iratolla's job was eliminated. He had burned so many bridges that nobody would have him and he was forced into an early retirement. When last heard from, he was attempting to peddle solar panels, an unlikely profession for someone with a preoccupation for obstructing rather than creating progress.

CHAPTER 17

Care and Feeding of the Boss

When the man affectionately known as Stormin' Norman Pearson (a/k/a Stormy, after the pit bull owned by one of my employees), became our regional administrator, my life began to change. I had been a supervisor for seven years and a division director for one year but I was not prepared for Norman.

Norman was independently wealthy, having made his money the old fashioned way – his daddy earned it. Daddy was a wealthy entrepreneur who was a major contributor to the Republican Party. Norm's desk was adorned with pictures of him and Ronald Reagan and other politicians. He had all of the political and industry contacts because of his family's business and had the gregariousness and self-confidence typical of someone born to privilege.

Our relationship did not start well. I had bypassed his formal swearing in ceremony because I was on vacation at the time. This was duly noted by his confidants and reported to him. Then I managed to fall asleep at his first managers' meeting. This was not out of disrespect. Unfortunately, the day before I was bitten by an insect while playing softball. A nasty rash broke out during the working day causing me to visit the building's health unit where the nurse administered a hefty dose of Benadryl. Norman's meeting was an hour later. My speech was slurred as if I had been drinking and midway through his meeting I was awakened by a poke in the ribs. When my eyes cleared I saw a roomful of people, including the boss, staring at me.

Like him or not, he made life exciting for all of us. Although we were originally mutual thorns in each others' side, he eventually became a supporter and friend. Wherever he went, chaos ensued because of his aggressive style and disregard for the laws and policies with which we were all attuned to follow. In my very first one on one meeting with him, he demanded that I put "For Rent" signs on one of our industrial buildings that he spotted from a highway and was told was vacant. The fact that the government was not in the real estate business, that it would have taken millions to make the building habitable for a private tenant, and that the law does not allow us to simply rent space out the way a private landlord would do, was irrelevant. This was typical of his demands. I explained that it would be more economical for the government to declare the property surplus and sell it. But he wanted to show originality by leasing "like we do in the private sector," no matter what the cost to the government.

An important rule of thumb in a bureaucracy is that the higher the level of participant in a meeting, the less will be the significance of the productivity. In our segment of the business, the top officials would meet to discuss allocation of parking spaces, groundbreaking ceremonies, press releases and other things important to politicians. Cost control or the structural integrity of buildings were a given. In fact, one of the first lessons a politician learns when they get involved with a real job is to distance themselves from any decision which can later come back to bite them.

Norm had a habit of not telling anyone about a meeting until it was time to meet. Then his secretary, the Lovely Lisa, would call and demand that you appear in his office instantly, leaving zero time to prepare. Not a good business practice. Often the meeting wouldn't even be in the building so you would be whisked away to be the lead responder in a meeting for which you were unprepared. This was before the cell phone era and it was beneath Lovely Lisa to call your office on your behalf to say you had been hijacked. Often I would disappear, leaving any appointments or legitimate business in a lurch, to go to a non-productive meeting about parking spaces or to listen to an unsolicited real estate offer from an influential party member.

Norm took his powers and ability to influence seriously, so any defeat was an ego deflator. For one meeting, I was told on arrival that we were going over to 90 Church Street, a Post Office operated building about six blocks away, to meet with the general in charge of the region for the U.S. Army Corps of Engineers. Norm insisted that one of his lackeys drive us there rather than walk. It was a power trip to arrive at our destination in a chauffeured Crown Victoria.

We were to be driven by one of the political appointees with no known skills, Melvyn "Duke" Sniderman. His nickname had nothing to do with legendary ballplayer Duke Snider. *Duke* was short for "Duke of Hurl," a title bestowed upon him when in an effort to be cool at a conference he had a little too much of the hard stuff and barfed all over the bathroom of our hospitality suite. The Marriott Wind Watch on Long Island requested that we take our future conference business to their competitor.

The United States Post Office at 90 Church Street is a monumental structure from the nineteen thirties. The back of the building, on West Broadway, contains a cavernous entry for postal vehicles to enter, load up at the interior docks and proceed around in a U-pattern back out to West Broadway. Because there were loading docks on either side of the driveway, there was no visual contact between the entry side and the exit side.

This building was not operated by GSA so Norm had no influence with any of the operating staff. As we entered the IN gate and approached the awaiting security booth, Norm leaned over Duke at the wheel and pompously and emphatically told the guard, "I'm the *regional administrator* of GSA and we're meeting with the *general*. What can we do with the car?"

"You can take it outside. Only postal *vee*-hicles here."

"But we're from *GSA* and we're meeting the *general*"

"Out!" said the barely-above-minimum wage rent-a-cop to the influential agency head and member of a prominent New York industrial family. "Just drive it around the turn and proceed out the exit."

Norm was now humbled by this blow to his ego. He told Melvyn, "Drive around the bend and we'll park it on the other side." As soon as we turned the bend in the *U* we faced the exit with another rent-a-cop staring us down, pointing to the street without saying a word. Stormin' Norman was defeated by a working stiff and now vengeance was more important than his meeting.

We were back on West Broadway and already late for the meeting, subject of which I was still not told. Norm barked commands at his driver. "Gimme the phone!" At the time we had bulky car phones but no cell phones. He grabbed the phone, punched a few numbers and a flustered Lovely Lisa answered.

"Patch me in to the PM!"

"Huh?"

"The Postmaster! Whoever is in charge of 90 Church Street."

After two or three circles of the block Lisa was able to get at least someone from the PM's office on the phone, of little influence, interest or with any desire for further abuse. Normie was on the phone for about six seconds when the other end clicked and went silent.

We finally made it to the meeting, while Melvyn was tasked to keep circling the block until called for the return trip. During this time our multi-talented driver succeeded in getting ticketed for an illegal turn and again for parking in a loading zone. Thinking he had the same privileges and immunities as his politically strong boss, he came close to having the cuffs put on him for abusive language. The caper ended up taking up valuable time of our legal staff to preserve his already tenuous drivers' license.

Oh, yes, the meeting. When we finally commenced the session before a cast of thousands, the purported issue was to perform some space alterations for the Army Corps of Engineer's District Office, which was located in our building, 26 Federal Plaza. This discussion could have been handled efficiently and promptly by underlings from both agencies. The meeting was entirely unnecessary until it was 95% over and the "by the way" came, as it always does in an otherwise unnecessary meeting. This time the "by the way" was a request for free parking spaces at "26" for some high ranking military personnel.

Understand that parking spaces are of such a premium, and carry so much prestige value, that people would kill for one. The law is very clear. Needless to say, in this area there was much intrigue and abuse, including a few building operational people getting fired for dispensing parking for a gratuity.

The meeting ended with Norman telling the general, "I'll see what we can do," and turning it over to me because there was nothing to be gained or lost politically.

There are exceptions to every rule, and as my career progressed I learned to accept this because fighting was fruitless and career-endangering. Of all of the nonsensical issues, parking privileges probably caused the most aggravation and animosity.

During a portion of my division director years, the person most responsible for assuring that we comply with the law was the primary abuser of privilege and rank. Our regional counsel lived in Brooklyn Heights. Most people there took the subway to work. But that was beneath him. He managed to secure an unpaid space which was assigned to and paid for by the Federal Labor Relations Authority, also an occupant of the complex. The space was free, a $200 per month value at the time. He did not pay income tax on the value of it as a benefit either, as anyone else would have had to do. This was a product of his friendship with the regional FLRA director and a courtesy within the legal profession. I was advised a few times to never question this apparent conflict of interest or double standard.

The general never did get his extra parking spaces.

*   *   *

Traveling with Stormin' Norman was always an adventure. It was like marching in a parade down Fifth Avenue and every side street at the same time. You never knew where you would be, whom you would offend or what promises he would make that you couldn't keep.

The first time I was scheduled to hit the road with him I made inquiry of another division director, who already had the pleasure. "Hold your confrontations until the afternoon" was the main piece of advice. "He usually eats a big lunch and tends to fall asleep in the car in the afternoon."

This was good advice. Norm was a bit of a chowhound. He liked fine food, as well as a nice glass of wine when warranted. In his company I learned to appreciate the expression, "a proper lunch."

Eventually Norm went on a diet for health reasons and this fine dining diminished. This was good for the restaurant industry because despite Norm's vociferous appetite, his restaurant manners were such that even Taco Bell didn't welcome our business.

Stories were legendary. He would routinely enter an eating establishment and grab whatever table that would accommodate his group and taste. When a flustered host would say, "Excuse me sir, but that table is reserved for a private party," he would plant himself down and announce, "We'll move when they come." He would give orders, make demands of the staff and loudly make comments offensive to the culture of the community. I don't know how many times we were embarrassed. In Puerto Rico, he was oblivious to those around him or the local culture. I heard "Fuckeeeng Gringo," whispered under many a Latino breath. Privately, our manager in Puerto Rico told me, "I would never take him to a restaurant to which I expect to return."

Stormy also had a habit of "inviting" lower salaried staffers at field offices to join his party for lunch. These are people who would traditionally brown bag it and now they were forced into splitting a check evenly in an upscale restaurant when they had a salad and the boss a full meal.

In one of my more memorable eating experiences we had visited a Federal Emergency Management Agency operation in northern New Jersey which had been set up by GSA for FEMA in order for that agency to provide emergency services following a flood. The local congressman was scheduled to visit so this was a perfect opportunity for a photo and some political mileage.

The politico never showed but upon our arrival Norm immediately attacked the table with the Red Cross donuts and coffee. That was embarrassment number one. He then became enamored with the FEMA disaster assistance manager who was charged with giving us the VIP tour. He thanked her for the tour with a magnanimous, "Let me buy you lunch" invitation.

Lunch turned out to be a drawn out affair in a local upscale beanery during which I and Norm's assistant (our high-priced driver) indulged in a salad while Norm and his invitee devoured a full-course meal. When the check came, since the FEMA person was "our" guest, Norm then commanded that the check would be split three ways, between himself, his assistant and me. Our meager five dollar salad ended up costing us enough to subsidize the meals of Norman and his lunch date.

After the meal he proceeded to demonstrate his government vehicle for his new friend, complete with sirens, flashing lights, fancy two-way radio and all other bells and whistles. Norman often used a fully equipped Federal Protective Service vehicle including a driver. When he played cop it always concerned me that while riding in his car someone might consider us *real* cops and would want us to step into an emergency. It wasn't unusual for him to have his driver put on the lights and siren so he could circumvent traffic for some dire emergency such as being dropped off at the airport or for a lunch appointment.

As much as local travel was an adventure, out of town trips made us all feel like his personal valets. He would order whomever he had designated as his driver, usually a manager who would have served the organization much better doing his regular job, to be out in front of the hotel at a certain time. No problem. He would stop at the first news stand and buy every paper available to check for Reagan articles or anything that might have his own name in it. As he finished each section he would routinely toss it over his shoulder to the rear seat, whether or not it was occupied. We never could figure if he meant this as throwing a free paper to someone he regarded as a poor slob in the back seat, or this was his way of discarding trash. Either way, we got used to being buried beneath a pile of papers.

*   *   *

Traveling with Norm was like a military drill. He would lead an entourage of customer agency and GSA people as if he was conducting a full-dress inspection. When he spoke the clipboards and pens would go into motion. He would promise anything to anyone and always get a word in for how the Reagan administration cared for the people.

His high level staffers, such as I, walked with him as if we were supply sergeants. The pecking order of respect was political affiliates and private sector people first; agency representatives at any level second, his own group of confidants and *yes* people third and the GSA managers at the bottom. I had been to more than my share of meetings where he would magnanimously tell a businessperson or a customer agency representative that his people weren't performing and he will be making changes, or he will demand an inspector general investigation to be sure that there was nothing crooked going on. All of the requested investigations/witch hunts revealed zero improprieties. In fact on more than one instance he was the one faulted for exceeding GSA's authority or budget.

There were several IG investigations about information leaks to bidding contractors which abruptly ended when it was learned that Stormin' Norman himself was the source of the leak. A particularly troublesome incident occurred when I made several unreturned calls to a Manhattan developer concerning his bid on a large lease. When I finally did reach him he told me, "Oh, I never submitted a revised bid because Norman told me you would be negotiating with us sole source." This might have been true; at certain times it makes sense to deal with only one vendor. But the last thing you want to do is to *tell* the person you are dealing sole source.

*   *   *

Norm had a habit of taking information from those who told him what he enjoyed hearing or those who generally lacked the knowledge, authority or experience to make a decision anyway. This was problematic when he would select people as confidants, keep them hanging around his office as gophers or drivers and then rely on them for a critical decision.

Take the case of Marty "Captain Video" Fitzpatrick. The Captain was a member of the Federal Protective Service which was scary enough because he had a contrived gun permit. He originally came to GSA with a recommendation from an uncle who was an ex-New York City deputy police commissioner. He reached a supervisory level in FPS without ever having actually been on the street, unless you count the time he locked himself out of his black and white while making an airport pickup.

He did, however, distinguish himself by being the subject of a front page *New York Times* investigative report involving GSA providing personal services to political heavyweights not associated with the agency. In Fitzpatrick's case it was his excellent chauffeur work on GSA time in a GSA vehicle to a number of Republican bigwigs. When he did an airport run for a Republican governor who was in New York for a campaign speech he solicited a letter for excellent services, which he posted on his cubicle wall as a prestige souvenir, causing someone else to drop the dime and trigger the investigative report.

Captain Video enamored himself to Norm because of his driving skill, especially when he blasted the sirens to skip through traffic. He constantly found himself in places of privilege while the real GSA managers and workers were left in the background.

There was the time Stormin' Norm had a meeting in the Brooklyn Courthouse with Andrew J. Maloney, the United States attorney for the Eastern District of New York. Attorney General Edwin Meese was scheduled to appear to discuss a few top security issues, including the Office of the U.S. Attorney's move to a new facility.

Because of the subject matter myself as the director of real estate and my boss Matty D were directed by Norm's secretary to go to the meeting in Brooklyn but to just wait in the hall outside of the U.S. attorney's office on a standby basis if needed. The Big Boss was going in his Crown Vic but we were to take the subway.

We sat in the hall like salesmen. We were never called to duty even though we were the two most knowledgeable people in the region on the subject matter. When the meeting ended the attorney general exited with his entourage, followed by Norm and then a smiling Marty Fitzpatrick. The driver was in the meeting but the assistant regional administrator and the director of real estate sat in the hall. When the entire group passed us as if we were maintenance men Fitzpatrick turned to us and said "You guys can go back now."

Matty turned to me and said, "Fitzpatrick said we can go back now."

My reply was a predictable. "Fuck Fitzpatrick. Once a prick, always a prick."

Fitzpatrick knew all the police buzzwords even though he was not a real policeman. His people were "on the job" and the chief was "in the house." When he told me once that he "had intelligence" about an imminent demonstration in the vicinity of our building, as if he had a private link to Police Plaza, I told him that I got the same information from WINS-AM (a news radio station) that morning.

A simple question was always worthy of a convoluted answer and a request for protective services was generally responded to with a list of reasons why it couldn't be done. No manpower; no funding; improper paperwork; untimely submission. By never providing a service one can never be faulted. Normally the requester would go over his head and the job would get done.

The feds acquired City of New York property to build the Foley Square Courthouse by friendly condemnation. When GSA actually took title to the site it was still utilized for parking by the New York State Supreme Court judges. Since parking is sacred, in the condemnation agreement for the land GSA agreed to construct a third level of underground parking in the new courthouse, to be used by city and state personnel, specifically judges and influential people. The city was to pay a fair rental. It cost the taxpayer more than ten million dollars for this intrusion further into New York's bedrock and the city never rented the space. This was another little slipup that our numerous investigators never picked up.

When it came time for us to request the city to vacate the lot so we could begin excavation, the judges who parked there were slow to give up this perk. At an in-house meeting we decided to post notices on the cars, advising that in seven days we would begin excavation and they had to vacate or risk being towed by the federal police. It was a polite note but on the seventh day Fitzpatrick was uncharacteristically proactive.

At 8:00AM (or 0800) he was already in my office, filled with piss and vinegar. "When do we take the lot? I have a squad ready."

"You can take your squad and go back to chauffeuring fat ass politicians. We're not *taking* any goddamn lot. If you would like to walk with me we can go over there and see if it has been cleared as promised. If not, the clerk of the court assured us that he will take care of it."

Fitzpatrick stewed. It was one of the few times in all the years I knew him that he was actually ready and willing to perform at least what he perceived as a police task.

Through it all, he managed to maintain a relationship with the boss. An efficient driver always willing to agree with the boss was appreciated by Norm. In effect, he was one of a team of incompetents that Norm often relied upon for advice, a fact that was often brought home to me.

One such instance was the matter of Uganda House, home of the Uganda Mission to the United Nations, which adjoined the United States Mission on First Avenue and East Forty-Fifth Street.

A crusty old pro named Roger "The Dodger" Murphy was my chief appraiser. Roger was conscientious but often unbending so as not to be second guessed as to his professional opinion. He had the power to make or break a deal with his opinions on value.

In this case the State Department was surreptitiously investigating the possible purchase of Uganda House. After the fall of the Idi Amin regime the building was up for sale. For years it was widely suspected that Uganda, from the other side of the wall, was spying on activities at the U.S. Mission. Since the Uganda building was higher than the U.S. building it was also rumored that Amin would routinely go to the roof and piss down on the U.S. Mission. The whole purchase discussion was hush-hush. Norm had been contacted by the State Department so that GSA might discreetly investigate the feasibility of this purchase. He and his staff loved this type of stuff.

Roger knew his business and I relied on his judgment. Since he appreciated my disdain for surprises, when Norm would contact him directly he would always fill me in on the nature of the discussion.

On this particular day Norm asked Roger to accompany him on a walk-through of Uganda House. Fitzpatrick was the driver on this mission to the Mission.

Later that afternoon during a lull in my office I was trying to figure out why I would receive a call from Peter O'Toole, as Liz's message had stated. When I realized that she meant Gene O'Doul I began to dial his number. At that moment Roger Murphy, red-faced and angry as ever, burst into my office.

"That prick! That fucking asshole! That moron! I felt like taking my dick out and pissing on him." I wasn't quite sure who he was talking about because any number of people might have fit the description.

"I've been in this fucking business for forty years! I've advised bank presidents and real estate developers. People trust me. They respect me!"

I was anxiously awaiting the climax of these theatrics.

"We walked through the whole fucking building. I had a briefcase full of comparables. I calculated the size of the building to the last square foot. I told him what other buildings sold for.

"So what does he do?" Now I realized he was talking about our boss and the Uganda Mission caper.

"We get back to the car, I go in the back and he turns to fucking Fitzpatrick and says, 'Well, what do you think?' It was like *I* was his fucking driver and Fitzpatrick had the forty years of experience!"

I calmed Roger down and assured him that he shouldn't take it personally. I am often treated the same way.

After all was said and done we never bought the building. The discussion ended as quickly and as quietly as it began.

CHAPTER 18

You Can't Keep a Bad Man Down

As difficult as dealing with Stormin' Norman had been, it was even more of a challenge to work with those who surrounded him. These were political appointees awarded staff jobs because of their family's influence or as a quid pro quo for campaign work.

Most fell into the classification of lackey. They had no ability or work ethic and had either a sole responsibility of being the boss's eyes and ears with the untrustworthy bureaucrats or they were political fixers who insulated the boss from any Hatch Act violation.[4]

One of the more annoying *Schedule C*[5] appointees was a young non-achiever named Lars Peterson. He had come with a congressional letter of introduction, a history of short term jobs courtesy of his wealthy father's influence, and a lot of baggage.

Lars had a way of screwing up royally but always resurfaced unscathed because he kept himself just far enough away from the real action and could always claim ignorance of the facts.

Our paths crossed a few times at staff meetings. I knew there was going to be a problem with him the first time he entered my office unannounced. Liz sheepishly came in to me and said, "A *gintleman* named *Lard* is here to see you." Needless to say, *Lard* became his handle in our office.

He entered my office accompanied by a pin-striped paisley tied slick appearing Republican who before even being introduced showed an aura of arrogance and confidence of one who thought he was entitled to something special because of his party affiliation.

Lars introduced me, followed by the anticipated, "Norman asked me to bring him to see you about the IRS lease."

It didn't take too much cerebral activity to know that he wanted advanced or privileged information about a major upcoming procurement. I glared back. "We'll be on the market in a few weeks. Give me your card and I'll be sure to get you the bid forms."

---

[4] The Hatch Act was designed to prohibit unauthorized political activity on government time or with government resources. Most appointees artfully skirt this fine line.

[5] Schedule C is a special Office of Personnel Management category for non-career and non-competitive political appointments.

In comes Lard. "Norman thought that you would look at some of Mr. Pinstripe's property right away." Remember what I said about using lackeys to insulate the Big Boss from trouble? "This might expedite the process." I now had another advisor.

After a few minutes more of uncomfortable probing it turned out that Mr. Pinstripe didn't own any property at all but was a real estate salesman with one of the larger New York brokerage firms, on the brink of unemployment or starvation if he didn't bring in a deal soon. I found out later that he was actually a friend of Lars with no connection to Norman, just an insinuation by Lars that Norman wanted this to happen.

I had a long standing rule that you can attempt to screw me once but in the case of Lard I couldn't let him think he would get away with this even one time.

When Pinstripe and Lars were leaving I called to Lars and said, "Would you come here for a second. I want to talk to you."

"I have to bring Pinstripe back to…"

"Now!"

I was clearly pissed. I put my nose uncomfortably close to his blond locks and whispered in his ear, "Don't you ever fucking walk in here again with a crony asking for a favor! We don't do business that way."

"Well, Norm said I should bring him to see you."

Now my voice was a bit louder. "Norman didn't say shit! He wouldn't ask me to violate a procurement regulation or the Standards of Conduct, something you should become familiar with before your Schedule C ass ends up in fucking jail."

As far as I can recall, that was the last time I ever spoke to him although our paths crossed a few times later because of his misdeeds.

Lars was a privileged political employee, not subject to the usual discipline or performance reviews. In the year of his employment he kept our legal, public relations and inspector general staffs on their toes so as not to publicly embarrass the agency.

He quickly decided that security would be his specialty. This was frightening. Coming from a society background with no experience and a history of underachievement, he now wanted to look into our security program and offer recommendations for improvement. This gave him a carte blanche to float all around the region "observing" security protocol and potential breaches. The scariest part of this was that he was awarded a gun permit without the usual training. We all figured that if he ever thought of actually using the gun he would shoot himself in the crotch first. As it turned out, his most serious misadventure with his sidearm came when he accidentally left it in a men's room stall. It was discovered by a mild-mannered accounting clerk who freaked out and wisely called the Federal Protective Service office in the building. The director, who had been through the drill of protecting Stormy's lackeys a few times, did a neat job in arranging history so that the event never happened.

One of Lard's early misadventures came when he decided to visit a civilian defense agency office in midtown Manhattan which had a GSA lease. He probably chose this location so he could first have a proper lunch at one of the fine Ninth Avenue restaurants. As the story goes he managed to get through the front reception desk by flashing his GSA ID and mumbling something about a meeting with the colonel. In his incognito mode he descended from the elevator, brushed past another reception desk and moved towards the stairs to check out first hand whether the area could be infiltrated.

Within about ninety seconds he was grabbed by two uniformed military police who, unlike Peterson, knew their profession. I'm sure the MPs showed restraint. There would be nothing an ill-humored and battle hardened MP would have enjoyed more than to wrap his nightstick around the balls of some blue-eyed draft-dodging pretty boy. After putting ten fingers against the wall, being frisked and removed of his unloaded weapon, he was cuffed and brought to a bare interrogation room.

This one took all of GSA's political and legal resources to free him. There was a call to a senator and a call to a general, followed by a call from general counsel to the judge advocate. He was eventually set free, based on a promise that he will never again carry a weapon and never enter a military office. Once again, the regional administrator could have been embarrassed by his trusty assistant but was nowhere to be found and was able to distance himself from this entire episode.

It would have been nice if it all ended there and Lars just faded away as most appointees do.

His unfortunate arrest was followed by the mysterious disappearance of some expensive electronic equipment which had been in his custody. Then there were the two government cars which he managed to total while on vague surveillance missions in places he should not have been.

Stormin' Norman was on the edge with Lars. He did not voluntarily hire him but was directed to do so by the White House. Because of his political connections and influential family he tried to keep Lars occupied and out of trouble but it was difficult. He had Lars sit in on meetings for him which was a waste because he rarely paid attention or offered anything of value.

At one staff meeting involving security he perked up when the agenda item was discussed concerning an upcoming peaceful demonstration which was to take place in front of our building. He announced to the boss that he will go "undercover" and infiltrate the group staging the protest to find out if they are up to any harm and point out to the police who needed to be arrested. He already blew his cover by announcing his self-declared mission.

The regional administrator and his bobble heads thought this was a wonderful idea until the deputy director of the Federal Protective Service, a retired NYPD real cop, pointed out that for this type of evidence, or testimony, to be valid the informant had to be on the NYPD informant's list, trained by NYPD and have a longstanding relationship with the group you are informing on. This was result of court decisions following the army's use of their own people to spy on peace demonstrators. Our legal staff also advised against this maneuver.

The regional director of Federal Protective Service, known as "The Constable" (more on him later) was not happy to be overruled by his deputy. Lard was not happy that his brilliant idea was trashed and Norman was upset that he now had to find something else to occupy Lard's time.

I forgot all about this interaction but when I returned from lunch a few days later I was reminded by the peaceful demonstration taking place in front of the building protesting Immigration and Naturalization Service's deporting some unfortunate recalcitrant.

Sitting atop a concrete planter in the Indian chief position was Lars, who had taken it upon himself to ignore the advice of all others. He thought he was unrecognizable but his fake beard and Fidel Castro hat must have been bought in the Dollar Store across the street. I was able to make a positive ID because I recognized his scruffy Payless simulated oxfords which were not coordinated with the khakis and the army surplus field jacket with a peace sign that he was also wearing. The Canal Street sunglasses didn't do a thing for him. All and all he looked like a moron. I approached within about five feet of him and stared him down. I would have liked to have said, "Hello, Lard," but since I hadn't spoken to him since that day in my office I didn't want to break the streak.

As we walked towards the building entrance I said to my lunch partner just loud enough for the undercover infiltrator to hear. "It's time for some of us to go back to real work. You can tell Lard that Greenberg said, 'Nice disguise, but you're still a prick.'"

The final straw with Lars came when he was evicted from his apartment. Unknown to Stormin' Norman, Lars had set up "home" in an infrequently used conference room in the federal building. He slept on the couch and refreshed himself in one of the men's rooms which had a shower. How he got his nutrition is anybody's guess. He probably crashed conferences and meetings in the name of GSA and hit the snack tables.

The one thing a political appointee cannot do is embarrass the agency or the party. Norm was tired of aiding and abetting the cover-ups for this clown. He was given about thirty seconds to resign or be fired.

* * *

Nobody epitomized the profile of a useless addition to the payroll and total slimebucket more than Nathaniel "Nate the Snake" Mendelsohnn. Nate had no skills, no scruples and no redeeming qualities whatsoever. Unlike Lars Peterson before him, he did not even have ill-advised ambition. All he had going for him was a recommendation from the senior senator of New York for whom he handed out campaign literature. Based on the content of his resume one would have thought he ran the campaign. Unfortunately when you took the grammatical and spelling errors into account, the likely conclusion was that it was written by an idiot.

Nate's purpose on Stormin' Norman's staff was to be his spy, tasked with finding out who was plotting against the King and reporting back. He was also the main political fixer - the sacrificial pig who would scout out a political favor so the King couldn't be accused of violating any ethics rules.

Since Norman was in a campaign to dump my boss at the time (with me to follow) one of Nate's early assignments was to be my boss's "confidential advisor." It was an oxymoron of sorts because how can you be a confidential advisor to someone who refuses to talk to you?

Nate was given a cubicle in the PBS management suite with no duties other than to attend all meetings, listen in on phone calls and trail my boss everywhere, including the men's room. This became a real charade because we took to having fake meetings discussing bogus topics, and then would have the real meetings after work over a few brews. We were planting misinformation all over the place knowing it would get back to Norman and then when we were confronted we would tell a whole different story, thus demonstrating that Nate was not doing his job right. At one point we even discussed a fake project involving a non-existing government agency in a property which likewise didn't exist. When word got back to Norm that the project was substantially behind schedule he called my immediate boss who acted totally bewildered and denied any knowledge of the project.

We were obviously on to the spy tactic and applying our own brand of counterspy techniques. The next day Nate was reassigned to the executive suite to continue wasting the government's money there.

My first personal negative encounter with the Snake was over an employment issue. What else? Political hacks are always trying to get their ne'er do well friends jobs.

I was sitting in my office one afternoon shuffling through some papers, alternately trashing the ones of minimal importance and redirecting others to staff members for action. My mind was really on figuring a way to get invited to a warm-weather conference. This was consistent with my oft-stated theory that every day out of the office adds a day to the end of my life. Maybe two days are added in the winter.

I was in fact practicing an early form of multi-tasking by also indulging in lunch at my desk. I was never the one to request personal tasks from a secretary, but Liz was going to the in-house cafeteria anyway so I asked her to bring me up a salad. I remember this distinctly because when she entered my office to deliver it I was in deep thought and she said I looked like I was in a *transom*. She volunteered that she was unsure what I wanted to garnish the salad so she brought a selection of dressings and some extra *gonzola* cheese.

While all of this was going on I came out of my trance and gazed through my open door where I saw someone sitting at the side chair next to one of the other secretary's desks. At first I thought the guy was a friend of Sarah, the normal occupant of that particular desk. The guy stood out because he was dressed like he was headed for a gig at the Lone Star Café.

When we made eye contact he waved to me, arose from his chair and sauntered into my office as if I actually invited him in. Something told me he was not here to ask me for directions to the library. He took advantage of my open door policy by introducing himself and handing me a one page resume while advising me that he was sent by Personnel for the job as a realty specialist. He said he was referred by Assemblyman Rodriguez[6] from Brooklyn.

---

[6] "Assemblyman Rodriguez" is the only elected official mentioned in this book with a fictitious name. I simply do not remember the real name, other than the fact that it was Hispanic.

Before I even sat down to talk (I couldn't just throw him out, although I would have liked that prerogative) I began to think of what this was all about. Firstly, he was sent directly from Personnel and not in response to any specific request, and; second, he was a referral by the state assemblyman, a fact he brought out to me many times in our "interview." All of these observations spelled trouble. While this dialogue was going on I was thinking of how I could avoid hiring this guy.

According to his resume he managed to graduate from a community college. After asking a few pointed questions I learned that he squeaked through with a D+ average and received his degree under a program wherein his professors were able to bring him up to graduation eligibility with some special testing and the requisite pre-coaching. There was no way I was going to hire him voluntarily. As if he wasn't unqualified enough, in the required federal questionnaire which accompanied the formal application for employment, he answered *yes* to the "Were you ever arrested?" question. Turns out that in addition to his superb academic credentials he also had a felony rap for weapons possession for which he got the usual suspended sentence.

This is just what I needed to round out my staff.

During our brief interview, with him resting his boots and leather duds on one of my guest chairs, I learned that he had been earning his living as a part-time musician. He explained to me the many reasons why he could have had a Grammy but it was "stolen" by other artists. What he did not explain to me was why he wanted to work for the government and how he could contribute as a realty specialist.

After he left he obviously stopped back in Personnel because I immediately received a call from the chief personnel officer, Percy "Non-action" Jackson. He was a mumbler as most people who give you a line of bullshit are apt to be.

"What did you think of him?"

"Think of who?"

"Mr. Cartwright."

"Hoss Cartwright?" Now I was pulling his chain.

"Um, ahum. No, Mr. Glenn Cartwright. The gentleman we just sent up to see you about a realty job."

"I didn't know I had an opening for a realty job."

"Well, um, ahum, Mr. Pearson (Stormin' Norman) would like to know what we can do for him."

"You can throw him out of the office, that's what you can do for him."

Another few ahems and ahums. "That's not the right attitude." Now an ultimate bureaucrat and proponent of the goal line stand was telling me I had a cavalier attitude.

I was getting annoyed. "Don't talk to me about attitude. I wish you would send me referrals that quickly when I actually needed them. I'm not hiring the guy. End of subject. You want him, you hire him. Make him a personnel specialist. He'll fit right in, especially with the cowboy outfit."

My government experience and Brooklyn street sense told me it wouldn't end there.

At eight o'clock the next morning I was sitting in my office listening to Liz describe her recent purchase of a new car. "I negotiated to the *kilt* and I think I got a real good deal." No argument there. She enhanced the experience with, "It took so long that I felt like I was on a *threadmill*."

Before the high-finance discussion got any further, in walked Nate the Snake. For him to be in the building at that hour meant he either slept there or this was something important. His shirt wasn't too rumpled so I figured it was the latter.

Since my previous interplay with Nate had clearly conveyed the message that I had no use for him I neither invited him to sit down nor did I offer him coffee.

He sat down and asked if I had any coffee in the office.

"If you're buying I'll send out." End of that subject. It was now time to separate the wheat from the shaft.

"I understand you interviewed Mr. Cartwright yesterday."

"*Hoss* Cartwright?"

Visibly annoyed, Nate snapped back. "It's Glenn. You know the name."

"We weren't introduced."

"Well, Rodriguez's office wants us to do something for him."

"Who's Rodriguez?"

Nate's turn. "You know who I mean. The powerful assemblyman."

My turn. "Well, first of all, if you ever took the time to learn how things are done here you would know that hiring is competitive (there are exceptions, as we both knew) so we can't just bring someone in, and even if we could I wouldn't hire him."

Nate's turn. "Well Norman wants it done. We have a deal with the assemblyman's office." Now it was the assemblyman's *office* as opposed to the assemblyman himself.

"I don't make deals. If you want him hired you sign your name to the papers. I won't."

At this point I couldn't be sure if it really was Norman who was behind this or it was a Nate side deal. Either way, it stunk.

Nate left with the admonition that my attitude was not a career-enhancing move. I seem to forever attract career counseling advice.

"My career or yours?"

My nose told me this still wasn't over.

Enter Carl Hall, careerist and sleazeball extraordinaire. Hall had been in a high management position on the administrative side and fully earned the nickname *Slime*. He was as slippery as the proverbial snot on a doorknob. This man was beyond all good or evil and was probably one of the few people I ever met whose funeral I would attend just to make sure he was in the box. Along the way he tried to derail my career as well as a few others in a series of personal power plays which had brought him to the position of acting deputy regional administrator. Most of his deeds, however, were directed against those least able to put up a defense. As a high-level manager, he also prided himself as a ladies' man, which he wasn't. His red toupee sat on the top of his head like a pepperoni pizza.

Slime's modus operandi was often to intimidate vulnerable young women with whom he had a supervisory relationship in an attempt to hit on them. As far as I know he never succeeded in his quests but in the pre-EEO days, most of the women were afraid to file charges. Slime wouldn't last one week in today's climate but it took a few years before several women were convinced by a small band of middle managers (including myself) to simultaneously file complaints. Coincidentally this came only days before Slime was to be promoted permanently to the very senior management position in which he was still designated as "acting." He went from Stormin' Norman's top advisor to a windowless interior office overnight, in order for Norman to distance himself from this character.

Slime never paid the piper because he apparently had a few things on some high-level people and ended up being permitted to retire before his hearing. One of the more notable accomplishments in my career was to go from the point of being sent to another purgatory at his behest, during which time I surreptitiously contributed to his rapid downfall by my uncovering all kinds of useful and lethal information, to become one of his many executioners. The inspector general had a field day with the people we convinced to give statements.

Anyway, since Nate couldn't persuade me to sign my name to the hiring of Six Gun Cartwright, Carl Hall, a/k/a Slime, entered the picture.

Almost an even twenty-four hours from when I was enjoying my salad with extra *gonzola* cheese, I picked up my private line to be greeted by Slime.

He was a master psychologist but I never fell for his crap. "Alan, would you mind stopping up to my office for a minute?"

Would I mind? Of course I would but I had to politely agree. "Sure, Sl.., uh, Carl." I knew the visit was not to invite me to the company picnic.

When I got into his office in the executive suite (this was a mere few weeks before his pending departure for less opulent quarters) I received a friendly greeting. This was a bad sign. I also knew he would be sharper than usual. He obviously had not gone to lunch yet since he was not exhaling whiskey fumes in place of carbon dioxide.

"Hi Alan, sit down." First he alluded to a nebulous event a few days before when the front office referred a matter involving a federal judge to me. "I like the way you handled the issue with the judge." This was the warm-up. Dealing with judges was routine so I waited for the other shoe to drop. Remember my "by the way" theory?

Then it came. "By the way, I understand you interviewed a candidate the other day for a job in your division."

"I didn't interview anyone." I knew his style so I was playing dumb to force him to come out and actually say what he meant.

"Mr. Cartwright."

"Oh, him. I would hardly call that an interview. He popped into my office on his way to the Lone Star."

Now he knew I was again spoofing him but he had to contain himself. He straightened his tie, coughed a few times, shuffled some papers on his desk and ran his hand through his ill-fitted topper, all telltale signs that now he was on the defensive. He began to explain everything in his usual roundabout evasive manner, using such terms as "management priorities," being an "equitable person" (whatever the hell that means), "the due course of political process," and concluding with the always vague "and henceforth thereafter."

My reputation has always been that I was rather direct, no matter who was on the receiving end.

"Carl," I said. "Don't bullshit a bullshitter. If you are trying to tell me that you want me to hire Cartwheel or whatever his name is, just say so." I wanted him to say *yes* or just nod his head so I can claim I was directed to hire this individual.

As usual, he never outright said anything. In this manner when something blows up he could claim "I never told you to do *that.*"

"Uh, this is, uh, what *top* management would like you to evaluate." Again, it was not a direct order.

Already having formulated a plan in my mind to sabotage this effort and not wishing to waste any more time I said, "OK, just have Personnel send up a referral list."

Fortunately I knew the process a lot better than the politicos or administrative types who never have direct responsibility for anything. I knew that there was an open end job announcement for realty applicants and when I request a referral list, Personnel panels the pile of applications and sends up referrals that are ranked by their panel score. The scoring matrix was based on a combination of experience and education. You can't pass three people on the list to hire anyone farther down and veterans get priority. I also knew that the Personnel Division was woefully short on resources for this process and they depended upon the operating divisions to help with the panels.

By that afternoon I called the head of personnel, "Non-action" Jackson, who was a disciple of Slime and almost as devious. I never liked to deal with Jackson, but when it was absolutely essential I made it a point to call him about five minutes before five o'clock with a crisis because I knew that at exactly five o'clock he flew out the door with the *New York Post* under his arm and it would annoy him to be detained. This time I asked for the referral list for this priority action. I was pushing him but he saw an opportunity to take credit for this special hire which I knew was never going to happen.

"Well, um, uh (Why to all bullshitters use a lot of *um, uh*s?), we need people for a panel"

This was just what I wanted to hear. "I'll give you the people for the panel. Norman wants this right away."

We set it up for the next morning. I immediately called three of my top technicians into the office, Fern "The Driller" Miller, Lady Rambo and Igor "Khrushchev" Krushelniski. These were my stars; I could trust them.

I explained that I needed a panel to evaluate realty applicants and there was a lot of interest in this hire. They already knew what I meant by that. "This has to be done quickly and .....properly, if you get my drift." They knew I was again thwarting *top* management. Without saying a word I put Cartwright's application in the front of my desk and made the thumbs down sign, gently touching the paper with the tip of my thumb.

"We get your drift," offered Khrushchev.

Thanks to the sterling work of my hand selected panel, Cartwright was rated tenth on the list of candidates, only because there were only nine other applicants. A referral list was sent to me by an unsuspecting personnel technician.

I took the list, interviewed the first three names and selected number two, all perfectly within procedures. I signed the paper and Liz hand carried it back to Personnel.

All hell broke loose when they saw they were finessed at their own game. First I received a call from Jackson who offered more career counseling. This was followed by the anticipated call from Slime.

This time he wasn't so polite. "Get your ass up here."

I told Liz that if I was not back in thirty minutes she should send a message that the chief judge wanted me right away.

When I walked into Slime's office he was seated with Jackson, poised for the aggressive.

"Alan, you don't have to like me but you *will* follow my orders. Don't substitute your will for my commands. Don't be an asshole."

I shot back. "You don't have to worry about me ever liking you. That won't happen. As far as your commands, I don't know what you're talking about."

"You were supposed to hire Cartwright." Jackson nodded affirmatively and offered a few unintelligible mumbles.

"I wasn't supposed to hire squat, besides for which you spoke in parables, never giving me what you call a direct order." Non-Action, meanwhile, shuffled a few papers, including the stack of applications.

I could afford to be a bit flippant because I knew Slime's days were numbered. The inspector general's report was about to come out, at which time Norman would be sending him so far away that *National Geographic* couldn't find him.

"Well, what do you want me to do? I don't want to rescind the selection. That would reek of fraud. Should I submit a new request?"

Some more parables were uttered. "If you feel that to be the administratively viable course." I left and took no action. Within days the IG report came to the regional administrator. Slime was given the choice of retiring immediately, or to fight the charges. He would probably have lost his case in view of the twelve women who had already given statements and the other credible managers such as myself who were prepared to testify on his drinking, abuse of power and unexplained absences on company time.

He was sent to a nondescript office far away from the executive suite, the very same privilege that my former boss had when Slime expedited his removal. He stayed around a few more weeks in obscurity before just fading away.

My only other contact with him was a chance passing in the hallway when I whispered to him, "Who's the asshole now?"

A few of his friends, including his protégé Jackson, took him to lunch at his favorite watering hole to celebrate his retirement. I chose not to attend. Instead I celebrated his departure in Chinatown where I got so bloated with chow fun that all I wanted to do was burp and pass wind.

Although Slime, Nate and Lard rank right at the top of my list of all-time sleazeballs, they did not stand alone.

An honorable mention goes to Parker "The Constable" McSweeney. The Constable showed up at a staff meeting one day and was introduced as our new Federal Protective Service director. The former director, a capable career person was now on special assignment. It didn't take long to learn that the Constable was another political hack in need of a paycheck. Originally with NYPD, he ended up as police chief of a small incorporated village in New Jersey where he succeeded in alienating local officials and his constituency by his absenteeism and general lack of any knowledge of modern law enforcement.

Now he was in charge of Federal Protective Service for the region. Fortunately he didn't get to do much security work, unless you consider arranging chauffeur service for the big boss and sundry bigwigs who came to town as law enforcement. The one thing he did well and did often was to attend conferences, usually in warm-weather venues and report back that "he discussed security with other police chiefs."

His surreptitious role was to dispense no-cost parking spaces in headquarters building to cronies, with himself getting the first space to park the taxpayers' black and white which he used to commute to work. He had little to do with the career people other than asking leading questions to get people to tell him what they thought of Norman and his band of merry men, which he would immediately report back to the boss. He was the intermediary in getting Lars his ill-advised gun permit. The Constable also introduced me to the term "poipetrator."

The lifers quickly determined that this was not a man to be trusted. One of the remedies for my immediate boss was to have his building managers provide monthly reports on use of parking spaces.

This became a constant *catch*-and-mouse (Lizzy's version of this well-known term) game for chasing the Constable and his friends and bouncing them from this valuable but unearned and illegal perk.

I had little to do with him except when our paths crossed at staff meetings. If you had a security issue you made sure he didn't know about it and referred it instead to his senior staffers. The one time I was involved with him personally when I was acting for my boss on a day he was out. "Acting" meant stopping in the boss's office a few times a day, signing routine paperwork and being available in the event of a genuine crisis. On one such day the Constable's secretary came into the office waving a training authorization for me to sign, explaining that Parker needed this back right away.

My Brooklyn instincts told me I smelled a rat. The boss had to approve all training because of cost and scheduling ramifications. On the one day the boss is out I get a request rammed at me to send him to a boondoggle seminar in Puerto Rico in the middle of January. How convenient. I refused to sign and I spent a good part of the rest of my day avoiding phone calls from the Constable.

When the real boss returned the following day the request for the Puerto Rico caper never resurfaced.

During the Reagan years, the government downsized considerably. Many unnecessary programs and procedures were gone overnight. There were frequent government-wide hiring freezes and many federal agencies were forced to streamline their operations.

Despite the streamlining, in GSA characters like Lars Peterson, Nathaniel Mendelsohnn, Carl Hall and Constable McSweeney always seemed to hang around.

CHAPTER 19

The Judges

It has been said that dealing with a committee of judges is like dealing with a mob, except that a mob is more organized and more predictable. Building a new courthouse was like designing a palace for a sultan with eleven wives.

The most frightening thing about doing business with federal judges is that, if you disagree with them, they have the power to look right at you and say, "Bailiff, hold this man in contempt of court!" You don't even have to be on trial for that to happen.

Don't think that there is no precedent for this. I have been threatened with contempt for failure to complete a building on time (as if I had control of weather, strikes, etc.), and failure to provide requested amenities for lack of a budget for the item (Congress determines how much we spend, not the judiciary or mortal bureaucrats like myself in the executive branch of government.). A colleague of mine was actually apprehended on the New Jersey Turnpike by a U.S. marshal at the judge's order because the wastepaper basket in the judge's chambers was not emptied that day.

Federal judges work hard and earn their salary. In private law practice they can earn many times their federal salaries, assuming they actually know the law. Most federal judges, upon reaching age seventy and mandated senior status, continue to maintain a full caseload even though they would in many cases receive their full salary by totally retiring. Nevertheless, something happens when one is appointed to the federal bench.

Whether it's a power trip or just a plain right of passage, when one reaches the federal bench the personality changes completely. I cannot count the number of times that I or an associate felt the wrath of a judge for an inconsequential transgression.

A wise army sergeant once reminded our platoon, "Don't sweat the small stuff." This is a good rule to follow in life but to a judge, it's not easy to determine what represents the small stuff.

Case in point. There was chief judge who insisted that a U.S. marshal water his daisies each morning. These are the same daisies that the judge personally planted outside of the courthouse. The daisies were ultimately stolen (probably torn out by the marshals) causing said judge to demand that the Department of Justice "conduct a full investigation."

Case in point. Another chief judge called a meeting (more like an inquisition) over GSA's inability to maintain and secure the district court's inventory of furniture. The judge sat at his bench, high above the lineup of GSA personnel which included the senior official in the region. After His Honor tore another orifice into a GSA building manager the chief clerk of the court sheepishly advised that it was court personnel who had removed the furniture to redeploy it to another court installation. We're still waiting for an apology.

I will not soon forget the judge who was feeling a bit warm during a trial. He summoned the marshal to bring the GSA building manager to his courtroom where he proceeded to interrupt his trial, put the building manager on the witness stand and grill him in front of a packed and sweating house. There was indeed a problem with the air conditioning, which was being remedied, but for his troubles my colleague was publicly humiliated and actually put under house arrest until the problem was resolved.

In another case the chief judge insisted upon a window behind the bench of his courtroom in a building under design because he wanted natural light. This was against the advice of the world-class project architect and anyone else with any common sense. Did I say that among their eccentricities, some judges consider themselves to be the great American architect? The result of this fiasco, as predicted, was that the natural light coming in from the aforesaid window prevented anyone from seeing the judge. The solution was to spend about $60,000 to have an artist create a custom designed and aesthetically pleasing fabric to install over the window. Ironically, the fabric looked so nice that architectural reviewers considered this an act of genius, with the judge of course, accepting all credit for this innovative design feature.

In a similar situation, there was a female judge who insisted that her newly created chambers in a renovated building face the side of the building with a great view but a church steeple across the street. We told her that the bells will disturb her. "Don't worry," she said. "My brother is a contractor and he can design another seal inside the window which will block out the sounds."

The bells disturbed her. Her brother's creation didn't work. What was her newest solution? "Tell the pastor not to ring the bells during the day." She ultimately came to terms with an hourly serenade.

I had a judge tell me to "go tell the city to get those people out of there," referring to a popular green market on New York City owned property near a courthouse. Apparently the sight of people enjoying themselves in the sun was an offense to tranquility of a courthouse.

There were other suggestions by the learned men and women in robes for which we created the illusion of studying in order to make an informed decision before rejecting. Included were such innovations as constructing balconies or patios outside every chamber so the judge could have a rest area with a panoramic view; recesses in the walls for doorknobs; raising the street outside to create a subsurface passage between adjacent buildings (the logic for this was to negate the need for a tunnel for prisoner transport although the judges originally thought the tunnel was for their own convenience); create exclusive parking under a nearby city park (knocking out subway service to the entire east side of Manhattan); and, as if I could forget, a redesign of the tower of a building in mid-construction to replicate a nearby building with a totally different design.

There was also the judge who was so disturbed at GSA because of an elevator failure which detained a defendant and his attorney that he substituted the time stuck in the elevator for the sentence. Not a bad deal.

Who can forget the frantic call from a GSA building manager after a judge demanded that he replace the toothbrush holder from his private bathroom because it didn't match the marble? I told our building manager that it would be cheaper for the government if he would just go up and brush the judge's teeth for him.

Those eccentricities were laughable but I was not laughing when one judge told us that the CIA was bugging his telephones and ordered that we prohibit phone company technicians from going into the telephone equipment room.

Nor was I amused when one judge demanded that we spend $500,000 to add a custom-locking closet to every robing room in the new courthouse – all forty-two of them – because his wallet was stolen due to improper GSA security. When he later found his wallet back in his chambers the issue was dropped.

I can't give the judiciary sole credit for what was perhaps the most ridiculous suggestion I ever heard. The United States Marshals Service was an accomplice on this. It was at a security meeting during which a marshal's representative suggested that instead of building the tunnel which had already been designed and was under contract, we should build a gondola over Pearl Street in Manhattan between the new courthouse and the Metropolitan Correction Center for the transport of prisoners. I couldn't begin to enumerate the laws, design and engineering principles or business logic that this would violate. It was so off the wall that there should have been no discussion. The marshal's person went on to say that the gondola would be used to transport prisoners between buildings. For added security, in case someone attempted a pot-shot at the gondola from the street to either hit or free a prisoner, there would be decoys in the gondola so the perpetrator would not shoot at the intended target.

After that one I headed straight to Chinatown to be a glutton and bloat myself trying to forget that meeting.

One of my personal highlights (actually lowlights) was to have a federal judge point a loaded gun at me. This was back in the seventies. If the same event happened in today's climate he would have squeezed the trigger, no questions asked.

For whatever reason, both Puerto Rico and the U.S. Virgin Islands are part of the New York Region of GSA and other federal agencies. Nobody really knows how this came about. Supposedly in the early days of the agency it was easier to get to Puerto Rico from New York than from Atlanta, which was actually the closest GSA office. There was never any real attempt to change this because a trip to Puerto Rico was always an ideal remedy to any winter heating issues in the northeast.

Because of the frequent unstable political climate in the islands, judges were paranoid about security and many carried a pistol. The security in courthouses was not nearly as tight as it is today and a lot of ornery people passed through their portals.

I was visiting the islands and getting an orientation tour of the spanking new courthouse in St. Thomas, located on a hill with a magnificent view of the harbor. Our building manager was escorting me. The judges, the building manager and the security force were the only ones with keys (now card readers are used) to the judge's private corridors which allowed the judges to enter and leave the building and their courtroom without traversing public areas, where they might encounter the family of a defendant who is about to be sentenced.

Judge Almeric Christian, who later had a courthouse named in his memory, was the chief. "Would you like to see the judge's chambers?" offered our building manager. "He's out of town. We can enter from here."

This was a big mistake. We entered his office through the private corridor and bypassed the reception area. Unfortunately the judge was *not* out of town. We passed through the secondary door of his chambers just in time for me to see a loaded Smith & Wesson pointed at my choking Adam's apple. The judge didn't know me from Adam or apple and probably would have fired if I took a step closer. Fortunately he recognized the building manager or he might have mortally wounded both of us.

As the gun slowly worked its way down, his words of wisdom, which I still think of every time I'm tempted to open a private doorway, were: "Don't ever come through that door again."

*   *   *

The Freedom of Information Act (FOIA) put a major crimp in my style. Because so much data is available to the media and general public through the use of Freedom of Information requests I learned the hard way to curb my appetite for writing editorial comments on official documents.

No project I ever worked on was subject to as many FOIA requests as the construction of the new United States Courthouse at Foley Square in New York.

As small pieces of information became public, much of it was either misinterpreted or misused. The early nineties was a time when court bashing was popular and many in Congress or the media were anxious to prove, real or fabricated, that the government overspends on luxurious accommodations for the courts.

When this project was in the design stage, the chief judge for the Southern District of New York was Charles J. Brieant, an outspoken and bombastic appointee of the Nixon administration. He was noted as much for his flamboyant Teddy Roosevelt moustache and outrageous dress as he was for being the most appealed judge in the district. The good judge, approaching his seventieth year and senior status at the time, was the original overseer of the project for the district court. I received an unforgettable management lesson from this one.

I always appreciated Judge Brieant, because when he made ridiculous statements to the press, it took them away from us. His take on it was, "What do I care? I have a lifetime job."

The judge had a fetish. He wanted every courtroom to have windows and he wanted every courtroom, judges' chamber and general office area to have at least one "operable window." This became known as the Great Operable Window Debate, which preoccupied the agency and had everyone with a particular agenda draw a line in the sand with no intent to compromise *their* policy. If there was ever an episode blown out of proportion this was it.

The judge kept talking about "That boob Jimmy Carter and his energy program." There had been a severe energy crisis during the Carter years and the administration had mandated that GSA should not cool federal buildings below 75 degrees. Judges of course, consider themselves exempt from any proclamation directed at the executive branch of government and there were constant confrontations between the court and GSA which, based on the Constitution, took its direction (and budget) from the Congress.

They would have liked to have had the ability to open windows when the buildings weren't getting full air-conditioning or if there was a power outage.

Allowing tenant agencies access to sealed windows was against policy for a lot of reasons: maintenance, energy management, safety and more.

One day I went to the old Courthouse at Foley Square for still another debate over the operable windows in the new courthouse. I rode up the elevator with our regional counsel. When we landed at the 28th floor, the elevator opened its doors about three feet above the landing, leaving a cavernous gap where one can easily plunge down the shaft from floor level. I don't know if it was fate or coincidence, but Judge Brieant was heading for the meeting at the same time and was in the corridor when the doors opened. He looked at us in our most precarious position and said something like, "Another GSA malfunction. Maybe before anyone gets you down we can discuss the operable windows."

This set the stage for the meeting. We eventually were rescued and as we headed toward the conference room the judge leaned in our direction saying, "Look, I'm getting those fuckin' windows if I have to go to the president to do so."

This time GSA's energy specialist was in attendance, sent from Washington by the commissioner of Public Buildings Service, to explain to the judges' committee why GSA could not permit the installation of operable windows. It represented a change order to the contract to the tune of about $200,000. But it was less a money issue than it was a power struggle between the commissioner and the court.

When we got to that issue the chief judge again reminded us, in a bit more controlled tone, "I will go to the president for these windows!"

The Washington man spouted the company policy again, as if it was a repetitive recording outside a carnival pavilion. This had been going on for months and was the subject of many memos and GSA conference calls. When he finished his spiel he added: "We just can't allow tenants to have control of the windows in buildings we operate."

Judge Brieant responded in an uncharacteristically soft tone. "We don't want access. The GSA building manager can have the keys to the windows. We just want a few of them to have the *capability* of being opened in an emergency."

"Huh?" said the Washington man. "Well, if GSA had the keys I don't see any harm in having a few operable windows."

Four months of political wrangling, nasty letters, internal conferences, personal animosities and power plays were over with a few soft spoken words. The whole debate involved a handful of windows which were now modified to open three inches inward at the bottom. Ah, the value of clear communications and a reasonable mind.

It was far from over for me. Because of a little carelessness on my part, the media latched onto this internal episode as if we had just cleaned out the treasury.

When Henry Smith of our project team wrote up the minutes of the meeting, he failed to mention the judge's eloquent pre-meeting plea. I told him in a tongue in cheek manner, "Don't forget to put in Judge Brieant's comments about going to the president." My intention was as a future memory jogger and to show how adamant the court was about this request. It made sense and was good business to comply with the request. We had already spent more money fighting the change order than the cost of the change itself. In terms of the magnitude of the project the cost was chump change and would be returned in the form of a satisfied customer. One power outage that shuts the court would negate any of our savings.

Unfortunately, the media later got hold of the whole caper. Through interviews and Freedom of Information requests they had enough fodder to rouse up the taxpayers and members of Congress to rally against the court's demand for luxury.

Inside Edition eventually ran a story about the purported overspending by the courts nationwide and it cited the new Foley Square Courthouse. Fortunately, some of the effectiveness was diminished because the Foley story ran between a piece on O.J. Simpson and a story about a six-foot big-boobed volleyball-playing model. I was watching this in the comfort of my den when the narrator cited the chief judge's threat to "go to the president," which came right out of Henry's meeting minutes. At that point I figured my career would be over by morning.

My telephone rang before the credits rolled off the screen.

"Hello, Alan?" came a female voice.

"Yes?"

"This is Mrs. Brieant. Hold on, the judge wants to talk to you."
Just about then I could have used some rubber pants.

Henry had a bit of a stutter to his voice and, after a few harrowing moments, from the other end of the phone came some gruff coughing followed by, "Hello, Alan?"

"Good evening, Your Honor."

"This is Judge B-b-b-rieant." My relief was immeasurable when I recognized Henry's voice and realized I was nailed by a practical joke

Strangely I took more heat from GSA than the court for the flippant comment which found its way to national television. Judge Brieant, who alternately treated me like a defendant, hostile witness or long lost son, never said a word about it.

Less than two weeks after the *Inside Edition* story, *Sixty Minutes* ran a segment implying mob influence in the New York City construction industry (there's a novel revelation). It featured a photo of a truck belonging to an alleged connected contractor parked at the project site with the inference that this contractor "built the courthouse." The photo of the truck was taken during excavation and superimposed in front of a completed building photo. You would have had to have been familiar with the project to realize it was two different photos.

The truck was actually rented by the alleged "mob contractor" to another party which was delivering steel rebars during foundation work. That was its only visit to the site. Even *Sixty Minutes* can mislead its viewers.

* * *

The operable window incident was but one of many instances of the judges' egos exceeding their common sense.

One of the more flagrant abuses of judicial entitlements had to do with the showers in the chambers caper.

For a brief period GSA was between Public Buildings Service commissioners. In one of those moves out of the White House that careerists become accustomed to not question, a high court administrative official was appointed interim commissioner, purportedly to enhance the working relationships of GSA and its biggest and most influential client.

During the six or so weeks in this relationship, the Courts Design Guide, a joint GSA-Court publication, was modified to allow such amenities as enhanced paneling in chambers and showers built into every judge's private bathroom in new court installations. Fortunately we did not retrofit every time a design guideline was changed.

There was much debate at our committee meetings as to whether this new luxury would be permitted in the forty-two chambers of the new building. Since the building was already fully designed and this million dollar amenity was never budgeted, the working stiffs of GSA vehemently opposed its inclusion. The judges, on the other hand, demanded it as an entitlement. Eventually we were worn down so much that our politically appointed regional administrator told us to "work it out." We requested a budget modification to accommodate this new requirement. Quietly, we hoped there would be nothing left in the budget and the issue would disappear.

While this crucial decision was being contemplated in D.C., other calamities occupied our time. On a sunny mid-day in lower Manhattan we were faced with a building collapse on the site of the office building portion of the Foley Square project. There were several old multistory buildings on the site, most of which were vacated or abandoned. However, there was always an issue of the homeless and illegal squatters.

Immediately after the collapse the scene was swarming with New York City police, fire and EMS people. Our own project management people, including myself, and federal protective officers were there. We did not yet know whether there were any fatalities or people trapped in the building. We also didn't know if utility lines, such as steam, gas or electric were in danger, nor could we yet assess the structural integrity of the still standing adjoining structure.

It was a very busy emergency response scene.

While I spoke with the local battalion commander, my eye caught sight of a judicial committee member with whom we regularly met on the unresolved shower issue. I assumed he had been passing by and just wanted to know what was going on.

"Good afternoon, Your Honor."

Without even so much as a glance at the collapsed building he asked, "Were the showers approved yet?"

I silently fumed but bit my tongue. "I'll get back to you as soon as we determine if there were any fatalities in the collapse."

"Try to get back to me this afternoon," was his only comment.

Luckily, there were no injuries or major damage. The new courthouse got its showers in each of the judges' chambers. As soon as the interim commissioner returned to the court, the design guide was changed to no longer authorize this amenity.

* * *

The Foley Square project provided an endless string of interaction with the Courts. We generally had bi-weekly progress meetings that were businesslike but could go from cordial to hostile in a heartbeat. If we took exception to one of the suggestions of the great American architects, or felt that a request was financially imprudent, it was like taking a kid out of Toys 'R Us. "We're entitled to this" was a frequent chant.

In fairness, the construction committee for the court, headed by Judge John F. Keenan, was generally responsive and timely, although we often didn't want to hear what they were saying. Judge Brieant was the chief judge at the start of the project and when his term was up he was succeeded by Judge Thomas P. Griesa. Sparks often flew but it was a successful relationship. Most important, the courthouse was completed with minimal surprises when the court took occupancy.

At one early meeting, the subject matter turned to the juxtaposition of the jury rooms in relation to the courtrooms. Judge Brieant insisted that they be located in a position which would have unintentionally prohibited jurors from entering and leaving the jury room without passing through the courtroom. Not a good idea. Even Judge Keenan, who generally remained reasonable and neutral in the disputes, came down on us hard for resisting this ill-advised suggestion.

The GSA delegation already was exasperated because we had just been flogged by another member of the committee who refused to understand why we could not excavate Pearl Street to build a secure parking area. Besides for the fact that the street was not federal property and there were statutes to enforce unlawful seizure, doing this on a street in which there were so many buried main utility lines would have severed water, sewerage and electricity for most of lower Manhattan. When we couldn't give a top of the head estimate as to what a caper such as this would cost, one judge replied, "So there are a few pipes in the street. You should be able to work around it. This is poor engineering."

With this as an opener, it was little wonder that we were less than receptive to the comments about positioning of the jury rooms. Judge Brieant was so adamant about this that he said he would consider us in contempt of court if we disregarded his command. With the incentive of wanting to return to our families that night we complied with the judges' request, only to revert back to the architect's original plan later when the committee realized that the chief's idea wouldn't work. "GSA should have told us this before we did it," the chief said.

After the meeting, I turned to my colleague, Project Engineer Charley Fraser and said something uncharacteristic of me. "I need to drown my anger. Let's go for a proper lunch."

Four of us headed to Forlini's on Baxter Street, an upscale hangout of the legal and political crowd. This was an upgrade from my usual wolfing of a sandwich or dirty water hot dog at my desk. As we approached Forlini's we discussed how hard Judge Keenan had come down on us, which was unlike him. Collectively we were rather annoyed at the judges, but they were judges and we were hired hands so we accepted it.

We ordered wine. Then the corner of my eye saw an ornament on the wall just above the tabletop. It was a small brass plaque with an inscription, THIS BOOTH IS DEDICATED TO THE HONORABLE JOHN F. KEENAN, US DISTRICT JUDGE.

This was just what we needed to forget our troubles. We drank doubles. It turned out that most of the booths were dedicated to distinguished members of the judiciary or prosecution, all of whom were regular customers.

The next time we went to Forlini's we requested a table. No booth.

Meetings with the judges were unpredictable. We never knew whether they would last an hour or a day. Often it depended on the court calendar.

At the conclusion of another aggravating meeting, Judge Keenan said, "Before we leave I would like to know if that episode in the ceremonial courtroom was somebody's idea of a joke."

We had no idea what he was talking about.

"Was it you or the construction crew that decided to put that lewd art in the courtroom?"

Again we drew a complete blank.

"Don't you know what I'm talking about, Alan?"

"No, Your Honor."

"Then let's take a walk and we'll see who knows what."

Mystified, a delegation of high powered judges and mortal GSA people walked to the under-construction ceremonial courtroom on the ninth floor. The judge pointed at the ornamental slab of marble framed with mahogany which was on the wall behind the bench. That was where the seal of the court would eventually be inserted.

We looked at it and looked at each other and still didn't know what the judge was talking about.

"Go a little closer," said Judge Keenan.

We looked more closely and then it hit us. "Damn," I said. "Now I see it."

The judge really did see something which resembled erotic art. The way this piece of marble was quarried and finished, the veins extended symmetrically from the center forming what looked like the outline of the legs, the pubic area and the breasts of a naked woman.

Now we had a real problem. This piece of art was not easily recognizable in the stone, but once noticed it would be a distraction in the courtroom. If *The New York* Post latched on to it, it would be front page news. The judges and GSA agreed that we had to do something.

This was easier said than done. The piece of marble weighed close to a ton, framed by very expensive mahogany. You couldn't just dismount it and turn it upside down.

GSA was declared innocent of any intent. Judge John Walker, the chief appellate judge, volunteered to head the committee to resolve this problem. We took photographs; we had brainstorming sessions; we went to other ceremonial courtrooms; we called in marble experts.

We brought back the rigging equipment, cut the stone into quadrants and scrambled the pieces. It now looked worse because the design wasn't symmetrical; you could see the seams. We put it back upside down, inside out ad infinitum but it looked out of place.

At the end of one of these meetings, our Charley Fraser said to the court's district executive, "Instead of modifying the stone, why don't we just modify the frame?"

The next day Judge Walker summoned us to an emergency meeting. We assumed it was related to erotic art.

As usual, Judge Keenan chaired the meeting.

"Gentlemen," Judge Keenan said, "our district executive has come up with a brilliant solution to the marble problem. Instead of modifying the stone, why don't we just modify the frame?"

When Fraser and I looked at each other with a collective, "Huh?" the judges actually thought this was news to us.

"Excellent suggestion," said Fraser. "I'll have the architect redesign the frame."

The meeting was over in three minutes.

In that ceremonial courtroom today you can see a lovely piece of marble in a frame behind the judge's bench. The Great Seal of the Court covers what previously had been the boobs and a piece of solid mahogany covers what had once looked like the pubic area.

This was not the last of our dealings with the tastefulness of art in a courthouse.

As the building neared completion, a committee of judges, with the concurrence of GSA's Fine Art people, decided that additional interior art was needed. A Maya Lin sculpture stood outside the building. Although it was in the budget, no further art had been commissioned because the judges were concerned that overspending on art would jeopardize some court amenities.

With the availability of surplus funds at the end of the job, it was agreed that instead of commissioning a new piece for the lobby, a replica of a work of art by sculpture Raymond J. Kaskey would be ideal. The piece, called "Lady Justice," stood outside of the new United States Courthouse in Alexandria, Virginia.

It made a lot of sense. The piece was perfect for the cavernous main lobby and the fact that it was a duplicate saved both money and the time it would take to commission a new piece.

Of course, nothing ever goes quite that smoothly.

One quiet morning I received a call from the regional administrator's confidential assistant. Ms. Anabel was a political appointee, reasonably qualified and with a mouth like a sailor.

"Alan, we gotta do something about the tits."

"What?" Anything was capable of coming from Anabel's mouth but why is she calling me about tits?

"The statue. Too much cleavage."

Then another round of jumping through hoops began. It seems that Judge Griesa was offended by the apparent low-cut gown to be worn by the statue. Too much cleavage was showing and the statue's nipples were visible.

Fortunately the sculptor was not an egotist and agreed to the modification rather than a claim that the government was interfering with public art. The recasting of Lady Justice for New York was not identical to the original in Virginia.

That was not the only problem. Due to its size and weight and the fact that it was installed after building completion, the lobby floors had to be steel reinforced. The piece was delivered from the foundry in parts because the entire statue could not fit through the entry doors. The huge arms and the scale of justice were assembled and installed on site.

The statue eventually became the backdrop for the official photograph of the building dedication. The judges, Senator Moynihan and some less influential politicians, government officials and anyone else in a suit who could fit into the panorama (including myself), cut the ceremonial ribbon with the ceremonial scissors, a set of which is now in my home desk drawer.

After the event, when the dignitaries discussed what a great job they did, my wife and I walked over to Chinatown for some beef and rice, with a hearty bowl of hot and sour soup. I needed a reality check.

*　*　*

Doing business with judges was like doing business with the Congress or your local parent teachers' organization. Nothing ever got done without at least a little intrigue, aggravation and give and take negotiations. It got so bad at one point that judges were fighting with each other and we had to have secret meetings with particular judges and the designers and withhold information from other judges.

After insisting that they be represented on the "art in architecture" selection panel for the new courthouse and spending what must have amounted to hundreds of hours choosing an artist, the judges decided that despite a public law providing for the same, they did not want any art in the building and ordered us to cease selection activity. The money was to be used for judicial amenities which were threatened by a possible shortfall of funds. It was not until much later that they agreed to include work by the world renowned Maya Lin on the exterior. The Ray Kaskey piece which eventually was installed in the lobby was outside of the program and was actually initiated by the court.

Another judge demanded we not install energy-saving fluorescent lighting in his robing room, stating that "no courtroom in the civilized world should have fluorescent lighting." This was after a team of judges told us we needed 80 foot candles of lighting over the pit area of a courtroom when engineering standards called for 60 foot candles and in reality 30 foot candles would have been sufficient.

During this interlude we were told that the architect's lighting consultant was "too young" for the job and that we should get an older person who would understand the judges' needs better. Fortunately reason prevailed when we did a tour of existing courtrooms and they got the message that 80 foot candles would have put the electric meter in high gear and would have caused the attorneys to sweat profusely while they questioned witnesses. We were accompanied on the tour by a gray haired golfing friend of the lead architect and all was well.

Most meetings with the judges were held in the courthouse. There was a rare meeting at our building when prospective artists were to make a presentation to GSA, the courts and the Municipal Art Society. Judge Griesa was a bit late and the meeting was delayed while our Fred Fortunato stood outside the room looking for him. When the judge alighted from the elevator and approached, Fred extended his arm for a hearty handshake. The judge promptly removed his coat and draped it over Fred's arm like he was the coat check boy. From that moment to the end of the project Fred endured merciless ribbing about his new trade.

When Judge Brieant passed away at the age of 85 in 2008, the White Plains Courthouse, where he spent his final years on the bench, was renamed the Charles L. Brieant Jr. Federal Building and U.S. Courthouse in his honor. Notwithstanding the aggravation along the way, I considered it a privilege to have worked closely with so many distinguished judges,

CHAPTER 20

My Fragile Children

As a manager I thought I was reasonably skilled at interviewing people and judging character. I take pride in the fact that I brought some good people to GSA. Over the years I was responsible for the hiring of hundreds of employees, either directly or by exercising my right to approve a selection by a subordinate supervisor. Along the way there were some real clinkers, which brought me to question my skills for evaluating talent as well as my often used Columbo theory about being guided by your instincts.

Take the case of Mindy Mermelstein and Maria Christina Scudero, who represented two of my greatest misevaluations of talent ever. Both were college graduates and had work experience. Mermelstein was working for New York City Department of Social Services, which should have been a clue right there. Scudero worked in a family business, which was another clue. It's easy to fluff a resume in a family business. Both presented themselves well and spoke convincingly. Mermelstein passed the interview process with not only me, but with branch chiefs Large Lewis and Uncle Miltie. Scudero was not scrutinized quite as closely but we congratulated each other upon our excellent efforts. Before either reported to work we were already suspicious that we might have erred in our judgment.

On Mindy's reporting date she was a no-show. About mid-morning I received a call from a staffer in human resources informing me that Mindy had called from Barbados where she was on a Club Med type vacation. She needed a week's extension prior to starting her new career. It was granted but I already didn't like what was happening.

When she finally arrived a week later she alluded to a new romantic relationship in the Caribbean which had prompted her request to delay her start. By the end of the first week on the job, the relationship went from a budding romance to a concern that she was not able to contact her beau, who made his living as a free lance limbo performer, or something equally outrageous. Then in my role as father-confessor I found out from our new princess that "I loaned him money and he was going to pay me back next week when he comes to New York."

Sure.

"Now I can't find him. He doesn't answer his calls and the hotel says they don't know where he is." Yeah, right again.

"I hope he's all right." Why shouldn't he be, with a new supply of cash to go along with his freshly cleaned pipes?

On the very first day of work she was given a set of manuals and directives to glance through just as an orientation. At mid-morning I happened to walk through the bullpen en route to Miltie's cubicle when I observed our new employee sitting on top of her metal desk, bare feet dangling, smoking a cigarette (pre-no smoking days) and sipping coffee. She was making casual conversation with her neighbor who tried not to listen.

"What's this all about?" I asked, pointing roughly to the spot where her ass, the desk and the cup of coffee converged.

She looked at me as if I had nerve to ask the question. "I take my morning break at 10 o'clock."

Oh, now I understand. "And I take my afternoon break at 3 o'clock. This is the way we did it at Social Services."

"Let's have a talk in Milton's office."

Milton, her branch chief, knew when it was time to put someone through his brand of a stress test. It usually didn't happen on the first day of employment but he made an exception in Mindy's case. He ran out of expletives in his zeal to explain that we didn't sit on desks, we didn't stop work at ten and three for a smoke and most of all, we didn't issue ground rules to our supervisor. It worked the other way around.

By the end of her first morning she already asked for the union representative. I wanted to fire her on the spot because we knew she was going to be big trouble but our HR cadets said we have to go through the process. Issue her a counseling notice, outline a performance plan and allow her sixty days to remediate any deficiencies. This is why as managers we would devote our efforts to making someone quit rather than build up a case to fire them.

As part of our training regimen, new employees received coaching from a senior specialist, technical training in a classroom and a series of rotating assignments in order to familiarize them with the entire organization. They start out by observing and assisting their coach and ultimately they receive tasks to complete on their own, starting with the very simple ones. This training plan was submitted to Ms. Mermelstein at the end of her first week, while her Caribbean romance was becoming as stale as an old piece of beef jerky. She took the one-page agreement home to study, as if it needed the blessing of her lawyer or next boyfriend.

On Monday morning Milton walked into my office. "I just wanted to show you what our protégé turned in." He handed me the signed training agreement with an asterisk at the bottom and a handwritten addendum. "I will comply with this agreement to the extent that it does not violate my civil rights or personal principles."

Milt and I nodded at each other. It was time for Plan B. Our strategy changed from "how we train her" to "how we get rid of her." We knew we would get little help from our human resources specialists. We had to make life so miserable for her that she would quit on her own.

Mindy lasted about thirty days. After four weeks on the job she had accrued one sick day, which she promptly took the day after it was earned, claiming the need for a medical appointment. At 4:30 PM that day she called Milton to say she decided to quit because the time in the office precluded her from devoting all of her efforts to find her missing man and her money. She regretted that she would not be returning to work.

We did not share her misgivings about leaving. Within the hour all paperwork was prepared and she was off the payroll, just in case she changed her mind over the weekend. I don't know if she ever found her beloved.

While this was going on we were blessed by another fragile employee joining our staff. Due to an uncertain budget we were periodically hit with a malady known a hiring freeze. This means no new accessions to the payroll, followed by a time frame where hires could be made only after receiving a formal waiver from central office. This kept staffers in Washington busy and put our HR sergeants in a regulatory mode, to their delight. The good news is that we always had advance notice of these freezes, which created a hiring frenzy before the effective date.

Another brilliant idea from HR was to expedite hiring in advance of the freeze. In lieu of calling in people for interviews for which there was insufficient time, we hired people based upon their application and the referral list from what was then known as Civil Service Commission. If they didn't work out we could always fire them during the probationary period. This was a real stroke of genius considering that getting hired under any circumstance was tantamount to a lifetime indenture. Unless you murdered someone on the premises in the presence of witnesses it was unlikely that our legal or HR staff would support a dismissal during that era ("We could get sued." was the usual response.). Even if a trainee did commit murder they would be entitled to a thirty day notice and a hearing.

It was because of this wonderful policy that we wound up with Ms. Maria Christina Scudero. Her interview was hastily arranged and short in duration. The freeze was coming and it was hire her or nobody. She was hired based on an unverified resume, no reference check and no documentation of her college graduation. When I suggested to our then-main man in HR that perhaps this should be done post-hiring in the event of a fraudulent application, the response was "We accept self-certification."

Maria started out without major incident but it only took a few days to find out that she lacked a most essential skill in our division, the ability to write coherently. Her learning capacity had its limits, and most discouraging, she was just a bit high strung.

She couldn't deal with smokers, abusive language, food or drink on people's desks, untidiness and anyone who approached her from the left side. Unfortunately we placed her at a desk in front of one Mr. Adolfo "Spots" Gomez, the ultimate slob who practiced all of the above. To boot, Adolfo had almost no hearing in his left ear so when he approached people from the rear it was generally from their left to take advantage of the good right ear. Since he sat right behind Maria and was wishfully trying to get into her pants, he constantly approached her from over her left shoulder. Adolfo had the ability to agitate people merely by saying "hello."

A few people who dared go to lunch with Maria found out that she would refuse to enter a crowded elevator and once inside the lift she would go to the rear with her back against the wall. In the beanery she wouldn't sit where there was a draft coming from the vent, real or perceived, she would not sit in close proximity to a rest room or serving stand, and had to sit so she faced the front door. She also couldn't deal with people who put dressing on their salad, put mayonnaise on their sandwich or drank soda from a can. If there were open soda bottles on a table she was always checking that the caps were screwed on tight to maintain the fizz. With these idiosyncrasies, her lunch partners slowly faded away.

It was little wonder that Maria became one of those for whom the term *high maintenance* was invented. This employee would not be trainable and would never produce squat for us. It was time for Plan B once again. Get her to quit or to commit an offense so egregious that we could fire her for disciplinary reasons, or at least threaten to fire her, to the point where she would resign on her own.

Maria had some past real estate experience which enabled her to fling around a few buzzwords or make people momentarily believe that she knew what she was talking about. Her ability to put together a government bid package for leased office space? It did not exist. Negotiating a deal to completion was out of the question.

One day, when we least expected it, our prayers were answered. My only regret is that I wasn't there so my accounts are from eye witnesses.

Adolfo's approaches from the left rear, sexual innuendos, and a desk full of butts and candy wrappers were again getting to her. After a particularly irritating "good morning" from Adolfo, she said something like, "Get your goddamn cigarette butts away from me. They stink. Get rid of the candy wrappers. You shouldn't eat candy anyway 'cause you're too fuckin' fat; and most of all, stay the fuck away from me." A brief pause followed. "And take a fuckin' bath 'cause you stink."

Adolfo was taken aback but given his lack of social graces, he had become accustomed to rejection. Without too much emotion he started to say, "Well if that's the way you feel it's your misfor...."

"Just fuck off asshole," was Maria's way of finishing Adolfo's sentence.

A crowd started to assemble. Adolfo was beginning to show some anger. He leaned forward at his desk and slowly rose until they were nearly face to face. He glanced down at her jugs.

"Fuck you, bitch!"

At which point she reached for the nearest object on her desk, her open purse, withdrew a wrapped package and flung it straight at Adolfo.

The package was an individually wrapped sanitary napkin. It bounced off Adolfo's head. They both went to retrieve it from the floor at the same time with similar thoughts, Maria to destroy the evidence and Adolfo to preserve it. The two of them were grappling, trying to pull the sanitary napkin, which had come loose from its wrapper, from one another when both ended up wrestling on the floor. The fight would have continued had they not cut the legs from under an aging colleague, Dean Callahan who was coming over as a peacemaker. With three people on the floor the concern shifted to Callahan, who was pushing seventy.

Dean ended up in the hospital with multiple contusions and a suspected ruptured spleen. It was the most serious workplace accident we had since Big Anthony "Cream Cheese" Cantalupo fell backwards into a dumpster for recycled paper when a typist who couldn't read his writing pushed his hand-written travel voucher into his ample stomach.

Somebody was looking over everyone here. It turned out that Callahan's spleen was bruised but not ruptured and the other injuries were superficial. But in the three days he was hospitalized for observation, thinking he was going to die, he used his meditation time to reconcile with his estranged family. The incident, if it didn't directly extended his life, allowed him to spend his remaining years at peace.

Maria couldn't take the pressure anymore and quit before the ink was dry on the paperwork prepared by investigators from the Federal Protective Service and the Office of the Inspector General. After a six month vacation to calm her nerves she later resurfaced with a New York City job as a parking agent (ticket writer). We heard that her application for a job as an air traffic controller was rejected.

Adolfo remained unfazed by the events in the same manner that he was unfazed by the requests that he occasionally complete some work. Within a few months he too quit, citing his acceptance of a position in private industry in the real estate department of a major insurance company. His immediate supervisor, Richard S, remarked that he would last two weeks in the private sector. He was wrong. He lasted but three days before being fired without having the opportunity to display his true level of incompetence. He asked us for his job back but that didn't happen. A cousin of his eventually helped him get a job with a municipality where he was able to hide until he was vested in its pension plan.

Adolfo hadn't been with us for too long, so there was no real going-away party for him. Out of common courtesy, however, Richard thought it would be appropriate if we had some event to mark his leaving and to wish him well, as long as it was far from us. It was at this event that I couldn't resist a quip or two and I did a few things which, in today's climate or if directed at a more aggressive person, would have generated a grievance or EEO complaint.

After thanking Adolfo for his loyal service - I often wondered how people say these things with a straight face - and before presenting him with a $25 gift certificate from Friendly's, I said something like, "We were planning to get Adolfo a stereo speaker......" At that moment I could see Adolfo's wife simmering with anger over my bad taste reference to the fact that he could only hear from one speaker anyway because of his hearing loss, and I observed some of my staffers practically choking to keep in their laughter. Adolfo didn't say a word.

Mrs. Gomez was an attractive, petite, soft-spoken and well dressed woman. She was as demure as her husband was crude. Her match with Adolfo was evidence of that well worn theory that there is a cover for every pot. Mr. and Mrs. Gomez gathered up his personal belongings from the desk, put the unspent candy bars in their pockets and waved their final goodbyes. As they exited I turned in Lizzy's direction and said just loud enough for some to hear "Call the building manager and see if they can send an exterminator to fumigate the area around Adolfo's desk." The cleanup of his desk would be the end of another unfortunate chapter in our division's history.

As disheveled as Adolfo might have been, he was no match for "Dirty" Harry Horowitz. I did not hire him but inherited him.

He was an architect and early computer expert whom we relied on to introduce us to the world of CADD (Computer Aided Drafting and Design). Architects have a reputation for neatness, meticulous planning and stylish grooming. Harry, on the other hand, was so unkempt that we were reluctant to let him loose with customers. He knew his stuff but his appearance and personal idiosyncrasies would turn a sixties hippie off.

Harry would sit at a presentation and run his filthy fingers through his long and uncombed hair. Then he would touch his mouth, his ear, pick his nose and twiddle his bushy eyebrows. He wore checkered jackets and wrinkled chinos which looked as if they came from the Salvation Army racks.

We had to tread lightly about telling our employees how to dress because our HR people were deathly afraid to pursue disciplinary action; they had been chastised for trying to "counsel" a female employee who had a penchant for going braless. Harry got the message when a group of his co-workers went to the Goodwill store and bought checkered jackets for 25 cents each and wore them to work one day which was referred to in the water cooler talk as "Harry Horowitz Look-Alike Day."

As bad has his grooming and dress code had been, that was not the most offensive part about him. He was constantly biting and chewing on his fingernails, to the point where his gnarled digits looked like they were sandpapered at the tips to prevent fingerprinting. He also had a slight speech impediment which caused him to slur his *s* sounds and spray in the process. If he told you he had *shcrambled* eggs for breakfast or it's a *shunshiny* day, you were in for a shower.

The final straw for Harry was when he passed wind at a staff meeting, causing the conference room to be vacated and creating a near panic in the halls when other employees saw people running from the room.

Under pressure from his peers to be a bit less offensive, he ended up leaving the government and setting up his own successful CADD consulting business, which he operated out of his parents' garage. Nobody would accuse him of not knowing his stuff. He capitalized on his knowledge of a new and rapidly growing specialty.

If Mindy, Maria and Adolfo were my only bad hires I would have considered myself a success. Unfortunately there were more.

Perhaps my worst hire ever was Reiner Schmidt, who quickly earned the nickname "Schmidthead." Compounding the error was the fact that I actually hired him twice, the second time selecting him over Fern "The Driller" Miller whom I later hired. She became one of my great performers. We're both retired now but for thirty years I have been hearing about this *faux pas*.

Early in my management career, the regional administrator asked me to spend a few months in Federal Supply Service ("FSS"), another segment of GSA, to help with a reorganization and to hire and transfer people into a new unit.

Reiner was one of my first hires. He came out of a respectable college with better than average grades, was well spoken, created a good appearance and from the interview, appeared to be motivated. We were pleased with the hire.

Within weeks he established himself as one of the better performers. A year later, when his name appeared on a referral list for a job as a realty specialist trainee, I hired him again without a second thought, thinking I made a major coup. The name "Fern Miller" appeared on the same referral list but all she received was the mandatory courtesy interview. Our personnel people were very adamant that if you interviewed one person on the list, which ranked the candidates, you had to interview all, even though you could not hire them all.

When Reiner reported for work after a brief vacation he sported a beard, longer hair than a conservative government office cared to tolerate, wore an army surplus field jacket and carried his stuff in a back pack. We were suddenly back in the sixties.

Reiner's grooming habits were only part of the problem. It became a never-ending game of "Catch Me if You Can."

We knew this guy would need some extra supervision so we sat him directly in front of Milton's office in the same space which was later occupied by our personal care product flinger and became known as *the ejection seat.*

Within weeks after Reiner's arrival I first became aware that we actually had a union in our agency. Either by declaration or election Reiner was the union president, unknown to me until a lot of traffic kept coming into our office. I was to quickly learn that it was the right of the union president to perform union business on company time and use the office's phone, equipment and typing personnel. Very few employees were actually union members because in government circles, the union had no input on major issues such as salary and benefits. The only union representation was on labor disputes, generally brought on by the malcontents and incompetents because the government provided this protection and because our personnel experts, not wishing to disrupt the equilibrium with excessive challenges, took an extremely liberal interpretation of the rights and privileges of our union representatives.

There was Schmidt, right smack in the middle of the office, conducting his union business while his coworkers went about their real work. We kept moving his work station, with an accompanying new telephone number, in order for him not to get overly comfortable. Each move was within visual range of Milton's cubicle so he always felt Milt's evil eye looking at him. Milton made it a practice of coming out and just glaring at him a few times a day. When he was able to take on simple tasks on his own we generally sent him to out of town projects because they were smaller and in his case, to get him out of the office. It was difficult to give Reiner even routine training exercises because he had no interest. It was hard to have him face customer agency representatives or business people because of his flower child attire. I was already warned by HR that I couldn't impose a dress code for fear of a labor action.

My patience with him reached its limit when I innocently asked a member of our typing pool if she saw a document I submitted in draft for typing. The response was something like, "I have it but Mr. Schmidt said I had to do a letter for him first."

"He *what?*"

If this happened later in my career I would not have blown my cool, but would have calculated my response. I was young and still a little naïve and less compromising as a manager then. I went completely berserk. I would never ream out an employee in front of others but in this particular case I couldn't control myself. Besides, Reiner was considered a burden and distraction by most of his fellow specialists.

I walked over to his desk and began shouting when I was about five strides away. In a rather elevated tone I said, "Look you little prick, when you become boss you can give orders around here, but that's never gonna happen because I'm gonna run your hippie ass back to *Haight-Ashbury.*" Heads turned as the octaves got louder. The exact words are a distant memory but I was often reminded that I set the Guinness and government records for use of the f-word in a paragraph, sentence and within other words.

I knew that all of my shouting and threats would be worthless unless I backed it up so I ended it with, "And your sorry excuse for a quarterly training report better be on time and written in at least first grade English or you can forget about getting your promotion." I was referring to a salary increment under training programs which was basically an annual entitlement until reaching journeyperson level. You get this unless you don't show up or don't complete your training reports. If the submissions were not timely or not equal to a Grade D term paper, HR generally recommended promoting the person anyway subject to future submission of the report. This was not the incentive managers appreciated and the malingerers pounced on it. The HR logic was that we did this in the past so that if we changed now and did not allow the same courtesy, a grievance could be filed. This is the kind of logic that put me at loggerheads with anyone with an HR mentality for most of my management career. For those in HR who bucked that defensive attitude and showed promise, I brought them into Public Buildings Service where their career advancement potential was far greater. This ticked off a number of former HR directors.

Within minutes of my outburst I received a visit from our head of HR. I expected this just as sure as a rocking horse has a wooden pecker. But I mistakenly presumed that it was to assist management with my issue with Mr. Schmidt. That notion quickly disappeared when it was suggested that the solution to the problem was for me to take a course in anger management. This set me off again, but at least it was inside my office although my volume extended to the far end of the bullpen. It was as close as I ever came to a physical confrontation with a fellow employee.

My relationship with Schmidt, the HR director and the PBS administrative person who honchoed such things as the training program became more strained than ever. As the director I seldom was directly involved with the work of trainees but in Schmidthead's case I personally attended his training reviews. The tide was turning because I made it very clear to all that despite the liberal attitude and past practice, I was not going to approve anything which was not at least passable and in English and that I didn't care if he never got promoted. I was clearly going to use him as a test case to remove an employee who doesn't successfully complete the two-year training program.

It wasn't necessary. Between my harassment, Milton's constant glaring and a few unsuccessful labor issues, he lost credibility with his own constituents. One of the happiest days of the year was when Schmidt resigned to accept a teaching position with the New York City Board of Education. Besides getting rid of an office distraction, it freed me from all of the time-consuming effort required to build a bullet-proof case to fire the person. He insisted on giving two weeks notice although I told Milton to tell him that two hours' notice would be just fine.

The management team decided that on Reiner's last day we should have a party *for* him but not *with* him.

Customarily, on someone's last day, they unofficially take the afternoon off. This worked well when we had retirement or going away luncheons because it enabled the guest of honor to bask in the limelight and leisurely fade out. From a more practical point of view, with a guy like Reiner, it made sense just to get him out of the office to limit the disruption caused by a disgruntled parting employee.

At midday the management staff gathered in my office. Milton brought in a cake inscribed with the words "SCHMIDTHEAD, GOING, GOING, GONE!" Etched into the whipped cream was an outline of a boot kicking someone in the ass.

While we were feasting on cake and sipping champagne brought in by Miltie we were visited by Ed Baron of the assistant regional administrator's office. This was the same Baron who insisted that we give Reiner the benefit of every doubt on his training reports, his time spent on union and personal business and every other source of aggravation for someone responsible for getting production out of him. Someone had apparently tipped the front office that we were having a celebration, with liquor (forbidden in a government facility) in my office.

Ed had a very worried look on his face. "You know that what you're doing is a violation."

We looked at him incredulously. "A violation of what?"

Ed: "You're making a mockery of this."

Me: "You let that prick make a mockery of us."

Ed: "Well, the big boss isn't going to like this."

Me: "Fuck the big boss. Have some cake, Ed."

Ed: "You're making fun of me."

Me: "No, we're making fun of Schmidt."

Actually I had a very good relationship with the big boss, who gave me carte blanche to do whatever it took to get Schmidt out. Later that year, with the approval of the big boss, we nominated Milton for the annual regional administrator's meritorious service award. The plaque read something like "For his dedication and managerial accomplishments...." We all knew that it was for his perseverance in making life so miserable for Reiner that he quit.

I never saw or heard from Reiner Schmidt again. Sometime after he allegedly began his teaching career one of my employees reported that he got in a cab driven by Schmidt in midtown Manhattan but Schmidt pretended not to recognize him.

*　　*　　*

Strange things happened at lunchtime. I don't know if it was the midday tranquility or a certain blue collar mentality which made people braver after a lunchtime brew or an off-site matinee. Maybe it was just a conspiracy to not allow me a few moments of peace to wolf down a sandwich or review paperwork.

One day I heard a commotion in the bullpen area. Through the powers of observation and my underground network, I usually knew who had issues and who was doing what to whom. I slipped a bit on this one. I knew Stacey Solomon had a married boyfriend. What I didn't know was that her man actually worked for GSA in a blue collar capacity. This princess-like young lady from a suburban family was the *schtup* of a Puerto Rican maintenance laborer. I quickly assumed all of this after the first angry "Mira, Mira!" from the aggrieved wife when she came to the office, baby in arms, to confront her husband's side squeeze.

By the time I got to them, the action was hot and heavy. The scorned wife did not bear any type of weapon other than her mouth so I didn't motion for anyone to call Federal Protective Service, although someone else took it upon themselves to do so. I grabbed another employee, Maria Sanchez, and whispered in her ear, "Start translating for me."

The interpreter's services were not necessary. Between the "I keel you *beetch*" and "when Manuelo come home I cut hees nuts off" I got the idea of what was going on. Maria, meanwhile, said something in Spanish to the señora and took the baby in her arms, with bib and bottle. This scared me because it freed both women adversaries for a physical confrontation. It would have been interesting and a few were already egging them on but a cat fight in the office would generate too much paperwork.

Through all of this Stacey said not a word.

I tried to cut off the passage between the two, hoping that my loyal troops would pick up the clue and also block access. It became academic because just then two rent-a-cops came through the door.

Rent-a-cops couldn't intimidate anybody and probably could not have stopped a fight without assistance; however, the distraction caused by the appearance of law enforcement authority calmed the señora. "Everything's fine," I told the lead square badge. I didn't want to get into another round of investigations. They quietly left after the intruder and her cub departed with one last look back and accompanying "Beetch!"

The office reverted to its usual noonday calm.

Stacey, the resident relationship advisor to the office, even with her untraditional relationship, transferred to another region after Manuelo dumped her to return to his *esposa*. Before long she took up with another blue collar maintenance person with whom she procreated and married.

Stacey never appreciated the occasional digs at her relationship with Manuelo. Milton and others would make it a point to mutter a "Mira, Mira," when she would walk by. Most of all, she didn't like Milt's frequent interruption of her Dr. Phil act to get some work out of her. The consensus was that she was the one who dropped the dime on our going away party for, but without, Reiner.

For every Stacey Solomon, who came from a privileged background, there was a Mamie "Black Pearl" Odum, from the mean streets. Mamie, too, provided us with lunch hour drama when she engaged in aggressive telephone dialog with her son or one of her boyfriends. Mamie was rough around the edges, yet her primary concern in life was to make sure her pre-teen son didn't go astray. Jaleel came home from school each day, assuming he actually spent the day in school, to an empty house in a neighborhood infested with gangs and drug dealers. Mamie herself had done time in rehab as a condition of her continued employment so she well knew the risks.

When we heard her loud and shrieking voice over the partitions we knew that Jaleel arrived home. She had a magical way of shifting from the perfect English she was capable of speaking to the dialect of the street. "Look *boy!*" would be a typical opening statement of her daily early afternoon telephone conversation with her offspring (of whom she openly admitted that she was unsure of the father). "I want your black ass in the house until your schoo' work is done. D' you heah me, boy? An' you call me if you leavin' the house!"

Her conversations with her son became predictable. What was not predictable was the behavior of her boyfriends. One quiet noonday I heard screaming from the bullpen floor. Either Elvis had entered the building or something was going down in the office. I slowly exited my bunker.

"He's got a gun!" I heard from over the bullpen partition. I went from slow to slower, motioning with my hands and lips to Lizzy to call security.

By the time I rounded the bend this ex-boyfriend was leaving, no weapon in hand. He was looking back at Mamie, exclaiming "ho'" a few times and threatening what he would do to the next homeboy to attempt to put their duck in his oven. Once more Mamie's afternoon productivity was cut, given the time she needed to tell Jaleel to not let anyone in and then to warn her current man to stay clear for a few days. We already saw Mamie arrive at work bruised after being struck with a flying mayonnaise jar thrown by a disgruntled suitor who caught her in the sack with someone else. I suggested that she keep a low profile for a few days.

When Mamie wasn't dealing with domestic abuse, child rearing, money problems and her everyday way of life she was a good producer in her support role. The problem was that we never knew if or when she would show for work, who was after her and what foreign substances were in her body. She had an unpredictable sense of humor. When I asked her once to follow-up on a lessor's missing tax escalation payment and to let me know the result she came into my office a few minutes later, she gave me a thumbs up sign and said a distasteful, "He has his money and he's as happy as a faggot in Boys Town."

There was the time we had visitors from Washington. It was after the normal quitting time and we were still meeting in the conference room. One of the attendees was Bill DeCourcey, a branch chief and Mamie's immediate boss. As Mamie was leaving around six o'clock she poked her head in the conference room looking for Bill with a question or some information. Bill had stepped out for a nature call.

Upon seeing that Bill was out she casually looked in my general direction and said, "Oh, DeCourcey must be shaking the dew from the lily. I'm leaving now. Please tell him the Pearl can't sleep with him tonight." She closed the door and left. There were some incredulous looks until the meeting participants realized this was New York humor.

When Bill came back in I gave him the message and the meeting continued.

*   *   *

Mamie Odum and Giuseppe Verdi DiGiacomo were about as opposite as any two people who ever worked for us. Mamie was the streetwise hustler and Joey D the naïve follower. Their paths crossed intermittently during the work week.

On a spring afternoon they were to interact in a manner which would link them together for the next few years.

Joe, in his relentless style, was badgering a typist to complete a letter he had hand printed. Little Vera, the typist, had enough of Joe and implored him to "just step back;" she would get the job done soon. Joe took her literally and did step back, unfortunately at the exact moment that Mamie was hustling back to her desk to take a call from her son. Joe's elbow met with Mamie's solar plexus causing her to drop to the ground like a duffel bag.

Mamie gasped for breath, tossed about and had a coughing spree. How much was caused by Joe's blow and how much was enhancement was questionable. When she recomposed herself she went to the health unit claiming shortness of breath because the blow triggered an asthma condition. The nurse advised her to go to the ER at the local hospital, or if she didn't feel that terrible, to go home and rest.

Joe volunteered to drive her home, which Mamie later said was more traumatic than the original blow. I gave them permission to take our government car. Joe drove over the Williamsburg Bridge and weaved in and out of traffic as well as columns from the elevated transit line. They traversed Broadway past the busy intersection of Flushing Avenue which was the unofficial Willamsburg-Bushwick border. Joe continued down Broadway, which skirted the Bedford-Stuyvesant neighborhood and eventually found his way to Mamie's place on Monroe Street. Joe honked his horn at slow moving traffic, causing Mamie to shrink down in the seat. These were uneasy times in New York City and the last thing Mamie needed was to be observed exiting a government car with a honkie at the wheel. All of this was lost on Joe, as were the dice and card games, beer drinking and powdered bags being exchanged on the sidewalks. Mamie declined his invitation to escort her to the apartment.

Mamie's streetwise instincts took over. Because she was injured on the job she decided to take her entitlement of time off under what is known as "Continuation of Pay (COP)." Employees were allowed up to thirty calendar days off due to an on-the-job injury. It was intended for people in law enforcement and hazardous positions but the general populace latched on to it. Mamie got a local pill pusher to give her a diagnosis of a respiratory condition coincidentally requiring a minimum of thirty days of inactivity. This was a common practice among malingerers who were able to feign injuries or amplify a paper cut to a case of acute trauma. I'll never know if Mamie was really hurt or faking it but I suspect the latter.

When I asked HR to challenge the Department of Labor's very liberal attitude in accepting these claims I got the same copout answer for years. "It is not our policy to question these claims."

The malcontents knew this game and they played it to the hilt. I had one employee who on ten occasions over a span of years managed to fall on federal property during working hours, with no witnesses. Each time he played it for the maximum COP. Each time we tried to deny him pay either our own HR or Department of Labor refused to challenge, thus validating his inability to work. When the person finally and mercifully decided to apply for a disability retirement because of his propensity to fall down on federal property, *then* our HR decided that he *could* work and held up approval of his retirement until he produced satisfactory documentation.

These types of incidents are what make federal managers take early retirement.

CHAPTER 21

"A Man Has Got to Know His Limitations"

Clint Eastwood as "Dirty Harry"

Young Shamus Walsh came to work for us as an intern at the peak of the Foley Square project. We needed all the help we could get and Shamus was a conscientious college student with enough basic knowledge of architecture that he was able to do such tasks as field inspections and maintenance of plan files with minimum supervision. Shamus was not born with a silver spoon and he knew the value of hard work.

Like many young people Shamus appreciated a good time and was worthy of his obvious nickname, "Famous Shamus." Without the benefit of dapper clothes, a fancy car or a budget permitting fine dining, he managed to attract an interesting assortment of lady friends.

Shamus began dating Disco Carol, a young topless dancer after a chance meeting in the library. Her profession belied her personality. The topless gigs were to assure her of college tuition and living expenses.

Her photograph, in working gear, adorned Shamus's desk in the rear of the office. It was out of sight of visitors but its presence offended the office administrative person, Christina, who always managed to remind us of her traditional values in addition to her readiness to file an EEO complaint for cavalier behavior or foul language in the office. Construction is not the type of industry that attracts Mr. Rogers's types, so it was often a challenge to be on good behavior around Chrissy. Although she had a sense of humor the sight of Carol's boobs in Shamus's desktop photo was more than she could manage.

In order to diffuse this potentially harmful situation before it left the office, the compromise was that Shamus put pink tape over the boobs and G-string, attempting to create the illusion that she was now wearing a stylish two piece bathing suit. It didn't make sense, considering that she was posing in front of a stripper's pole, but everybody was happy.

One quiet Friday, Shamus brought Carol to the office for his afternoon shift. They were going to dinner to celebrate the end of finals and then he would drop her off at work.

Since the office was devoid of people, with Shamus and I as the only staffers actually in our small quarters, Carol occupied Chrissy's front desk. She made herself comfortable alternately with a book and online computer games. She looked anything but a member of her chosen temporary profession.

What could possibly go wrong?

From my private office, I heard conversation in the front. Peeking out from the bunker I saw our esteemed regional counsel, Sweet Caroline Taylor, in the office, along with the regional administrator's chief of staff, Stephen ("Don't call me Steve.") Stevens, and a matronly looking lady whom I found out was Anna May Buford, GSA's new general counsel who was visiting the region. Caroline was showing her around. Since Foley Square was such a high profile and politically sensitive project, to say nothing of the potential for major litigation if things went wrong, she brought her up unannounced, to meet the staff. The only thing I knew about her was that she was politically connected and was an ordained minister in some Alabama church.

I quickly sized up this potentially embarrassing situation. We had Caroline once again trying to blow her own horn. We had Stevens who would like nothing more than to hang me as payback for my smart-ass attitude and a previous incident for which he tried unsuccessfully to suspend me. Rounding out this trio was our bible toting general counsel who just might make the connection between the woman at the front desk and the photo on Shamus' desk. They already assumed the traditional view that Disco Carol was a secretary. None of them had ever been to my office so they had no idea of who was the real secretary.

Carol knew none of them. None knew Carol. Carol didn't know me. They asked for me by name and Carol drew a blank. She was up to her tassels in a computer game but instinctively knew that she didn't want to get her boyfriend in trouble.

I knew the drill for high-ranking official visitors. They walk around the office glad handing, making small talk and telling how much the administration was doing for the people. I got to the front just in time to divert attention from Carol.

"Why don't we show Ms. Buford around the office?" Mr. Stevens sensed my discomfort and did what he could to keep me in a state of anxiety. I turned to Famous Shamus and with my right hand made a quick rotating motion in a feeble attempt to get him to ditch the picture. At the same time the phone rang in front of Carol. She answered with an unbusinesslike "hullo," further signifying that she had no business acumen and had no idea of the names of the inhabitants of the office.

Caroline encouraged Carol with, "Take a message." Caroline always enjoyed telling people of lesser status what to do, especially if it was something they would have done anyway.

Meanwhile, with attention diverted to the phone, my rotary motions became a frantic arm waving and silent mouthing. "The picture!" Shamus got the point just as the entourage approached his desk. Since he could no longer turn the offending photo face down without highlighting it he merely tidied his desk by sliding a thick set of rolled construction plans over to the side, obstructing the view. Without missing a beat I introduced him to the parade with a tag line, "Shamus is a bright, quick thinking young man. He can go places in this organization."

With a flick of the wrist one problem was averted. This didn't take anything away from an unfortunate incident several months earlier. Mr. Stevens was still seething from not being able to nail me for the prior event. His self directed charter was to find technical, judgmental or procedural errors for which he could administer either a disciplinary proceeding or negative input to the annual rating process.

Our Foley Square project was nearing its substantial completion. It was still on schedule and within budget, a definite exception to the usual project. I almost gave Stevens all the ammunition he needed to interject that one element that could have negated all of our successes.

Charles Fraser, the senior project engineer for the new courthouse, was a hard working, highly skilled individual and a tough negotiator. Although he was gruff at times he was a straight shooter with a sense of humor and had the respect of his peers in government as well as the team of contractors on the project.

As he approached his sixtieth birthday, the staff and I decided he should be honored with a unique ceremony. Exactly who made the suggestion is a matter of opinion, or how well the blame is deflected, but we decided it would be cute to do something just a little risqué. Obviously we weren't thinking of the standards of conduct or using much common sense.

"Ever Ready" Freddie Fortunato of our team had a connection with a young stripper who handed him her card at a party in New Jersey. She was a pro and not a college student like Carol. By the time we made the arrangements we had our staff, another ten or so of Charley's friends in GSA and a few of our hired technical experts all interested in attending. We would stage this as part of an expanded project meeting in the office.

I knew Chrissy would want no part of this given her straight-laced style so I explained what was happening and she chose to take a late lunch and stay clear. She was not the type to let her values spoil somebody else's fun.

When the meeting began Charles distributed the agenda and we discussed a variety of issues including the amounts due at the next payment request and the costs to settle some pending change orders. Charley was a notorious ballbuster when it came to change orders, which contractors typically use to run up job costs.

Charley was once again working himself into a fever, barking at the general contractor's representative that $25,000 was too much for adding ten duplex electrical outlets on a single floor, despite the claim that this would require a lot of work from multiple unionized trades. "Bullshit!" Charley's favorite reply to any proposal, whether fair or not.

The proceedings were interrupted by the slow entrance to the room of a studious looking young woman with a briefcase in hand. With her hair in a pony tail, big dark rimmed glasses, white blouse and plaid skirt, she could have passed for a parochial school student.

"Mr. Fraser?"

"Yes?" Charley actually thought she was from one of the contractors and was delivering paper work.

"Library police."

"Huh?"

"Yes, Mr. Fraser. We tracked you down at your place of business. You never responded to our letters or the calls at your home."

"Dunno what you're talking about." Being a rather perceptive man, he was beginning to suspect that this was a put-on.

"Well perhaps I can refresh your memory. You never returned the three quilt-making books you borrowed."

"Do I look like a damn seamstress?"

At this point the young lady released the pony tail to reveal long, flowing blond hair, put aside the glasses and leaned across Charley with one boob practically in his face. She nodded her head towards Freddie who reached out the door to bring in her boom box.

The music began and the young woman worked on Charley's memory by first putting one knee on his chair between his legs, running her finger down the side of his face and with one magical motion, removing her matronly blouse to reveal a bare chest save for sequined tassels on her boobs.

There were about a dozen people around the table observing this reclamation of library property. Charles now understood that this was his birthday greeting and drew his cheek a bit closer to the pulsating breast but was careful not to touch. At this point she said that it was time to blow out the candles and began a sensuous "Happy Birthday" while at the same time somehow attaching the candles to a holder affixed to her nipples. She shut the lights, lit the candles and invited Dave to make a wish and blow them out while the music blasted "Light My Fire."

The attendees, all male, forgot that they were in a federal building and depending upon their position, could lose their job or contract over this peccadillo.

We sobered up in a hurry. Our lookout, Freddie, stuck his head in the room and waved frantically. "Stephen Stevens is coming down the hall with Murray the K." His nickname came from *Murray the K*, a long gone New York disc jockey. The DJ's real name was Kaufman. Our Murray's last name was Kirschenbaum.

We now had the chief of staff and the human resources chief heading in our direction like two huskies at the Iditarod, liking nothing more than to hang the favored Foley Square team. I came about as close to a pure panic as I ever did in my career. I waved at our entertainer and pointed at the box. "Cut it!"

Someone had blown the whistle on us and called the front office. To this day, we never found out who did it. We also never admitted one ounce of guilt, nor was there one iota of evidence ever presented to implicate anyone, thanks to the code of silence by the attendees.

The birthday singer obviously encountered situations like this before and reacted like a true professional. In the time it took the two joy boys to walk the length of the hall to our office, and then go through Freddie's stalling tactics while he blockaded the entrance, the situation was under control. "Hi, Mr. Stevens, it's so nice to see you up here. What can we do for you? Have you toured the new building lately? We would love to take......"

"Where the hell is Greenberg?" I could hear the bark from inside the conference room.

Freddie's temporary diversionary tactic was all that was necessary. Our entertainer went from a near bare-ass stripper to a part of our project team in seconds.

Fred was a veteran of these types of situations, having been caught in a compromising position with a female staffer in a storage room once. The inspector general had planted a camera in the room to nail suspected in-office drug traffickers. That never happened but Freddie's indiscretion gave them something to do. He also had a minor issue of photographs which circulated of him and another female staffer in a hot tub. There was no GSA discipline with that since the hot tub was not on government property. But Freddie's wife was not pleased.

At my first panicky wave our library cop had cut the boom box and pushed it under the conference table. She put the frumpy glasses and parochial school blouse back on. There was no time for the plaid skirt so she stuffed it in her briefcase, put it against the wall and took her place at the conference table, on the side which faced the door where our interlopers now stood. From her location, only her upper body was visible to Stevens and Murray. She did this without even singeing her fingers when she put out the candles which were still attached to her nipples and were under the blouse, looking something like the lines from an ill fitting bra. To complete the transformation she grabbed a pencil to twiddle while Charles quickly resumed the meeting. She looked the part of a young architect.

When Mr. Stevens and Murray the K finally got past the road-block and entered the room they expected to see a very punishable scene. Both were experts in the "Penalty Guide" and frequently advised us of this. All they saw was a group of people talking serious business and an enlarged Primavera project schedule pasted to the wall. Since Stevens and Murray never came to any of our meetings except to convey bad news such as "You're one dollar over budget," or "Your EEO report is late," they really didn't know the cast.

This was fortunate. Our guest architect was sitting across the table with her fluffy blouse and a G-string, with our collective careers within her control.

"Alan, can I see you?" said Mr. Stevens, looking around the conference room for some shred of evidence of the alleged events. I know he would have said more but for the presence of what could have passed as a real librarian.

"Sure." I got up and walked out. "What's happening?"

He looked at me seriously and pointed to my private office.

When we arrived in my office he coughed and let out a few sighs before getting any intelligible words out. "Alan, I was told that there was a naked woman in the office."

"What office?"

"You know what I mean, your office."

"No, I don't know what you mean. Are you accusing me of something?" Fortunately I knew that the project team would have a lapse of memory and nobody would ever admit to what they had seen.

"I'm just saying that if you did that, it constitutes a serious violation of the standards of conduct and you can be punished for it."

"Punished for what?"

"Inappropriate behavior." Murray nodded in agreement.

Now Stevens was getting upset because with every stonewall answer the evidence in the other room was diminishing.

"What's inappropriate? We've got a project meeting going which you are now interrupting and you're accusing me of inappropriate behavior. You might think I'm an asshole but that doesn't constitute inappropriate behavior."

I slowly drifted from the entrance to my office to a position standing behind my desk, forcing my accusers to face me, with their backs to the door. This created a less welcoming environment for visitors and more important, allowed our birthday singer to gather her gear, exit the conference room and disappear into the hallway.

It occurred to me, however, that someone might have witnessed the coming and going of our guest and could cast suspicion on my story.

"Well, something was going on here or the front office wouldn't have been called." Steven S. said and Murray nodded again.

"OK, if you really want something I'll 'fess up. Somebody really was here." My face was drawn and dead serious.

"Tell me about it."

"It was for Charley's birthday."

Stevens said, "Yes, go on." Murray nodded.

"A singing telegram."

Now Mr. Steven's neck was bulging in the absolute belief that I was spoofing him. "Bullshit."

"Yeah, that's what it was. A singing telegram. The team wanted to do a fun thing for Charley."

Stevens earned the nickname "Uneven Steven" for his ability to surreptitiously obtain negative information about someone or learn of a flawed project and then spring this at the most inopportune time to embarrass or punish a staffer. When I said the word "team" Stevens saw another opportunity to set the trap. "Who paid for it?" I knew what he was thinking. If we accepted a gift from a contractor he could press for a violation.

"We all did."

"Who are *we all?*" Now the balance was shifting. It was he who was panicking, thinking that he came up with nothing and I could turn around and file charges against him. Not that I would. I was skirting a career-impacting disaster.

"The staff." I was thinking of hinting, but not saying, that the contractors contributed, just to agitate and give him something to waste his time over, but if I did that he would have had the inspector general over us like syrup on pancakes. They would have been under orders to pursue the "investigation" until they found something. We had better things to do with our time.

Stevens and Kirschenbaum walked out. By the head shaking and body language it was as if they said, "We'll get you yet."

It wasn't over.

Fortunately others had more of a sense of humor without the desire to nail me, or anyone else, and Stevens' efforts to push the issue were thwarted.

I found out from my immediate boss at the time, Matty D, that the issue was brought up at the next regional administrator's staff meeting. The reaction of the female RA at the time was a yawn. I was told that Stevens at least wanted to suspend me for a few days but was reminded that there was a due process and considering there was no evidence, no admitted witnesses, no way to pinpoint me as ringleader and that I was rather popular among my peers, the likelihood was that the whole case would embarrass the agency more than me. This was cemented when the IG later told me that the only thing that upset them was not being invited to the birthday celebration.

After all was said and done, there were lessons to be learned from this. When someone is out to hang you, you shouldn't be giving him the rope. We escaped on this one. More specifically I escaped, because I was the senior official and the events were in my office. Clint Eastwood was right on when his *Dirty Harry* character said "A man has got to know his limitations."

When Charles retired a few months later, we took him to Chinatown to celebrate.

*   *   *

There was another incident, this time off hours, which also could have triggered an early retirement, or at least serious disciplinary action.

One of my well documented passions had been the sport of running. Over the course of my running years I had run more than seven hundred road races of distances from five kilometers (3.1 miles) to the full 26.2 mile marathon.

On a particular fall Sunday in New York, not long after I became the big boss, the New York Road Runners Club sponsored a five mile run, which started at the United Nations Building, proceeded down the FDR Drive on Manhattan's east side and ended downtown at Battery Park.

As with many large running events, a big inconvenience is the lack of pre-race facilities. No matter how many porta-potties are there, it is never enough. For male runners, there is usually a way to improvise, although this becomes a challenge in urban locations.

My running buddy, Norman (not Stormin' Norman) Schimmel, and I took one look at the line by the potties set up on United Nations Plaza and realized that this wasn't going to work.

"Let's piss behind one of the office buildings," he suggested.

Sounded like a plan to me. "OK, find one," I said.

He proceeded behind a residential tower on East 45th Street, went down a service alley and called back to me. "Right here is good!"

I started to walk over and just as Norman was about to relieve himself. I realized where we were and made a dead stop.

"No, don't. Not here!"

He gave me a quizzical look but refrained from his immediate mission. "What's up?"

I had to stay where I was and not come any closer, because I realized that we were at the back of the United States Mission to the United Nations, a building occupied by the U.S. State Department and owned and operated by GSA. By virtue of my job I knew that there were security cameras all over the place, some hidden from view and some powerful enough to determine if I was wearing my Nike or Adidas running shoes.

If I had gone a few steps closer or worse yet, if I had actually urinated against the building, my career would have ended on the spot. I would have been cuffed by the State Department Police and my picture would have ended up not only on the police blotter but likely on the front page of the GSA News for the world and all of my peers to see. I could just imagine the caption, "Top GSA Official Gets Relief at Mission."

We ended up doing our thing instead at the adjoining Uganda Mission and considered it a political statement.

CHAPTER 22

The "Judges"

It didn't take me too long to learn that there are judges and there are "judges." Federal judges have a hierarchy of their own. Beneath the United States Supreme Court you have judicial circuits and within each circuit there are districts. Because our region encompassed New York, New Jersey, Puerto Rico and the Virgin Islands, the district courts in the region were parts of circuits based in New York City, Philadelphia and Boston.

Appellate judges consider themselves superior to district judges in that they have the power to overturn lower court decisions, but nevertheless they all belong to the same fraternity. Under the same courthouse roof are often found bankruptcy judges and magistrates who carry the title "judge" but are considered second class citizens by the district or circuit. There are certain specialized courts, such as Court of International Trade or the U.S. Tax Court which are part of the judiciary but within the hierarchy they are kept at a distance by the circuit or district.

Herein is where we get to the category of "judges." Some individuals carry the title "judge" but do not have the power, influence, privileges or immunities of judges. They do have the same ego. They *think* they are real judges and tell their friends they are judges but they are mortal public servants like the rest of us. They are not even part of the judicial branch of government. This classification includes immigration judges, or representatives of the Equal Employment Opportunity Commission, Federal Labor Relations Authority and a host of others, which can at best be called hearing examiners or administrative law judges.

Whenever a new courthouse is constructed you could depend on one or more of these groups to recommend their inclusion since "We're all part of the judicial family." This idea is usually quickly dismissed by the real judges.

As a mid-level manager I had a lot of dealings with a unique group of pseudo-judges who were part of the Social Security Administration's Hearings and Appeals subdivision. Their role was to adjudicate disputes arising out of denied claims. SSA maintained offices throughout each state for appellants to present their case, apart from the regular Social Security field offices. The hearings judges had an important job and made decisions which impacted people's lives.

The "chief judge" walked around as if he had the same status in life as a real chief judge. In any discussion about their office space, they would urge upgraded variations from the agency's own guidelines because "we are all federal judges."

One of the more irritating characters I dealt with was a "chief judge" named Joseph C. Cardinale.

Our relationship did not start very well. My subordinates began referring to this pompous windbag as "Jose" after the St. Louis Cardinal's infielder Jose Cardinal. He was referred to as "Jose" so often that we forgot his real name.

This charade went on until one of my technicians wrote, and I unwittingly signed a letter to *Mr. Jose* Cardinale. The subject was a field office in Long Island, which was already the source of confrontation because the "judge" had previously required that this office be relocated from an urban area where his clients lived to a suburban office park near his own residence. In our typical "we're not happy until you're not happy" fashion, GSA refused, citing additional rental costs as well as Executive Order 12972, originally signed by President Jimmy Carter in 1976. It stated that government policy when locating federal agencies was to "..make maximum use of existing federally controlled facilities" and "..give first consideration to a centralized community business area and adjoining areas of similar character." This was generally interpreted to mean, "Find the worst possible space in the most unsafe areas."

What I remember was being called to Stormin' Norman's office where the judge sat in waiting. Before I had both feet in the door he demanded my firing for not referring to him as "The Honorable", for addressing him as Jose instead of Joseph, and for showing "misfeasance and malfeasance" by continuing to offer inferior and unacceptable space. Apparently he was not a baseball fan and didn't understand the significance.

"GSA can't continue to treat the judiciary with such disrespect." We were merely doing what we perceived as our jobs at the time. This is why we were called "space cadets."

"Oh, yeah, I'm sorry about the Jose thing. It slipped by me. The typist must have been thinking about the *outstanding* baseball player by that name. I often get called 'Hank' the same way." This momentarily diffused the disrespect issue when he convinced himself that we actually called him "Jose" as flattery. I felt good about my diplomacy skills.

Stormin' Norman, who never said no to a political appointee, especially a Republican, said, "What can we do for the judge? He needs better space than you offered."

I felt like saying, "What can we do? We can throw him out of your office. The last I heard, his Bureau of Hearings and Appeals was not part of the judicial branch of government."

What I actually said was:

"Why don't I go out with Jos.., umm, *Judge* Cardinale myself and see what we can show him." This scored me a few points with the boss. It also meant I would meet him on Long Island where I also lived and could sleep an hour later. Despite my enthusiasm, when it came to blowhards like the good "judge" I would have preferred another visit to Dr. Not So Feinstein.

The result of all of this persiflage was that to circumvent the urban policy issue, Social Security Administration concocted a consolidation scheme for several offices which would have now put the geographical center of the area served under the new alignment of offices, right smack near the judge's town, assuring that he could take a leisurely drive to work each day with an up front reserved parking space and the knowledge that he was imposing justice on the American people.

Just when I thought I was done with him my own poor judgment caused the dragon to raise its head again.

I had been in New Jersey for a meeting with some real judges in Newark. When I returned late in the day, rather than return our division's assigned car to its regular indoor parking space I seized a curbside spot on Worth Street, adjacent to our building. These were also reserved for specific government vehicles. I wrongfully assumed that whoever was assigned the spot had gone home. My plan was to come back after I left work, remove the car to the garage and then get on the subway to Penn Station.

That was another big mistake. It turned out that "Judge" Cardinale was returning to the city that day from his Long Island haven to attend a ceremony and I had parked in the space under a street sign which said RESERVED FOR HEARING AND APPEALS JUDGES. When the judge saw the space occupied and then saw my name on the dash he went berserk.

He flew into my office like he had just caught me in the sack with his wife. *"Where is Greenberg?!"* I heard from the reception area, wishing I had a side door through which to exit.

Lizzy got as far as "Who should I say is call...." when the judge stomped through the door of my private office.

I already had an idea of what was coming. In one of the finest examples of how to sweat the small stuff and overreact to nonsense he began spewing, "This is the ultimate act of disrespect! I should hold you in contempt! I demand an apology! You took my parking space."

Unless I misunderstood the law, he had no authority to make good on the contempt threat. "Hey, what's up, judge?" was my quiet reaction.

"I'll tell you what's up. You are an ingrate. GSA will pay for this."

"Pay for what?"

"When will you learn to respect the judiciary? This is malfeasance and misfeasance (again)! I could have you arrested for *trespassing!*" I went from contempt to a misdemeanor.

Now I was getting irritated.

"Well, *Your Honor,* first I'm sorry I took your parking space. I thought the judges left for the day. And sec..."

"Don't think for us. We think for ourselves. That's why we're federal judges!"

"Well, *Your Honor,* now that you bring it up," I began as I reached behind me for a thick volume entitled *Annual Report of the Administrative Office of the United States Courts.* "I have the courts' annual report of workload here and strangely I see nothing about hearings and appeals judges. Not one word. I thought you were federal judges?"

This was the "Ah Hah!" moment where I knew I had crossed the line and was about to inflict irreparable damage. The "judge" was doing more than a slow burn. The issue shifted from a parking space to one's ego. "*Lookit!* We are judges, whether you like it or not. There's a proposal to make us part of the federal court system!"

A proposal? By whom? Certainly not by the real federal judges. They were very protective of their turf. They wouldn't invite a hearings and appeals judge to have coffee with them, much less sit in *their* courthouse. These types of "proposals" are usually generated by, or are the wishful thinking of, those who will benefit most. Consistent with all other self-serving proposals, this madcap scheme went nowhere. Twenty-five years later and the hearings and appeals judges are still not part of, nor will they ever be part of, the judiciary.

"Judge" Cardinale stayed around a few years longer. I had few dealings with him, although the roast chicken episode provided a break from the tranquility.

Norman called me to his office one day to advise that H&A had roaches in their Jamaica, New York office. This truly was an issue for the regional administrator who received an irate call from "Judge" Cardinale. The protocol would have been for the local office to call the GSA building manager who would have had the problem exterminated immediately. But no, the chief had to go to the top.

Now I, as the division director was told by the RA to personally check it out. I couldn't "pass the book" as Liz had suggested. After telling Storman' Norman that I'd get right on the case, I delegated it to Sam "The Sham" D'Amico, a creative and unpredictable realty associate.

Sam's report said the apparent cause of the rodent infestation was "an employee roasting chickens on a rotisserie in the break room." He further reported that the trash from the mini-Boston Market was left uncovered and food products were "exposed, unrefrigerated and stored in an improper manner." To top that off, Sam also observed that the cooking equipment, the use of which was prohibited in our lease because of safety and energy consumption issues, had frayed wires, was left dirty after use and in general "posed a hazard to employees." Sam suspected that the offending employee was not doing this solely for himself and a few office friends but was running a side business in the office.

When I got Sam's report I merely wrote a one paragraph letter to the judge, report attached, stating that we were pleased to be of service.

Cardinale was not the only H&A ego I had a run-in with.

There was a stretch in time when we had an extraordinarily heavy Social Security Administration workload, which included the many public contact offices as well as H&A locations. To expedite completion of these leases we borrowed Social Security staffers to work with us, given their familiarity with the agency's needs. H&A was a perfect example of how you could spend the most time, effort and aggravation on the smallest projects.

Every location was a major project even though the amount of space was relatively small. SSA's administrative group had to get approval of any decision from the chief H&A "judge" and the senior "judge" at each office, which generally required input from all other "judges." Their most important concerns were usually the sizes of their offices relative to each other and the proximity of free parking.

We had monthly progress meetings with our staff and the SSA staff. Generally I chaired them and as long as we had no uninvited guests the meetings were productive.

On the morning of one of our scheduled meetings I had strolled to the men's room. While doing what people do in such places and observing that the stalls and fixtures were suffering from severe wear and tear, I heard the rattling of someone barreling at great speed into the room. It was Wilson P. Thorn at his hyper and nervous best.

"Alan, are you in here?"

"Yeah, what's up?" came from behind the stall door.

"Liz is looking for you. She's got a judge on the phone."

Incredible. "Tell her to tell the judge I'll call back. I don't handle government business in the crapper."

This was a play on an often repeated rule of conduct for my subordinates. I would tell them, "I only do business on the carpeted floors of the division." Translated, this meant "Don't nail me in the men's room, at the coffee wagon, walking down Broadway or at Subgum Louie's, my favorite Chinatown beanery. The only exceptions are true emergencies of which I am the sole judge."

Willie came back a minute later. "Liz said Judge Kelly had to speak to you *now* about the Riverdale lease." I never heard of Judge Kelly nor was I aware of a Riverdale lease.

When I finally emerged to take the call I found out it was not Judge Kelly but "Judge" Keller and it was not the Riverdale lease but the Riverhead, Long Island lease.

The "judge" first admonished me for not coming to the phone sooner. Then he said he heard there was a meeting today and he planned to attend to get to the bottom of the problem with his lease. I was not aware of a problem. I had never previously met "Judge" Keller but when the meeting began I needed no introduction. He stood out like a cockroach on a lunch counter. While most of us were in shirtsleeves and loosened ties, he was attired in a heavy wool herringbone sport jacket on this summer day, a scarf around his neck and what I guessed were driving gloves. If he were a few years younger, a little thinner and without the rug on his head he might have passed for a Gatsby-era playboy. To us he looked like a damn fool.

He actually had no authority, not being even the ranking judge in the Riverhead office. Nevertheless we gave him the courtesy to join the meeting and speak.

I chaired the meeting and graciously offered to review his project first. Translated that meant "State your business and leave."

The specialist handling the project said that a new leased location has been approved by SSA and that a lease should be signed within a week, pending some further negotiations, and that the space should be ready for occupancy in 120 days. No magic or intrigue. What could the "judge" possibly want?

Then the fun began. The "judge" began to speak, and speak, and speak. He spoke in parables and innuendos without anyone really knowing where he was going. He spoke of deriving his authority from the Constitution; he mentioned the integrity of the entire Social Security system; he spoke about equal justice whether you were in the cornfields of Kansas or the inner city of New York. He referred to GSA with terms like "perceptively oppressive" and "outside the parameters of reasonability." Mercifully he finally concluded with something like the popular "and henceforth thereafter."

Nobody yet knew what he was talking about. Most of us started to squirm as if we were in gastric distress. As the senior official it was up to me to end this nonsense and get to the point.

"Your Honor, please tell me where are we going with this?" I asked.

"The point is that our new Riverhead lease is the product of a sweetheart deal between the GSA representative and the owner."

At that instant my attitude changed as I stopped treating him like another politically connected clown. He was a loose cannon who could cause harm with his accusations. "Judge, I suggest you offer evidence of this and be prepared to discuss it with our inspector general. Otherwise, this meeting is over."

"Perhaps we should discuss this in private."

That was the last thing I wanted to do with this crackpot without the benefit of a witness. "You opened up this can of worms. If you want to discuss fraud, waste and abuse in GSA there is a protocol. You can go to the IG or, at your option, Department of Justice. However, since you made an allegation against my people, it is now my obligation to bring this to the IG myself for further investigation."

"Oh, no, no, this is not necessary. We can handle it here."

He then went on with a rambling story about overhearing a men's room conversation coming from behind two adjoining stalls at 26 Federal Plaza. He saw two sets of shoes moving about and one kicked what looked like a brown paper bag ("undoubtedly filled with money") from one stall to the next.

By this time all of the people at the meeting were aghast and wondering how this would all end. They also recognized that I was now putting the judge on.

"Well, how did you know what was in the bag and who was behind the stall?"

"It was the wing tipped shoes. The GSA people always wear wing tipped shoes."

"Oh, I see." Now I had all I could do to muffle the laughter.

"And who kicked the bag?"

"It had to be an owner. I know that's the way you do business." Now I knew I was dealing with paranoia.

I leaned on the intercom button in the conference room and asked Liz to send in the leasing specialist for Long Island.

When Denise "Twilight" Lampert entered I asked her how we're doing on the Riverhead lease. Without hesitation she said, "Fine. It should be signed this week."

"Good. By the way, nice shoes."

"Twenty-one ninety-five at Payless." Then, taking a line from Lizzy's dictionary, she said, "They're *stimulated* leather."

That effectively ended the confrontation. The "judge" did, however, cross the line from strictly business to personal with the accusations and I couldn't simply let it ride.

I called Social Security's head administrative person, and strongly suggested that an apology would be appropriate. Eventually we received a letter from the regional director thanking us for all of our efforts and offering a vague, bureaucratic damage control type of statement. It was worthy of the best Madison Avenue PR firm.

To this day I don't know what the "judge" was inhaling at the time to create all of this fantasy. What I did find out was that he had never wanted to move to the new location because his status with the chief "judge" would relegate him to a rear office facing the parking lot as compared to his previous location – one with a garden view and a short walk from his favorite bagel store.

CHAPTER 23

The Sport of Negotiating

People have written volumes on negotiating, calling it an art, a science or whatever else they choose. Some have made millions on their negotiating skills, often by writing books like the *Idiot's Guides*, conducting seminars, selling tapes or finding other ways to pry cash from people's pockets.

My guidelines are very simple. Be prepared, know your opponent and understand that if you squeeze blood from a stone you may lose in the long run. I've seen my share of construction projects go down the tubes because the margin of profit was so tight and the contingency allowance so low that one unforeseen event could be the difference between success and disaster. Cleaning up after a contractor goes belly up is not pretty and it is very costly.

One of my guidelines: First make sure the parties you are negotiating with have the authority to make a decision. Remember my woeful tale of our negotiations with the City of New York, only to hear after we came to a meeting of the minds, "Now we have to submit it to the Comptroller's Office for approval." Then we started negotiating all over again, with new issues.   •

Let's go back to my theory about learning from everyone. My unlikely source in this case is none other that the great Ozzie Smith, former major league shortstop. When he was interviewed on the day he was inducted into the Baseball Hall of Fame a reporter asked him for his secret of success. "It's all in the preparation," was his reply. How true. Know your strategy and know the strengths and weaknesses of the opposition.

Business is the same. Nothing can be worse than going into a negotiating session unprepared. Your opposition will sense this immediately. I always believed in keeping an outline before me. At a very minimum you should include the starting point, your objectives and your limits beyond which you either had no authority to negotiate or business sense would dictate that you would not negotiate.

On another sheet you should have talking points to validate your position. You should know your opponent's style. If you're going up against an antagonist you know you will have to do some stonewalling without being intimidated. If it's your style you can show an aggressive tone at the right time but pick your spots or your effectiveness will be lost. When the dialog gets aggressive think of what Michael Corleone said in *The Godfather.* "Don't hate your enemy. It affects your judgment." Remember that everyone is different and don't take things personally. It's strictly business.

Another guideline: Don't be swayed by a good guy/bad guy scenario or self-serving endorsements. For sure, you've sat in a car dealership sandwiched between a salesman and a manager/closer reeking of cologne. You felt like saying, "If this is such a good deal then *you* buy the car." Or perhaps, "If you're losing money on this deal how do you stay in business, with volume?"

Finally, make a note of things you can give, especially those which you didn't want anyway. As long as your opposition *thinks* you are giving up something it will help you.

One example of this strategy was written by basketball star and former United States Senator Bill Bradley. In a book he wrote after his playing career he cited his contract negotiations one particular season. He wanted more money from his team, the New York Knickerbockers. Management was willing to budge a little but demanded that the contract stipulate that the Knicks would get twenty percent of all endorsement money earned by Bradley. What the Knick negotiators did not know was that Bradley had a personal rule that he would *never* endorse anything. "No problem," Bradley said. "You can have twenty percent."

Bill got his raise and the Knicks got twenty percent of nothing.

Whether you are negotiating for business or for personal issues the principles are the same. Only the stakes are different. I considered Foley Square the ultimate late-night no-money-down TV infomercial, the difference being that Foley Square had more zeros after the dollar sign.

*   *   *

A conference I attended in Denver, Colorado is a perfect case study.

On one of the nights of the conference the Colorado Rockies were playing against the New York Mets. Most of us had never been to Coors Field in Denver so a group of three decided to go to the game that evening. Remembering that when the Rockies first opened for business Coors Field was a hot ticket, we were apprehensive about getting last-minute seats.

We set out via taxi for the ballyard and got an earful from our driver. From under his Stetson he told us a few pieces of information that we didn't know but were essential for a successful negotiation. "Don't go to the box office," he lectured. "The scalpers are going to get burned tonight. Make your deal at game time when they're stuck with tickets."

He told us that the Rockies were not drawing as well as they used to draw and, most important, the Denver Broncos of the National Football League were playing their season opener the very same night. As an added kicker, the Broncos were ceremonially retiring the jersey of their great quarterback John Elway. This assured next to no interest in the Rockies' game.

"Don't let them bullshit you," was the cabby's final advisory. He earned himself a larger tip with this hospitality, proving he knew how to negotiate also.

We had time to kill so we stopped at a watering hole for a brew. This was a pleasure venture but in business I would *never* go into a negotiating session after alcohol or a heavy meal. That's the surest way to lose your edge.

Twenty minutes before game time we sauntered back to what amounted to an outdoor flea market for tickets. Since I was the senior person I was selected as the negotiator. We laughed off the first scalpers' offer of seats "behind the dugout" at a mere ten dollars above face value.

Eventually we found ourselves talking with a scalper who was a reasonable businessman. He didn't insult our intelligence and he recognized that his product was losing value every minute.

We saw that there were far more sellers than there were buyers and this guy had a lot of tickets in his hand. "Twenty-five bucks each. That's face value. *No premium!* Front mezzanine." He knew we would never pay even face value but at least it wasn't an insult. It was a starting point.

I learned when I was young that when a man is starving you don't have to offer a steak. He will take a hot dog.

"Two bucks each" was my counter offer. He feigned being offended by the offer but he knew that it was two dollars more than he would have if the tickets weren't sold. It was now seven minutes to game time. He put his hands in the pockets of his jeans, spit through the gap where one of his front teeth had been and rolled his eyes upward as the drool slithered down his western snap-button shirt.

After a little give and take and hearing how we were taking oatmeal from his baby we settled on five bucks each for the tickets. We were happy. He was happy. I truly believe that if we waited until the first pitch was thrown we could have had all three tickets for five bucks but being greedy is not good negotiating.

This deal had a little of everything. We were prepared, albeit not until after the cabby's advice. We knew our opposition. He was stuck with these tickets and had to make a deal. We knew our objectives (five bucks a ticket), we didn't fall for the self-serving endorsements of the first scalper and in the end everyone came away with something. We all agreed that this was a textbook example of negotiating principles.

The game sucked.

* * *

Not too long after the Denver deal I had the opportunity for another sports negotiation, but this time it was a sellers' market.

On February 27, 2003 I was scheduled to take an afternoon train from New York to Washington for a conference starting the next morning. That morning, skimming through *The New York Times,* I realized that the Washington Wizards of the National Basketball Association were playing that evening. I'm not a big basketball fan but this was Michael Jordan's last season and this would be my last chance to see him play in person.

By coincidence, our group was staying at the Monaco Hotel, only a block from the MCI Center where the Wizards played. I decided at 7:00AM that I had to go to this game, but it wouldn't be easy. To make it even a tougher ticket, the Wizards were playing the Houston Rockets, featuring the amazing rookie Yao Ming.

I arrived at the hotel just an hour before game time. Unlike the Denver incident, this was a case where tickets would get *more* valuable as game time got closer.

None of my associates cared to join me so I was on my own. It was a cold night with a light snowfall. The ticket situation was worse than I could have imagined. There was nothing available, even from scalpers. Between Michael Jordan and Yao Ming, the demand for tickets was enormous. Ming had attracted a huge Asian contingency to the game which made the tickets even tighter.

I walked back and forth a few times and saw that this effort was fruitless. Then I stood inside near the pickup window in the event that I could overhear someone say they had an extra ticket for sale. It was fifteen minutes before game time and I had all but given up.

Then it happened. My powers of observation and my New York street smarts kicked in at the same time. In the ticket lobby I spotted a gentleman with a big envelope and sporting a name tag which read *Washington Chamber of Commerce.* I made a quick analysis. We have a group outing here sponsored by the C of C. A lot of tickets were reserved for non-basketball fans. Others will stay away because of the sprinkling of snow. In any event, his envelope looked pretty full minutes before game time.

"Howya doin'?" I stated in my distinctive New York drawl.

"Fine. Name, please," as he opened the envelope ready to dig out a smaller envelope with my ticket.

Too bad I did know the names of any of their members, but that would have been dishonest. "No, I'm not in your group," I confessed. Then I went to work. "Washington C of C?" I said. "I think my ex-boss is the head of that group." I knew that wasn't true but it started the conversation.

When I mentioned the name the fellow said, "Oh, no, he's not with the Chamber of Commerce. He's with the Board of Trade." I knew this but now I had a friend.

We exchanged back and forth pleasantries while I was eying up his ticket envelope. Plenty left. I couldn't really just ask for one. That would almost be begging. I figured that we could make a deal which would make everybody happy. I also figured that whatever deal we made, the money was going to him and not the Chamber.

"It looks like you have some no-shows," I nodded in the general direction of his envelope.

"I'm afraid so. I guess not everyone is a fan."

"Would the Chamber consider selling me one?" I specifically asked the Chamber to sell me the ticket, not him, in order that he not feel like he was making an unauthorized side deal.

He thought about it and again looked at the pile of tickets, some of which would be wasted. "Well, these are hundred dollar tickets. At club level." He rightfully assumed that I'm not a hundred dollar ticket person, for any sport, which was confirmed by my less than enthusiastic silent response.

"But, maybe we could do better."

"I was really just looking for an upper-level twenty five dollar ticket," I replied, thinking that this guy didn't realize that he was sitting on a scalpers' mother lode.

We settled on fifty bucks which was a fair amount for both sides, at least in my opinion. He didn't know that I was prepared to pay scalper prices. I would remember seeing Jordan, a man of incredible skills, a lot longer than I would remember the price of the ticket.

It turned out to be a good deal because for my fifty I got to see a great game and since I was with the Chamber's specially invited group at club level I also got a complimentary dinner in their private suite.

This was another example of negotiating a deal in which everyone comes away singing.

CHAPTER 24

The Joker is Mild

Practical jokes have always been a part of my repertoire. I never forgot some of those great practical jokes between my two early friends, Large Lewis Levine and Don Paolo Rossini. It's like a magician always respecting the Great Houdini. Keeping cognizant of my principle that one needs a sense of humor to survive in the cruel world of the bureaucracy business, I always seized the opportunity. When I became a senior manager I was often able to set up the opportunity.

One of my best had to do with a bogus reorganization, which had some of my top staff in a traumatic state until they reached the end of the memorandum and noticed that it was dated April 1st.

A job vacancy opened up when my director of property management accepted a position elsewhere in the organization. The job to be filled was perhaps the most critical and visible of all of the high management positions because the incumbent was responsible for day to day operation of our buildings.

There were several highly qualified in-house candidates. I knew it would be a tough selection. New York Danny was one of the favorites for the job. He had been an excellent district manager and had a good relationship with his customers.

Several other highly qualified candidates declined to apply. New Jersey Byron didn't want to commute to downtown Manhattan. Upstate Marvin, likewise, wanted no part of the scene. He and his family were very satisfied residing in frozen Syracuse, New York. Long Island Willie was happy in his staff role and didn't want the responsibilities of a division director. Gifted Glendora ran our Long Island office and lived on the island so she had no desire for a change.

The only serious applicants were Danny, the odds-on favorite, and Queensboro Neil, who was a long shot but had the spunk to apply. He was working in Manhattan anyway.

I began to plot my little surprise when I saw the list of applicants, or more important, the non-applicants.

After detailed paneling and screening, Dan was selected for the job. This was almost a foregone conclusion but we went through the motions of due process. Since the selection was made in March, April Fools' Day would be the perfect time to strike.

I composed my memorandum at the close of business on March 31st. The general thrust of the memo was how the current GSA administration favored mobility as management development tools. I cited how the region supported and encouraged this concept.

With that opening salvo I announced that there would be immediate changes in the assignments of the region's managers. The two out-of-towners, Byron and Marvin, were to be reassigned to the regional office, just the place they wanted to avoid even with a promotion, as branch chiefs. Glendora, who loved her suburban post of duty, would receive a special projects position in the region. Willie, who loved the comfort of the region, will now *take full charge* of the upstate territory. The good news was that it would be his decision if he wanted to work out of Syracuse or Buffalo.

While the readers were choking on that, since Neil had just purchased a house in eastern Long Island, I announced that he would take over our Newark, New Jersey office. Figuring that I hadn't done quite enough damage, I also announced that Socrates Papajohn, who was becoming complacent in his division director chair, would be a special assistant to the person he disliked most in the organization and would be replaced by the person he thought was angling for his job.

Since I knew my managers checked their BlackBerrys in the evening, I held off pressing the "send" button until morning. A joke is one thing but I didn't want anyone to lose sleep and I preferred not to create any domestic disharmony, alcoholism or potential suicides. I also didn't want any midnight phone calls.

I released the e-mail to all of my management personnel at 7:30 AM. At 7:33 AM Queensboro Neil appeared at my door in a near catatonic state and close to tears.

"I j-just s-saw your memo."

Playing oblivious to Neil's issue I cheerfully replied, "Ah, glad you liked it. I think this will be great for the organization and the individuals."

"B-but I just bought a house on Long Island. How can I commute to New Jersey?"

"Ah, no big deal. It will only be about two and a half hours each way to Newark. Every day."

By this time my private line was ringing and I recognized Long Island Willie's number. I turned to Neil and said, "Let me take Will's call."

"Hey, Will, what's goin' on?"

"Good one. You got me."

Now I was thinking quickly. Neil didn't have the benefit of hearing Willie's side of the conversation.

My reply. "Well that's great, Will. When do you want to report upstate?"

"Huh? What are you talking about? This is a joke, right?"

"Yes, Neil is here right now and we're discussing his new assignment."

Neil was sweating and his knees beginning to buckle.

From Willie's side. "Oh. Now you want me to be part of the prank. Give Neil a break."

"Okay, 'bye Will."

I hung up the receiver and turned again to the startled Neil. "Willie loves it."

Neil is an intelligent man, and as an ex-cop had plenty of street smarts. No way would Willie have loved this arrangement.

"Are you really gonna do this to me?" he asked, as if I was meting out punishment.

"Neil, did you read the whole memo?"

"No."

"When was it dated?"

"Today."

"What's today?"

Silence.

"The date?"

More silence. Then Neil lit up like a kid with a bagful of Oreo cookies. He was saved. No Newark. With a heavy sigh he said, "Good one." and left the office knowing he was finessed.

My private line lit up again. This time it was Glendora, who said "My jaw dropped so far that I caught a mouthful of flies."

"Glad you liked it," I told her. "Gotta go."

George Hochberg, Socrates Papajohn's friend and ranking staffer, appeared at my door. "What the hell did you do to Solly?"

"Huh? Nothing. Why?"

"He's ranting all over the office, 'What the fuck is Greenberg doing? No way am I doing this!' He's a raving lunatic."

"Oh, it must be the memo," I calmly said, pushing a hard copy across the desk to him. "Read the last line first."

He muttered, "April 1st. OK. I know what's happening." He glanced over the rest of the memo, smiled, stroked his beard and pushed it back to me. "Good one. Keeps people on their toes."

Few enough recognized the April Fools' connection to prevent the chain of nervous protest calls to me and a series of rumors throughout the office. The "Is it true?" calls and the people who avoided me during my stroll towards the men's room accelerated.

Years later, during a post-retirement visit to the building, I was told, "We haven't had a good practical joke since your reorganization memo."

* * *

Our good friend and associate, Julio Giampetti, eventually outgrew his Geppetto nickname but never his propensity for difficulty. With marriage and a family his attention shifted from the ladies to various get rich quick schemes. Of course none worked out, costing him hard earned money each time. His inner salvation came from his hope that one day he would score big in the Lottery.

All he did was to present an opportunity for a devastating practical joke.

One Monday he called in sick. When another associate, "Crash" Helmut Wolff (he acquired his nickname after multiple mishaps with government vehicles) checked Julio's cubicle for messages and mail which might need follow-up, he discovered that he left two lottery tickets for the prior Saturday on his desk. Like every other lottery purchase, these tickets were now worthless, but Crash thought it would be nice to string Julio along for a while so he went down to the newsstand and bought a current ticket with the previous week's winning numbers and substituted it for one of Julio's original tickets.

When Julio walked in the next morning his reaction was beyond description. "Yes! Yes!" came over the cubicle wall. He was dancing up and down the aisle, alternately announcing his resignation and inviting all to his soon to be new home for a big party. Things were getting out of hand.

When he decided to tell his wife the good news we had to put and end to the elation before the damage was compounded. Helmut suggested he look carefully at his tickets before doing anything irreversible. When he discovered the date discrepancy he went ballistic in trying to find out the perpetrator of the joke. When he found out it was Helmut he mounted a physical attack until he was stopped by peers. That saved him from going from instant millionaire to unemployed in a heartbeat.

I had to intercede on this one. He eventually calmed down and replaced the threat of physical harm to Helmut with a promise to get even. Helmut didn't stay on the job long enough for Julio to retaliate.

*   *   *

A person who I considered a friend throughout my management career was Theresa Patino, who worked her way to the position which could be loosely called communications officer. Through many organization changes and management purges her title and official responsibilities often changed, but her role was always to sift through the bullshit and be the agency spokesperson (or speechwriter for the political figurehead) on tough issues. She had to balance responsible reporting with political whims.

Theresa was often pushed aside in favor of politically appointed congressional liaison types who came and went with each administration. Even when she was put in the background, such as when one of our regional administrators decided to place her in the role of internal event planner and bring in a large-boobed former television weathergirl as media liaison, she always kept a sense of humor. She remained in the background but bailed out her less knowledgeable string of replacements.

During my spell as branch chief in charge of several court construction projects, my prankster instincts struck.

Theresa routinely received faxed news releases from all regions and central office and passed paper copies around to the managers (fortunately this procedure has since changed to electronic copies, saving a few trees and an hour a day of copy time). At any given time she had a desk full of agency bulletins, ranging from a groundbreaking in Idaho to a child care center opening in Chicago (politicians love to be photographed at child care centers) to a water main rupture in Minnesota.

One day when I was in a mischievous mood, with the wizardry of the computer I did a cut-and-paste operation and managed to come up with what looked like a letterhead from the Office of Public Affairs in Washington. Copying the style of the usual release, I issued an almost real looking bulletin, dated April 1st of course, and inconspicuously slipped in into Theresa's inbox. Then I sat back and waited.

Theresa is quite astute and she suspected something amiss when the GSA "contact" was listed as one Dan B. Cooper (Remember the disappearance of DB Cooper?).

The GSA News Release began with a grandiose announcement, credited jointly to David J. Barram, GSA administrator, Senator Daniel Patrick Moynihan and Michael D. Eisner, Disney chairman and CEO. A joint venture between Disney and GSA was formed in order to convert the historic General Post Office in Brooklyn into a vertical amusement park. If that wasn't shocking enough, this change of plans came during the design phase of a $200 million renovation project to convert the building to a federal courthouse. The announcement continued by lauding this partnership as the federal government's first *intentional* venture into the amusement business.

The announcement continued by proclaiming that "the building's imposing Romanesque towers will be reconfigured as Mickey Mouse ears over downtown Brooklyn." I added that the interior courtyard will be used as a state of the art cartoon studio. As a classy touch, the announcement confirmed that the IRS commissioner committed that agency to be a major exhibitor and that "taxpayers will have the opportunity to win prizes ranging from tax abatements to teddy bears at booths staffed by IRS personnel."

Theresa, about to put this announcement through the usual distribution, was smart enough to verify the accuracy of the information with her bewildered counterparts in Washington who scurried to find out what this was all about.

Upon flipping to page two and reading the fine print she breathed a sigh of relief when she saw one of my nicknames with the admonition that if this April Fools' announcement goes anywhere I can likely be found at the Shady Pines Retirement Community.

*   *   *

I was not immune to being on the receiving end of more than a few pranks.

As a trainee I was instructed that the only people who could sign outgoing correspondence are the branch chiefs or division director. All correspondence had to be approved by the section supervisor before going to the typing pool and when it was typed in final form the carbon copy had to be initialed by the author and section supervisor before going to the boss for signature. Correspondence for the signature of higher-ups had a predetermined format and a checklist of initials.

When I became a manager I understood why this was necessary. The bosses were responsible for their subordinates and many could not write English if their career depended on it. Of those who wrote in a reasonable form of grammatically correct English, some used one hundred words when ten would do. Nothing would infuriate me more than receiving something for my signature written by a college graduate and initialed by a supervisor, which was in a foreign language, or didn't address the issue.

When I later became responsible for hiring people, I was more interested in their communicative skills than their technical expertise. Through a training program they could learn the business, just like I did, but if they couldn't communicate properly they were wasting everyone's time.

The protocol for anything for my signature as division director was that it would first be proofed and initialed by the author and that person's branch chief. I would check this before even reading the correspondence. Branch chiefs were allowed to sign correspondence also, so many outgoing letters were not seen by me. In order for me to keep aware of everything going on, we had what we called a reading file. This was a chronological file of all outgoing correspondence. My first task every morning was to skim the prior day's reading file. Correspondence bearing my signature also went in the reading file, which was available for the reference of everyone.

I usually meticulously read everything put in front of me for signature. However I trusted my branch chiefs' abilities and judgment, so if one of them was in a rush to get something out and I didn't have the time to read it, I might have said, "Is it OK for me to sign?"

One such instance had to do with a routine letter to the Department of Labor offering them leased space near John F. Kennedy Airport, in response to their request. I was glancing through the reading file copy of this letter that I had purportedly signed the prior day without the benefit of reading it. There was no issue until I reached the final paragraph.

Please note that by your acceptance of this space you will waive any right to a future claim against GSA or its agents and employees. As explained to your representative, Mr. Archibald Bonsiglio on site, this building was constructed on a landfill over a former gasoline storage facility with known carcinogens in the soil. Those exposed to these contaminants in the past have reported side effects such as enlarged genitals and a craving for take-out Chinese food.

Very truly yours,
(stamped signature)
Alan L. Greenberg
Director, Space Management Division

My associates have always commented about how seldom I show anger and how calm I can remain in the face of a crisis. They knew something was up when I stormed out of my office screaming, *"What the fuck is this?!!"*

In the three seconds it took me to reach Branch Chief Milton's office, I calculated that I was fifteen years from early retirement eligibility and no matter how lofty I described my duties on a resume any prospective new employer would be curious about why I was dismissed from a secure Government job.

Miltie seemed to be expecting my visit and deadpanned my appearance.

"What's up?"

"What's up!? My career is up! Yours is too if you don't retrieve this fucking letter before Labor opens it." I waved it in his face and he studiously put on his reading glasses to review it.

"Oh, yeah, the big genital thing. I should have mentioned it."

"You should have mentioned it! That's all you have to say?"

"No big deal. As long as we tell the truth up front we can't be held responsible. I cleared it with Legal. Pearlie spoke with Archie before she wrote it." Miltie tugged at his reading glasses again, not showing the slightest bit of nervousness.

I didn't believe what I was hearing. "Just what do we tell the *New York Post* when someone sends this letter to that rag?"

At that moment Pearl the Earl, a technician noted more for her big jugs than technical skills, walked into the cubicle stifling an ear-to-ear grin. Miltie lightened up also.

I knew I had been taken. They got me big time with their practical joke. Pearl held the real carbon copy of the letter I had signed, identical save for the paragraph about the risk to the genitals.

I walked back to my office with a sheepish grin on my face, causing everyone around to wonder how I could go from a raving madman to laughter in sixty seconds.

The business lesson to be learned from this episode was to never ever sign anything without reading it. The second lesson was that when someone nailed you once you had a marker and sooner or later that marker should be called in. It's a matter of respect.

* * *

When Motor City Smitty (Henry Smith) nailed me with the bogus late night call from the chief judge after the unfortunate *Inside Edition* episode about the judges' windows, it was payback for a stunt I pulled a few years earlier.

I had assembled a hand-picked staff for the Foley project. That was a rare advantage in government. At the time Smitty was a supervisor in the Real Estate Division. With him coming to me, it meant a promotion to a GS-14 grade and the departure from an organization in which he was getting stale. Smith was a person of routine and had difficulty accepting changes in procedures and technology. The world was passing him by. He was a hard worker and very loyal which was just what I needed for the project.

We had a small office and a small staff early in the job when Smitty left for a two-week summer holiday. He knew that during his absence we would be having a briefing for the commissioner from Washington and he also knew that when he got back, I would be away for a few days at a regional management meeting. But it was vacation time and this was strictly on his back burner.

During the two weeks he was away the commissioner and his entourage came and went without incident. However, the profile of our office changed. Hy Lowe came on as project engineer for the office building to compliment Mel Reed who was that building's project manager. During this time frame, Christina, our administrative assistant got sick and was temporarily replaced by a young woman named Blossom, who came with a great sense of humor and a pronounced West Indian accent. We also borrowed Shelly from Real Estate Division for temporary assistance to help Smitty work up the tenants' space programs. She sat at Henry's desk when he was on vacation.

Concurrently, Matty D, our boss, requested that I bring my entire management team to the conference.

The picture for Smith was that when he returned to work he would find an empty office, except for a few faces who he didn't know (Hy and Blossom) and a face he did know (Shelly) who was now positioned in his cubicle. Hopefully, he would have remembered that the commissioner was there in his absence.

The script went well. When he arrived he saw a new team in place. On cue, when Blossom saw him bewildered she said, "Oh, you must be 'Enery. Good mornin' mon."

Smitty checked the room number to be sure he was in the right place. Then Blossom continued her memorized spiel. "The commissioner was here last week and was not very 'appy mon. Alan, he was transferred to Washington. Charley retired suddenly and Mel was put on another project. The commissioner said he was putting new people on the project. Chrissy, she quit in a huff and *Zhelly* is in your place. I was told to send you to the *ARA* (assistant regional administrator)."

Smitty's corpuscles were bursting so he couldn't think logically. If he did, he would have realized that Matty D, the ARA, and his management staff were all at the conference in Hartford. The "Acting ARA" was a fellow named Jose Goldstein who was actually at a lower grade level than Smitty but was the most senior person around and available to act in the absence of the other managers. Jose was also in on the joke.

From what I was told, when Henry Smith arrived at "the ARA's office" his ears and nose were so red from elevated blood pressure that he could barely function. When Jose gave him the orchestrated news he nearly went into shock.

"The commissioner wanted a clean sweep. You're back in Real Estate." To Smith, this was like a life sentence. He had burned his bridges when he left and now people who he trained would be his bosses. To ease the pain, Jose added, "The commissioner wanted you sent to the motor pool out at the depots but Matty convinced him to *let* you go to Real Estate." Now it was a *privilege* for Smith to go back.

While all of this was going on, Charley, John and I were tooling up I-95 towards Hartford, listening to drive time radio and oblivious to the caper we concocted.

My cell phone rang. When I picked up both Hy and Smitty were talking simultaneously. Hy was in on the joke. "What kind of a place is this? I'm here a week and there's a total change of staff. I hope it wasn't a mistake taking this job."

Henry, meanwhile, was stuttering, as he did when he was nervous or upset. He thought I was in D.C. "Wh-wh-what's happening here? I have to go back to Real Estate?"

"I understand the commissioner *agreed* to let you do that," making it seem like a privilege rather than punishment.

"What can I do? I can't go back there. Everyone is pissed at me."

Then I faked a little anger. "You son of a bitch! You get a message that all of us are either fired or shipped to pasture and all you think about is yourself. At least you have a job and don't have to move."

"B-b-but I don't——."

"Never mind." Now I was concerned that he might be going into cardiac arrest and I had better ease off. "Go back up to the office and tell Shelly to change her desk. She's gonna help you with the IRS space program. We're all still there. This was a joke. Charley, John and I are at the conference. Christina is out sick."

Dead silence. He apparently did not share our sense of humor. Before hearing the click he muttered, "It may take me years but I'll get you for this."

It took three years. The bogus late-night call from the "judge" was a calling in of the marker. We were even.

* * *

One fellow who used to annoy people by just being around was Dapper Danny "Tex" Ritter. In his day Danny was the best dressed person on the engineering staff. He worked his way up to team leader more on his appearance than his ability. He bought his suits at Barney's, had his shirts custom made and wore the finest designer silk ties. His shoes were highly polished wing tips. Even his belt had a designer buckle. He was a sharp contrast from the polyester suits and schlock store ties which were common in Federal Plaza. He wore fedora hats and carried an English style umbrella at the hint of a shower. His hair was slicked back with Vitalis and he always wore the finest accessories such as 14-karat cuff links with a matching tie pin. He retained the smallest trace of a Texas accent from his youth. A man who carried himself about like Dapper Danny Ritter could easily fool a naïve political appointee into thinking he had far more ability and ambition than he really possessed.

For all of sartorial splendor, he wasn't worth a damn as an engineer.

On a particular cloudy autumn day he pissed off one of his junior technicians by sitting quietly at a meeting while the junior tech got raked over the coals by the division director for a judgmental error which was done at Dan's direction. The technician, who eventually went on to become a branch chief and would have been Danny's boss if Danny was still around, did not want to be an asshole by pointing fingers so he did the next best thing. He wanted to subject Danny to the same embarrassment so he would think twice before hanging a subordinate out to dry.

The technician found a carton in which a tabletop copy machine had been shipped. This was before bubble wrap so inside the carton was a generous supply of shredded newspaper for packing, with the constituency of confetti.

He took Dapper Dan's big umbrella where it hung next to Dan's London Fog raincoat, loosened the prongs from the casing and methodically shoved the confetti into the half open umbrella. When that was done he neatly closed it up and placed the umbrella back on the coat rack.

The word I got on what happened next is that Dan left the building at five o'clock (he never stayed later than five) and, seeing the precipitation outside he unfastened the prongs as he was exiting the revolving door, and pressed the release button when he was outside. Upon opening the umbrella he was doused by an avalanche of shredded paper. Because of the rain the paper stuck to his soaking wet tailored suit and fedora, making him look like he just came through a cheap carwash. This was an offense to his normally impeccable appearance.

Furious, Dan re-entered the building like someone gave him a hotfoot. He went back up to the office to avenge this little misdeed. He wasn't sure who did it but had a pretty good idea. First he went to his desk to remove the haberdashery brush to touch up his suit. Unfortunately for Dan, the same perpetrator had anticipated his next move and removed the upper right drawer from his old wooden desk, put a cardboard over it, then flipped and replaced it, gently removing the cardboard. The net result was that when Dan opened the drawer to get to the brush, all of its contents fell out and landed by his wet feet.

Now he was ready to kill. He kicked the offending drawer aside and like he was doing the long jump, took a few steps and leaped at the technician, grabbing him by the throat, threatening to cut off his air supply if he didn't confess. Fortunately, surrounding co-workers who did not run out at five o'clock came to the rescue.

The technician never confessed. He did, however, bring assault charges against his supervisor which he said he would consider dropping after his next rating.

The technician went on to bigger and better things. Dapper Dan cleaned his suit and continued with life. Until his retirement he was known as the Austin Strangler, in deference to his Texas roots.

CHAPTER 25

Nothing Succeeds Like Failure

I can paper my entire house with the collection of training and special achievement certificates that I accumulated over a career. You name it; technical matters, ethics, affirmative action, management by objectives, etc.

It was never really important how much you learned in a training class as long as someone could certify that you passed the course and were somehow qualified for your job. Nobody ever failed a government training course. That would be a reflection on the instructor and the person's supervisor would then have to devise a remedial plan.

It was easy to take and pass courses but to do something so egregious, so bizarre, or just plain so stupid that it makes it as a case study in the ethics training manual takes some extra effort. With that in mind we come to the case of Ludwig the Latvian Lover.

Under normal circumstances Ludwig would have been written off as your garden variety asshole, but he was constantly in a position to do damage or embarrass the agency, wittingly or not. A "Washington type," he was as ubiquitous as horseshit, popping up when least expected. Every time you thought he was finally gone he would show up on another project.

Ludwig epitomized several of my theories for prosperity in the bureaucracy, particularly "Nothing succeeds like failure." Ludwig worked his way through the system applying every technique imaginable. He talked a good game, created motion and havoc before backing away from an issue which would be left for someone else to solve. He never put his balls on the table so he could never be nailed for a wrong decision. Ludwig succeeded in spite of himself. He had a way of getting into new programs, filling the odd spot in a reorganization and always being the body to be spared if someone had to represent the agency at a senseless seminar.

Through a combination of dumb luck and default, Ludwig found himself as a startup manager for another new computerized tracking program supposedly designed to help the government manage its inventory and finances better. Like many programs, PACE

(Property Acquisition Computerized Entry) started out as a harmless nuisance, destined to run out of steam as soon as its political backers did their damage and left the agency. Due to Ludwig's desire to delegate all responsibility so he could point a finger if the program failed, this small project, which started by operating out of a former file room, grew into a monster.

From an initial four-person staff, what was known as "Ludwig's project" now generated to a fifty-person staff, mainly spinning their wheels as the project gathered moss. Through Ludwig's leadership most of the people were taken out of productive capacities and placed in make-work situations. Ludwig continued to talk his good game, lulling the politicos into a belief that they would come away with a masterpiece, while the crusty career veterans waited for the inevitable explosion. Fortunately, Ludwig did himself in before the project took the agency down.

Ludwig loved to travel, a trait common to those with a fear of staying still long enough to be nailed for something. He decided that he had to personally visit the facilities of all bidders on the information technology contract he would eventually administer. It didn't matter where. Silicon Valley, New York, Texas; his only regret was that the Request for Proposals ("RFP")required "Buy American" compliance so he could not visit potential European bidders. Ludwig worked in a vacuum, thus although he was the so-called executive in charge, he never bothered to invite, or at least inform, any of his subordinates who actually had some technical knowledge of the process.

When Ludwig checked into a Marriott near Dallas-Fort Worth International Airport he found several messages waiting for him. This was pre-cell phone and BlackBerry.

Big Georgie, his boss from National Capital Region, had called. "What are you doing in Texas?" Ludwig tossed that message.

His secretary left a message that Georgie was upset that Ludwig skipped the weekly staff meeting and hadn't bothered to send a substitute. Not that Big Georgie needed Ludwig, or wanted him there, but it was one way to keep a lasso on him. Ludwig tossed the message.

Then there was a curious note from an Arthur "Tex" Parker, a vaguely familiar name, requesting a return call and perhaps a drink and dinner meeting that day. Ludwig recalled that Parker was one of the principals of the company he was about to review for their capability to produce the software system he was purportedly in charge of procuring.

Ludwig accepted this Texas hospitality like Pavlov's dog.

They didn't meet in Billy Bob's but the atmosphere was the same. The Towne Pumpe was filled with good ole' boys named Hoss, Buford or Billy Ray. They were backslapping, and taking down Coors Silver Bullet like it was water and they were in the Mohave. By the time the Texas-style steaks came Ludwig's head was so disoriented that they could have served him Texas palomino instead of prime beef. He had already violated almost every paragraph of the Standards of Conduct which permits acceptance of a modest meal at a working dinner or a social drink but prohibits gluttony and repeated acceptances of meals and alcohol. In his mind he had merely broadened the interpretation of a working meal.

Tex Parker and his procurement chief, Hoss "Big Gun" Remley were having as much fun as Ludwig. They were joined at the table by "Amazing" Grace Lynn, introduced as Parker's administrative officer. She apologized for being late and explained that she had to do some last-minute juggling of Parker's schedule. She was a late-thirties attractive blond with implanted Texas-sized boobs, smartly dressed in a two-piece mini-skirted suit, a fine set of leather Texan boots (made in China) and a Dallas Cowboys-type Stetson, also made in China.

Between the Coors, the beef and the skin, Ludwig was barely aware of his purpose in Texas and completely oblivious that he was on government business.

After sloshing down a post dinner amaretto neutered with a generous portion of pecan pie the group staggered into the evening and Tex miraculously navigated his vehicle back to Ludwig's Marriott digs. They were feeling a bit sorry for their distinguished guest who was now as bloated as the Pillsbury Doughboy and not thinking clearly, given the enormous amount of food and spirits consumed.

Tex and Big Gun thought of their dinner accomplice merely as a commodity and a conduit to a lucrative contract. All of the parties knew that this was not a low-bid situation; there was judgment involved. Contrary to popular belief, government contracting is not simply a numbers crunch but in the case of high-tech or unique products and services it is a "best value" situation, where a vendor's experience and technical capabilities can be equally or more important than mere price. The boys figured that if Ludwig returned to Washington happy, it would enhance their chances at a windfall.

When Ludwig entered the Marriott lobby he spotted a familiar and desirable face in the form of Amazing Grace Lynn whom he just left at the Pumpe. She was sitting on a lounge chair, mini-skirt closer to the crotch than the knees. She had driven her own car over to the Marriott out of a motherly instinct of sorts to be sure Ludwig found no other distractions and didn't wander into the night again before turning in. He could have embarrassed himself further, but more important, could have jeopardized the contract. She had to keep this meal ticket relatively intact.

"Maybe we should have some coffee and talk this over." Grace nodded in the direction of the coffee shop.

By this time Ludwig was so captivated by this Texas beauty that he began the mandatory recital of his life history and current position. It was the usual tale of being stuck in a marriage for the kids' sake and his wife no longer understanding him. Indeed it was difficult for anyone to understand him.

He was now undergoing a metamorphosis in his mind from an inebriated servant of the people to a great lover. Grace did nothing to negate the image.

What happened later was subject to whose report of the case one chose to believe. Ludwig awoke in the morning with a Texas-sized hangover and Grace's perfumed scent still in the air. As time went by the story got better. Some reports alleged a pair of opened handcuffs left on the nightstand. Other accounts included a generous supply of body oils on his torso. Whatever the real story, Ludwig was in for some difficulty but was still too naive to recognize what was happening.

There was a note on the desk pad next to the phone. "Have a good day. Call me next time you're in town. Love, G." Her home telephone number was written right under the Marriott logo. While that lustful message was still sinking into his brain the phone rang, sounding like a jackhammer. Instead of Grace it was Big Georgie himself telling Ludwig to get his sorry ass back to Washington before sundown.

Between the hangover, the interlude with Grace and the message from his boss, Ludwig had difficulty concentrating on the plant tour. The pint of grapefruit juice he had at the complimentary continental breakfast (for which he billed the government the cost of a more elaborate spread) didn't clear his head at all. He still thought he found true love and fantasized about it on the plane ride home.

Once Ludwig had graced the Texas bidder with a plant visit he had to give equal time to the other bidders, hence he made less adventurous trips to California, Long Island and the Beltway. The most exciting thing he was able to do on these sojourns was to sample the restaurant offerings of the areas, mainly solo.

The memory of the night in Texas with Grace continued to preoccupy his mind. Given his flair for braggadocio he was a bit careless about those to whom he mentioned this adventure. One thing was clear. He wanted to go back and was hoping that the Texas bidder would be a finalist.

His wish came true through contrived circumstances. He couldn't justify another official trip to the area based on the project. That would be gilding the lily and even Ludwig didn't think he could get away with it. After scouring the schedules of the various government training contractors, he found a "Claims in Government Contracting" course being offered by a vendor in - where else? - Fort Worth, Texas. He had a good point here, because if this contract ever came to fruition, and Ludwig had anything to do with it, you can be sure there would be an abundance of claims.

Upon his arrival he dug out the scrap of Marriott paper and dialed Grace's number. She was aloof when it came to discussing the bid or anything concerning Tex and the boys. She was, however, quite willing to meet him for dinner and whatever might follow.

Again, what transpired depended much on who was telling the story or which investigative report you read.

They met at the Marriott bar, the scene of Ludwig's original triumph. She conspicuously avoided anything resembling business talk, other than her own business enterprise.

"Ludwig, my dear, in arranging this date we never did discuss the business aspects."

"That's fine. I'm not here on the contract issue. I'm here for training so it isn't necessary to talk business. I never told Tex that I'm even in town."

She looked at him apprehensively over her green apple martini. "I don't think you quite understand the picture."

Ludwig stared beyond the mascara into her contact-lensed blue eyes with his customary look of bewilderment. He couldn't help thinking of his last encounter with Grace just a few floors above where they now sat.

Grace leaned forward showing some cleavage between her implants. "Ludwig, we didn't discuss what this date will cost you."

"Don't worry, Sweetie. We can go to whatever restaurant you want." His mind was already set on waxing up the old rocket to cap the evening.

"You still don't understand, do you?" Now she was getting a little impatient. She adjusted her blouse, closing the cleavage a bit. "Ludwig, I am a business person and there is a fee for my escort service."

The picture cleared in a hurry for Ludwig. Even he was able to finally understand quite clearly that his wonderful conquest was a high priced hooker hired by the vendor on his last trip. As if this wasn't a big enough blow to his ego, he *was* smart enough to know that he was in deep trouble. His career could be in jeopardy, his already failing marriage was as good as over, and, under the right set of circumstances, he could end up doing hard time if the services received were considered a bribe.

Ludwig miraculously got away with his transgressions, once again succeeding by his failures. Nobody could prove a direct connection between the services received and favorable treatment for the contractor. The fact of the matter was that Ludwig never *knowingly* accepted the gratuity. He actually believed he was the great lover who conquered the beautiful Texan.

As usual, it was the contractor who gave Ludwig up. Their "best and final" offer was disqualified for late submission after they relied on Ludwig's assurance that it would be accepted if submitted via regular mail. It was received a day late and appropriately not accepted by the contracting officer.

Ludwig's punishment was more the embarrassment than anything else. He became known in the agency as "The Lover" and his saga became a case study in the Office of Government Ethics Training Manual.

When the project was abandoned, all of the team members, including Ludwig, received commendations for their efforts.

A few years later Ludwig, who was available and expendable at the time, came to New York representing the commissioner to "help" us award a sensitive lease in Manhattan. He came and went at will, probably saw every show on Broadway and sampled every theater district restaurant. He offered no help at all other than to remind us that "The commissioner considers this the highest priority."

Ludwig drafted a lease contract, or I should say he had someone else draft it for him, which was so restrictive that nobody in any degree of sobriety would ever bid on it. After six months of spinning wheels in New York he returned to Washington where he announced how "I pulled the region's chestnuts out of the fire."

It took another year to undo Ludwig's "help" and finally award the project.

*   *   *

As if Ludwig didn't leave me with enough grief, my waning days as real estate director featured the unexpected arrival of Ms. Caryn

"Skin Tight" Barton. When you're subject to political whims you expect the unexpected and illogical.

One afternoon while riding with Stormin' Norman back to the office from one of our regular floggings from the Eastern District judges at the Brooklyn courthouse, he hit me with the surprise. We had been traversing the Brooklyn Bridge in a cab driven by a guy named Mohammed who had been in America for two weeks and now had his hack license. It happened right after Mohammed cut off a late-model Oldsmobile tank and received the finger from the female driver. I told Mohammed that the gesture was a New Yorker's way of saying, "We're number one." He grunted and muttered something in a foreign tongue which probably meant "I'm surrounded by American idiots."

"Alan, there's someone I need you to hire."

My mind started to race, thinking this was step one in hiring my replacement and sending me out to pasture.

"It's a White House referral. She's an accountant but she won't be on the financial staff. Find a place for her in Real Estate."

Translation: someone with political backing needs a job. For me to try to fight this would be as advisable as doing deep knee bends while wearing spurs.

"White House referral" is a term career managers learn to live with but never quite accept. It means someone with marginal ability and often no scruples but with political influence or something on someone that the administration wants to go away. In this case it was a former staffer during New York Governor Mario Cuomo's administration. She annoyed some high-ranking state officials by repeatedly leaking information to the media about alleged but never proven steering of contracts. The governor's office fired her for inappropriate behavior (unauthorized statements to the media). Unfortunately, with enough publicity, perception is more dangerous than fact. She worked for a Democratic administration in New York State but her political roots were on the Republican side. This was during the Bush Sr. administration. State politicos and a particular senator from New York wanted two things to happen. Her improper dismissal lawsuit had to disappear for fear of further embarrassment, and she needed to be given a job. Hiring her into an agency known at the time as a hideaway for political hacks was the perfect price for her silence. Her deal included a government career appointment, and a promise from her to do nothing to embarrass the Republican administration. It was a great example of bipartisan cooperation of the parties.

This was pre-Google so I had to rely on manual research of newspaper indices to get further information. I knew I was in for a treat or a challenge, depending on your point of view. My ace staffer came up with newspaper articles and records of State Assembly hearings with her as the star witness. There was even a congressional hearing because one of her never proven allegations involved misuse use of federal grant funds. No matter how much experience I had and how high up I was on the food chain, if it came to a battle I would be no match for a White House referral. Knowing that I was on shaky ground, I had two tasks at hand. Keep her out of the way of important business and don't let her end up taking the job or promotion of a deserving careerist. I knew this was super serious because I had a call from our national budget director informing me that central office would be funding this position. It doesn't take a genius to figure out that when central office volunteers funding on a personnel issue, someone is getting a political favor.

Nothing happened for a while and I thought the whole thing had gone away. Then, on a day I had taken off to be at my daughter's college graduation (at which, ironically, Governor Mario Cuomo was the keynote speaker) my pager beeped just after the caps were thrown in the air.

When I called the number back I recognized the voice of our budget director and I knew that he was not calling merely to wish me a good morning.

"Ms. Barton is ready. We need a starting date."

"Whatever she wants is fine with me. Cut the papers and let me know."

I soon found out that she would start in two weeks but would then take time off for medical leave to undergo surgery. The first thing I thought was that this was a scam for health insurance. In the federal government new employees are eligible for health and life insurance on day one and there is no exclusion for pre-existing conditions. Not a bad deal. I remembered back to when I was forced to hire a very pleasant gentleman in his seventies. Unknown to me he was already on limited time with a cardiac condition. He signed up for all available optional health and life insurance coverage since insurability was not going to be challenged. When he passed away within a year his wife received life insurance proceeds of five times his annual salary. In Caryn's case, I called the administrator's chief of staff who orchestrated this deal and was as slick as they come politically. I said: "If this was an insurance rip-off to cover her surgery please tell me now so I can resign before the attorney general nails me for complacency." He assured me that was not the case but that it was an interesting thought. To this day, more than twenty years later, I am not convinced that I was not correct.

As soon as we agreed on a starting date I received a fax of a position description for her. She was coming in as a "senior financial advisor." I found it strange that someone carried a "senior" designation their first day on the job. She had an accounting degree although there was no indication that she ever became certified or for that matter, ever did any real accounting work. She was to be a Grade 14, which is high up on the salary chart. The description of her position was less than a page for this high paying job, yet a data entry clerk had a description several pages long with detailed performance specifications. The PD specified that she was an advisor on financial issues, a field in which she had no proven experience, and it included an inexplicable paragraph with an asterisk and smaller print which said that this position was not part of the financial staff and the incumbent was not authorized to make "binding financial commitments or policy revisions." What that meant was anybody's guess. What was perfectly clear was that I now had a senior advisor who was not empowered to give advice. This whole thing meant that although she was paid a branch chief's salary I could never rate her as a poor performer because she had no real duties for me to measure. Only in America.

No sooner had I digested this information than I received a call from Norman, who was always anxious to please Republican elected officials.

"Is everything set with Caryn?"

"As set as it's going to be, but can I at least see a resume and interview her so I know what to do with this high-priced talent?"

"I'll see what I can do."

I received a call from Human Resources saying Ms. Barton would be coming in to speak with me next week. By the flavor of the conversation it sounded more like she was coming to interview *me*. Jennifer from HR brought down a two-paragraph resume with just her name on the top. She asked me to get her address and telephone number when she came in so HR could set up a personnel folder.

The day of reckoning arrived. She showed up decked in a natty business suit with all of the proper accessories, her face glistening from lip gloss, her eyes highlighted with eye shadow and mascara. After thirty seconds of conversation I was convinced that given a choice I wouldn't hire this person as the aforementioned data entry clerk. With her reputation I knew I would have to watch my back and not let her be privy to too much proprietary information. I asked her what she did at the Office of the Comptroller in New York State and all I got was rolling of the eyes, gazing out the window and responses like, "I made sure everything got done right." This was not encouraging.

I wrote her West End Avenue address on the resume - there was plenty of space - and bid her adieu until her first day. Before she left the outer office something hit me like a ton of bricks.

I was to meet my wife that afternoon for a medical appointment. By coincidence, her doctor was in the very same building where Ms. Barton lived. After asking for her address, all I needed was for her to see me standing in front of her building. It would be the fastest sexual harassment complaint in history, or an arrest for stalking. I called my wife and told her not to wait outside of the building for me. I'll explain later. When I left the office I went to Canal Street and bought a pair of knockoff designer sunglasses for five bucks, a New York Yankees hat for another five bucks and headed uptown.

The two years that she purportedly worked for me was a game of intrigue and angling. Her post of duty became upstate New York and she rarely came to New York City. It turned out that West End Avenue was actually her mother's apartment. She lived in a small town outside of Albany. She was generally on "special assignment" to the regional administrator performing a variety of politically-related tasks to appease upstate politicians. The few assignments I gave her were on special initiatives out of Washington, particularly those which I suspected would be going nowhere.

At Stormin' Norman's request I made her available to assist our Property Disposal Division, whose actions are always subject to political scrutiny. Once a month she submitted a report that summarized her work with a list of potentially excess properties which she accumulated by joyriding through the state making windshield observations. In reality, she received her information from public documents, confirmed it with the technicians, took her ride in the country and then wrote a report which essentially said, "Yeah, this is excess and now the people who know what they're doing can take it from here and make a deal for the government. Let me know when it's done so I can tell the boss about *our* success." For this and her financial non-advisory services we paid her a GS-14 salary.

So I had a high priced senior financial advisor who was precluded from taking part in real financial issues, and was now spending her time burning fuel in the rural areas of New York State.

Fortunately, I was relieved of my Real Estate Division duties and put on the Foley Square project so I didn't have to deal with her that long. Although she thought she had a career position, on the day before Bill Clinton's inauguration, her resignation was accepted. She was not aware that she submitted it the day she was hired, a required protocol of political appointees.

The last I heard of her, she was peddling time shares in the Catskills.

Myself with Senator Daniel Patrick Moynihan in April, 1991 at the announcement of construction awards for the Foley Square projects. Apparently we both used the same optician. *Courtesy of General Services Administration.*

With Senator Alfonse M. D'Amato in 2003 at the renaming of the Long Island Courthouse in his honor. *Courtesy of General Services Administration.*

In my fashionable 1975 suit and long hair, receiving an award from Bob Bogardus, my boss at the time. The certificate was probably for 100% attendance or completing a training course (not Basic Supervision). *From the author's private collection.*

With my friend "Adderw" at still another award presentation. Note the 1976 bicentennial wall plaque. *From the author's private collection.*

Our archaeological contractor, "Big Ed," explaining to concerned high level suits why the African Burial Ground dig should be his lifetime meal ticket. The author, at left, is obviously thinking, "What, me worry?" *Courtesy of General Services Administration.*

Remnants of the Santeria ceremony. *The Chief* provided spiritual fulfillment followed by some New York size rodents to the Broadway site. *Courtesy of Robert Collegio.*

The new Brooklyn Courthouse. The project and the judges within acceler-ated the end of my career. *Courtesy of Hosain Hashemi.*

Some of my fans bidding me adieu. *From the author's private collection.*

PART FOUR

The Twilight Years

CHAPTER 26

Another Round of Wisdom

Before talking about my career wind-down process, which was like an extended illness followed by a State funeral, I would like to pass on some final words of wisdom, important for survival anywhere in the business world.

In almost all business situations, <u>time is money</u>.

There is nothing new about this. Time is your most expensive resource. When a construction project is delayed or extended for a minor change there is nothing minor about it. The real cost is not in the change itself but in the time extension. Let's say you financed $300 million of hard construction costs and your construction period interest is at 5.75 percent. By delaying a job a single day because of a small change or a questionable administrative decision you are adding close to $50,000 in construction period interest. Add the contractor's overhead and general conditions and that can be *another* $5-10,000 a day on top of the interest. I pass this on because on more than one occasion a judge or other high official would want a last minute change and they couldn't understand why we would resist. "It's only a few outlets. What's the big deal about a two day delay?"

The big deal is that the cost of the outlets may be $500 but the cost of the two day delay could be $100,000, which the taxpayers must ante up.

R-E-S-P-E-C-T

As in the Aretha Franklin hit song of the same title, everybody deserves respect, regardless of their station in life, skill level or aspirations. We are all different so as long as someone is hardworking and loyal they deserve your respect. This does not change my prior statement that you only have the right to f* me once.

I don't have enough fingers to count the number of times I've seen unqualified political appointees enter a position and fail to respect the loyal careerists. One of my ex-bosses would openly talk with other appointees referring to the employees who had the capability of making or breaking him, as "the bureaucrats" as if it was "us" vs. "them". Needless to say, respect is something to be earned and it is not earned merely by your position.

When enough people keep telling you that your fly is open, then you better look down.

This came from Bruce Willis in one of his *Die Hard* movies. Some people just never get the message. A word to the wise to a manager would be to listen to your employees, your superiors and your customers. It always amazed me when a manager got fired or moved and it came as a shock.

If it's a shock, you haven't been listening.

Always tell the truth, but you don't necessarily have to tell <u>all</u> of the truth.

I referred to this earlier in regard to the many investigations in which I was a subject, or should I say a suspect. For the record, let me again state that I was part of investigations because I never shied away from difficult or controversial projects.

Not telling *all* of the truth is really just another way of saying that in business you should always keep your options open. Don't give away your strategy or proprietary knowledge and if you have your own business don't be cavalier with your trade secrets.

When I was the contracting officer for one of the courthouse projects in the New York area I had an issue with Louisiana Clem, the regional administrator at the time. We had thirty days left on our option to make a construction award. The date of the award would not have impacted the schedule because the property had to be conveyed to us first. All Clem wanted to do was to be able to call the chief judge and say an award was made, under his administration. Since we didn't have clear title at the time, and were not 100 percent sure that we would get title, this made no business sense. In the worst-case scenario, it could have been a costly embarrassment. If the property owner knew we made the award what would incentive have been to maintain the price?

Reason eventually prevailed and an award was not made until the final day of our option period, which coincidentally was the day we knew we would actually acquire the property.

Never sweat the small stuff.

To put it a different way, I paraphrase the title of a Donald E. Westlake book: "*What's the Worst that Can Happen?*"

This is as much a lesson in life as it is in business. It never ceases to amaze me how people can agonize over nonsense. On the job I couldn't help but think of our associates who survived life threatening illnesses, or our brothers and sisters fighting in some hellhole in the Middle East. With that as a backdrop I couldn't get overworked by a minor protocol or procedural breach. If your train is late, your coffee is cold or your printer doesn't work, it is all fixable at minor cost and effort.

If the worst that can happen in a situation is that your team lost, the sun will still shine tomorrow. When I was a New Yorker I lived in an area where there are a lot of princesses in designer jeans with high heels who talked on their cell phones when they pulled their Lexus out of the day spa parking lot. When they went bonkers over service in a restaurant or how bad their nails looked (not from washing dishes) I just shook my head and was thankful that I was not coming home to them at night.

You can't teach table manners to a shark.

We have all encountered people, often our bosses, who are crude, obnoxious, opportunistic, sadistic and a few more superlatives. They take pride in humiliating people, being overbearing or just plain ornery. Sorry, but in this case you can't fight fire with fire because you will just aggravate yourself. Accept people for what they are because personalities rarely change. You are probably better off just doing your job and at least act as if you're not intimidated.

One of the more obnoxious people that I had to deal with was a court senior administrative employee who thought he had the same privileges as his boss, the chief judge. He would interrupt meetings with comments; finish people's sentences; badmouth anyone and everyone; and dismiss participant's comments or suggestions with sarcastic laughter. He even had the audacity to ask me when I planned to retire when

I had not yet made that determination myself. Finally, a subordinate of mine did something that should have been my task. "If you want to work together we could have a very successful project but if you continue with this attitude the project team will not be able to keep meeting with you and the failure of this project will be your responsibility."

After the usual denials that he was the cause of the problem and a phone call demanding that I remove my subordinate from the project, the meetings continued. About a year after I was gone my subordinate told me that he had to hit the refresh button on the ground rules again.

Write it down! You never know when you will need the information.

Documentation is important in this litigious society.   What I really had in mind was more like writing down tidbits of information in case twenty years from now you want to write your memoirs or become a "fun guy" like me. I used to keep two sets of records. One was the official record for documentation and Freedom of Information Act purposes and the other was for me only, never to see the light of day. Our auditors and lawyers would have choked if they knew this. Do you really think I could have remembered all of these stories?

"It's all in the preparation"

I mention this in summary because it is an important principle. In the chapter on negotiating I went into more detail.

You can't go into any situation unprepared. You've got to understand what the other guy wants or needs, as well as what you need and your negotiating objectives and limitations.

While I cite sporting examples, the difference is that in sports it is a win-lose scenario. In business it has to be a win-win outcome or sooner or later all parties suffer. You've got to know what the person on the other side of the table is thinking and what it will take for *all* parties to go away singing.

CHAPTER 27

Life at the Top

It was fun being the big boss. It wasn't an ego or power trip for me but more the satisfaction of being able to get things done using management skills and the authority of the position. I was able to quickly break logjams or use the position to initiate action.

Like a baseball manager, you begin planning for your demise on the day you're hired.

At the top, more so than ever, perception was far more important than reality. I kept thinking of what Woody Harrelson told Wesley Snipes in *White Man Can't Jump*. "You think that how you *look* is more important than whether you win or lose."

One message that hit me early on was the GSA administration's passion for improved customer service. Our technical and business capabilities were a given but our ability to keep a customer happy and coming to GSA on a voluntary basis was another issue. I had no dispute with the concept of our emphasis on customer service. In fact I thought it was long overdue. The only issue was that by definition a customer had money to spend. When our so-called customers got wise to our inside workings, many made unreasonable demands on us, without the requisite funding because they knew that rather than make a customer unhappy GSA would underwrite the request. This was especially critical if it happened while the clock was ticking on a construction project. This was another way of gaming numbers because we were in effect buying favorable responses to the Gallup surveys done under contract to GSA to measure our performance.

At the top, a person is more detached than ever from reality. I spent less time on the details of a billion dollar construction program and a four hundred million dollar operating budget and more time on twisting numbers or appealing to my people to participate in the savings bonds or suggestion programs.

At quarterly management meetings a team of the uninvolved would tell my people how to get out from under construction projects which were behind schedule or over budget while the administrative types blew their horns about the speed in which they answered congressional letters or advertised a personnel request. When our largest project ran into construction difficulties - the general contractor went belly up - our ratings were doomed to failure, but since HR responded timely to two congressional letters the prior month all of their management benchmarks were met. I always preached that the business of the organization should be where the resources go and everything else is support so it would appall me when I couldn't get adequate engineering support for a major construction project but elsewhere there was a full time committee studying the "work at home" program or another ill-fated reorganization.

Timely accomplishment of your mission is assumed. It's all of the ancillary functions that can make or break the boss.

"Work at home" became a buzzword of the new millennium. Advanced technology and modern thinking in the workplace made this possible. In our case, the *act* of working at home became the unit of measure rather than the actual fruits of home labor. We constantly reported on *how many* worked at home but never on the productivity. I never objected to the idea of work at home because it kept good people on our payroll, such as young parents, but I did object to the concept being more important than the results.

One of the original incentives for working at home had been to conserve energy and reduce traffic. In New York City, 99 percent or more of employees come to work by public transportation so the entire argument became moot. Nevertheless, countless hours were wasted at meetings developing goals and standards or preparing reports on how much participation we had in the program and how much energy we saved. This generated grievances from people who claimed that they were unfairly denied the opportunity to work at home. The fact that they were secretaries, protective officers, building managers or custodial workers was lost on them.

The work at home program was not alone when it came to waste of management time initiatives, or schemes which became the tail wagging the dog.

For example, there was the "How Much Did You Save Today" campaign. Each week we reported on cost savings initiatives. Things got so outlandish that people were reporting savings due to using self-service gas pumps for government vehicles; utilizing both sides of copy paper; eliminating speaker phones; canceling magazine subscriptions; or, eliminating field trips which they weren't going to take anyway.

Another program worth mentioning had to do with paperwork. The amount of paper generated while reporting how much paper we *saved* as result of the "Paperwork Reduction Act of 1995" could have caused the Mohave Forest to become the Mohave Desert.

* * *

At the top, you become privy to information not available to the general public. Sometimes you have to ask yourself, "Why?" Some of this information is of no strategic value other than to possibly allow someone to blow their own horn.

One such instance came when we were told to stand by for a major announcement from the Office of the Inspector General. This could not be good news. The only time the IG seeks publicity is when they nail some sorry SOB for putting his (or her) hand in the till. We were all wondering who it could be this time.

Then the press release hit the news wires. The IG, quite by accident, solved a fifty-year-old "missing persons" case. They acted as if they found Judge Crater.

When the old federal courthouse in Newark was torn down many years earlier, it seems that the concrete eagle which proudly stood at the base of the flagpole disappeared.

Notwithstanding the IG's bulldog perseverance for a half century, the missing eagle was actually in the neighborhood in plain view for all of those years.

It turned out that the widow of the owner of a demolition company decided to sell the family home years after his passing. This ornament was cemented in place in her backyard for the entire time, which I suppose made her an accessory to the crime. She went to the local courts asking if somebody would please take the eagle.

A New Jersey magistrate took up the cause and demanded that the federal government pay for moving this ton of cement to a more appropriate place, such as the new Martin Luther King Courthouse in downtown Newark. The eagle was no longer federal property and GSA could not magnanimously foot the bill for moving and re-installation.

The funding debate went on while the IG investigated in order to get to the bottom of the mystery. Eventually private funds were raised for this effort while the IG absolved everyone of any charges of criminal possession.

Within a year after being installed at its new location some whacko came by one evening and chopped off the head of the eagle as well as several other historic statues around the city.

The IG has not solved the latest case.

* * *

One of the skills I learned going up the ladder was to know when to distance myself from something destined to bite you in the ass.

There was a program of computer giveaways that our politically appointed PR people wanted the public to believe was great and charitable.

On the positive side, we were always near the cutting edge of technology, so our equipment was up to date. This frequently left a surplus of used equipment on hand. By the time the equipment left the custody and control of the government it might have been serviceable but its value was little more than junk.

In comes the magnanimous donation program. Regulations prohibited allowing employees to take or purchase this equipment for personal use (although it is permissible to take home new equipment for business use), and putting the stuff in a dumpster required enough paper to endanger a few forests.

Donating to a worthy charity for educational purposes was another thing. This was cool.

In lower Manhattan there were many schools and religious organizations which would benefit by a gift of used but serviceable computers. They would even volunteer to pick up the equipment. Ah, but this was too easy. Generally our administrative and political gurus would find a remote school in San Juan or Ponce, Puerto Rico to receive this second hand junk. Shipping via Fedex already cost more than the value of the equipment, compounded by the need for photo ops. A high level representative of the region, accompanied by an administrative or PR person would make the journey to the tropics to formally present the equipment in this massive deception of the public. Everyone gloated at the pictures in the San Juan *Star* and the GSA newsletters which suggested the generosity of the government to underprivileged youngsters.

For the cost of this boondoggle, the feds and the recipients would have been better off had we just written a check for new equipment. As I said, perception is greater than reality.

* * *

At the top, I often thought about how nice it would be to once again sit down at a project meeting or negotiating session and do something real.

Besides manipulating numbers for measurement tools I spent a lot of time preparing for building dedications, attending conferences and presentations which minimally impacted our program and in which I was not an active participant or simply listening to someone's spiel about how we should again reorganize. (I exclude working sessions with my counterparts from this category.) On the plus side, I kept piling up frequent flier miles and hotel points.

During one of my own manager's conferences, which I tried to limit in size, frequency and duration, as part of my introductory remarks, I made a few observations:

- It is only necessary to go to about 10 percent of the events marked "Must Attend."

- The job has a lot of responsibility and influence, but you don't really *do* anything which adds value.

- Nothing is so trivial that it can't cost you your job.

It was a bit of a put-on, because it's a leader's role to manage by putting the right people and resources where they will produce the best results. It was also my way of saying the person at the top would be worthless without the dedication and skills of the subordinate staff.

As the Big-Ass Boss I ate a lot of banquet chicken, attended many dedications and conferences, presented and received awards on behalf of the region, and resisted redecorating my office knowing that I would be gone before the furniture ended its useful life. I represented my region or the agency at congressional hearings, funerals, holiday parties and press conferences. Although I didn't look for it, I ended up on C-Span and in the *New York Times* a few times.

Oftentimes I felt like the patriarch or protector of our family of four hundred. When I called it a career my only regret was that I couldn't do it all over again.

CHAPTER 28

The Beginning of the End

For all practical purposes I began to see the end of my career coming when I was promoted to the top stripe in the region.

As I indicated at the outset, the position became available when my predecessor made the mistake of trying to go head-to-head with a political appointee. He lost the battle although he ultimately won the war.

I was selected for the job as the last man standing who was eligible, reasonably qualified and willing to take the position. There were few people amenable to putting themselves at risk towards the end of an administration. Given that I was in the twilight of my mediocre career and contemplating retirement anyway, I had nothing to lose.

When someone achieves the status of senior executive in the federal government it is with a clear understanding of the rules. Unlike most career positions, as a member of the Senior Executive Service ("SES") you are vulnerable to transfer on a moment's notice. In the event you don't get along with your boss or the higher ups in the administration, this is your problem and you accept the risk. Who is right or wrong has little bearing. Unless you are willing to incur substantial legal fees, a senior level person has less of a forum to seek justice than your everyday lower-level malcontent.

I came into the job near the end of Bill Clinton's second term. My appointment was ratified during a Democratic administration (although it was a merit promotion, not a political appointment). If the Democrats stayed in power my risk was that if I didn't do well I could be abruptly transferred, downgraded or disciplined, even if the criteria for such action was arbitrary. With the Republicans in power the added risk was that if any one of many new political appointees didn't like me personally I would be out. I had the customary ninety days to ingratiate myself to our new leaders.

Unlike other qualified candidates, I was willing to take this risk because I was already contemplating retirement in the not too distant future. If things didn't work out I simply wave goodbye and fade off into the Sunbelt. Nobody would get hurt. It was a win-win situation all around. To put it another way, I could be sacrificed.

When I started my new job I announced to my senior staff that I would set no timetable for retirement. In my own mind I knew that when it was time to go I would know it. Nor would I hang on long enough to be carried out feet first.

My selection was generally well received by subordinate managers as well as the proletariat. I had always been a "workers' boss." The fact that a streetwise native son was in the top seat rather than a young go-getter with no New York experience was another plus. Anyone who knew me was aware that I was not going to act like a power-hungry jerk. In my first managers' meeting after my name went on the door I made it very clear that since I had little to lose, if they felt the need to offend anyone, they should ask me to do it. I also told them that I might piss a few people off but I would not hurt anyone. This became abundantly clear when I had to remove a few managers from their positions. This hurt me to do but I saw to it that there was no salary loss and no humiliation. I made sure that they ended up in positions which were essentially a better fit than their old job.

*   *   *

A year into the job, world events changed the course of our focus and altered the lives of millions.

When the first plane struck the World Trade Center, the explosion was deafening. Our office was only a few blocks away. Information was sketchy but we all knew the building evacuation procedures and we all knew the protocol for activating our emergency control center.

I and several others were looking out of a sixteenth floor window at the burning north tower while trying to get some intelligence as to what was happening. When we saw the fire start to rage in tower two after the second plane hit, we all knew what was going on. Our view was surreal. We also knew that Federal Plaza was a known terrorist target because it housed the FBI and that terrorists plan multiple simultaneous attacks. Years earlier, a plot to destroy Federal Plaza was foiled.

The evacuation began instantly and by that afternoon our command center in Manhattan was in full operation, assessing damages and beginning the task of finding over a million square feet of replacement space for law enforcement agencies which had been housed in and around the World Trade Center.

In my many years as a manager and frequent speaker, I acquired a reputation for starting presentations with a joke and lacing speeches with humor and satire. September 11th became a very notable exception. In any of the subsequent 9/11 presentations there was no levity whatsoever. It was at least six months until I regained some semblance of my own sense of humor.

Our reaction to 9/11 could be the subject of an entire book. Suffice it to say that I was proud of the way my many dedicated associates responded to the crisis.

A subsequent development would have been humorous under any other set of circumstances.

A few days after 9/11, while we were in the command center operating on a 24/7 basis and dealing with destruction beyond imagination, I received a call from our White House-appointed public affairs director in Washington. She was the one charged with turning any kind of news into the administration's advantage. "Can you get me a fact sheet of what's going on?"

Another fact sheet? We were on the phone multiple times a day with the administrator and his top staff who in turn kept the Congress and heads of impacted federal agencies apprised. Because of equipment outages involving the phones and the computers we were channeling all information through the commissioner's office. Now a PR person wanted us to stop everything and send more fact sheets.

"Look, Miss Becky (she hated when I called her that), we have a war going on here. I don't have time to do PR bulletins."

"Well I thought we could get the agency some good publicity on this one. We could get a TV news crew in to do interviews."

I was dumbfounded. Remember what I said about *where you sit is where you stand*? In the middle of a rescue and recovery operation I had a glory-seeking White House appointee trying to score points for the administration with photo ops. I lost count of the expletives from my mouth before I actually hung up the phone. The only other contact I had with Miss Becky was when our paths crossed at groundbreakings or other ceremonies. Like most Schedule C appointees, one day she just disappeared.

As for myself, I never expected to become a wartime general in the closing years of my career but that was exactly what happened. The pressures and emotions became so intense in the weeks immediately after 9/11 that I made a preliminary decision to retire soon, although I kept it to myself. We were dealing with the business of replacing space, combined with paranoia to the extent that every time the sound of aircraft was heard, or someone dropped a heavy carton on the floor above, someone would think we were being attacked. The anthrax scare came shortly afterward so if someone left a bag of soap powder around there was a near-panic. I could have walked at any time but that would have sent the wrong message to our employees.

In early 2002 I was feeling better emotionally and our people were doing an excellent job with the recovery. I gradually decided that I will stay beyond my initially contemplated departure date. Thankfully I had announced it to no one. Young Bruce had become regional administrator and we got along well. Slowly work was starting to be fun again. Nevertheless, I knew in the back of my mind that my time will be limited. I wasn't getting any younger. The 9/11 pressure and the every day job duties were difficult. I was traveling extensively for agency senior management strategy sessions and getting the feeling that I was doing little more than accumulating frequent flyer miles and sampling restaurants.

The year 2003 started with a January senior management meeting in Oklahoma City. The highlight of that meeting was that on the night of President Bush's State of the Union address, a group of us had scored tickets to a Rolling Stones concert and bypassed the speech, a slap in the face to our commissioner, who was at the conference and invited the group to dinner and then to listen to the president's address with him. I knew then that by putting the Stones *Forty Licks* concert above the president, my job attitude was slackening. I was not even a Stones' fan.

For reasons known only to career civil servants, the end of the year is the most common time to leave. My wife and I had agreed that 2003 would be my last year. I discussed it with nobody in-house, preferring to hold my announcement for a strategic time. Good thing. I shortly amended my thinking to the end of January, 2004, knowing that some key negotiations would be happening late in the year and I owed it to my people to stick with it to conclusion. I didn't want people who knew I would go at the end of the year to wait me out on key issues. I anticipated making my announcement in late fall, allowing me a wind down period and giving GSA ample time to install a replacement.

Now the calculating began. Early fall came and I decided again to defer. February was a short month. Why not painlessly extend another month and boost my pension another few bucks? Besides, our event calendar was forming and in February I saw two conferences to which I would be invited or be obliged to attend. A U.S. Marshal Service conference in Florida and another GSA specialty conference in Texas were among those on tap. I saw warm weather and two blowout conferences, the ingredients for an easy month. Any conference in which I am a mere attendee rather than active participant was considered a vacation.

February quickly became March when I found out that the next project managers' conference was to be held in Seattle in mid-March. Project management was always dear to me and this would be a chance to say goodbye to many friends who would be attending from around the country. Besides, Seattle is nice any time of year.

By early 2004 I still hadn't given my notice, but I was expecting to dog it over the next few months so I thought I owed the organization the courtesy of ample notification. This would allow the replacement process to start and would enable me to ease out, rather than sprint to the finish.

The indecision and the wear and tear of my years at the helm were impacting my family life. While I traveled and stayed at nice hotels and enjoyed fine dining my spouse was at home, rattling around the house. Winter made it even less comfortable. This was brought home to me in a very eloquent manner one cold February day.

I had just flown from a meeting in Fort Worth to St. Louis where I had a meeting the following day. I arrived in downtown St. Louis, a city I had never been to before, in the late afternoon. At dusk I walked to the St. Louis arch, managing to catch the last tram of the day to the top of this monumental structure. At the top, I was in awe of the view from the small windows and decided to share my enthusiasm with my dear wife.

When she answered the call from my cell phone I began, "You will never guess where I am. I'm at the top......"

That's as far as I got. Uncharacteristically, my wife's voice barked through the phone. "I don't give a flying fuck where you are! I'm stuck in the house with three feet of snow on the ground and you don't even have the sense to call me until now! You can stay in St. Louis or Dallas or Detroit or wherever the fuck you are!" *Slam.*

I thought about that overreaction while enjoying a fine dinner with wine and decided that I better finalize my departure before I end up spending my retirement living at the local Y.

By late February I told Young Bruce that I would be leaving at the end of June. This was another big mistake. Now I advise people that instead of the four months' notice that I gave, I should have given four hours' notice.

As I found out, once you are a lame duck in a high profile position your status and influence diminish faster than puke passing through a vulture.

*   *   *

In my last year on the job things were beginning to unravel and I would have been naïve not to notice it. Some could be blamed on my leadership, or lack of leadership, and some of the miscues could be attributed to events beyond my control. Either way, it was my responsibility to run the region successfully and with a positive cash flow. That was not happening. Our relationship with a major customer, the courts, was deteriorating as were several large court projects. My personal relationship with some judges and their subordinates (who thought they had the same clout or privilege to be just as obnoxious) was seriously strained. I didn't see any short-term improvement coming regardless of the effort of myself or the region.

There were some definite advantages to my having ascended to the top position relatively late in my working life. If you do well in such a situation, as I did the first few years, people say "this guy is a great manager." If you do poorly, as I did in the latter stages of managing my fiefdom, people don't get mad at you. They just say, "Ah, it's a pity. He's really too old to do this job."

Another factor which wasn't helping the situation was that the agency was going through a major reorganization. My thought on reorgs never changed. Consolidations are almost always an opportunity to create a *larger* organization with more jobs at higher grade levels. They are great for the travel, hospitality and government consulting industries. Politicians continue to believe that if an outside consultant with a million dollar contract but no knowledge of the real workings of the organization makes a recommendation it is more authentic than the opinion of mere civil servants.

The extent of the changes, which were completed after my departure, were mind boggling and resulted in massive new hiring at high levels and relegating other high priced talent to lesser roles. The government has a lot of job retention rules, preventing arbitrary removals or using reorganization as a tool to eliminate certain positions, only to replace them with higher priced talent doing the same thing. There are, among other protections, things called bumping rights, so if your job is eliminated you can bump someone at a lower level at no loss in pay. This goes on indefinitely until the last bumpee, a janitorial temp making minimum wage, ends up losing his job. Political appointees often fail to understand this in their zeal to create their own legacy.

The Court deterioration, the reorganization, and my being saddled with Washington appointed "advisors" was compounded by the normal aging process, all of which left me less capable physically and emotionally to deal with these issues. It was definitely time to go. No need for another survival act. This was reconfirmed by some simple math. I was under the original Civil Service Retirement System. With 38 plus years of service and a year of unused sick leave my pension would be almost as much as my take-home salary. Not a bad deal.

CHAPTER 29

The Grand Finale

Being a lame duck in a presumably powerful position is a mixed bag. Outgoing presidents use the time to heal wounds, grant ridiculous pardons and put people in jobs which exceed their own term in office. Others do their best to line up future employment to take advantage of their prestige and insider knowledge and connections.

In my case, the moment I made it known that I would be leaving, my powers, authorities, initiatives and dignities were slowly stripped by the political barons. This is a rule of the bureaucracy. Like a former World Series manager whose team is now mired in last place I would have been naïve not to think that change was due. I just made it easy for everyone. Based upon the way I was treated after giving notice, if I were to do it again I would steadfastly refuse to retire, then fight my inevitable transfer to purgatory and settle everything with a nebulous job for another year working out of home or some outpost where I would never be seen or heard from again. This would have been a nice transition from the frying pan to retirement but my conscience told me I wanted to leave with dignity and to provide a smooth transition.

By coincidence, right after I announced my retirement, GSA announced that my boss, Young Bruce, go-getter that he is, was being reassigned to the central office as chief of staff to the administrator. The prior, soon to be indicted, chief of staff, had moved to greener pastures at the Office of Management and Budget. Bruce was moving into an important position but I was suspicious, given my mistrust of politicians. My nose again told me something was wrong. *Nobody* in a political appointment would sell the family home of three generations and move his growing family to Washington within months of a presidential election. If George W. was defeated in the upcoming election, Young Bruce would be out of a job. No sane person would do what Young Bruce was doing without a guarantee or promise somewhere.

I liked Bruce, but he was moving too fast for his own good.

There had been several changes of heart before I finally told him that I planned to retire. The way I handled it violated my own rules of business. I gave more than four months' notice. In retrospect, I should have given two weeks notice, or better yet, two hours. That would have been consistent with my business principle of never closing out your options, which I did the moment I gave my notice. Bruce accepted my retirement notice like a Labrador retriever pouncing on an errant tennis ball.

I jokingly told YB that if I changed my mind again he has my permission to fire me. I suggested a recruitment plan for a successor with the hope that my replacement would be identified before I left so that I could assist with the transition. I also made it clear that although it was time to fade out, I had plenty of energy left, would not be leaving town so quickly and would like to be called upon for part-time consulting work in view of my experience and knowledge of the organization. With such an arrangement, I would keep my head in the business world doing something I liked in a familiar setting and the government would get an inexpensive additional resource. All was good, or so I thought.

My offer to help was spurned. About two weeks later Young Bruce called me to his office where I found him and his loyal deputy huddled together with serious looks on their faces. His deputy was a career person and when a career person is put in an awkward position by a politician you can see it in his eyes. They never look right at you and their body weight shifts from cheek to cheek. The person is thinking less of the task at hand and more about when the score will be settled for betraying the trust of the family of lifers.

It turned out that Bruce was thinking of making some organization changes and my timely departure announcement was the perfect opportunity. He informed me of his impending move to a new position in Washington, which I already knew, and that the new regional administrator, Young Tiffany, would be appointed quickly, which I also already knew. Political appointees often underestimate the information network of careerists. Since I was leaving he preferred (I should say *commanded*) that the new person work with someone who remained, to assure a smooth transition. That made sense to me. He suggested (Did I say *commanded?*) that I step down early so that my top assistant could assume my job on an acting basis until a permanent selection was made. I had no real problem with this, but I wanted to do it on my terms. Young Bruce, however, insisted that *he* make the announcement and requested that I remain silent. The incentive, or quid pro quo, according to YB, was that "I have some thoughts about consulting work for you, if you get my drift." Being a team player, I went along with the suggestion/command. This would give me some well-earned wind-down time.

My ego was hurt but I wanted to continue as a team player. Bruce had made those vague references to send some consulting work my way if I cooperated. Believing Bruce's sweet talk was another mistake on my part. His deputy sat there silently and later conveniently remembered nothing of the conversation.

Young Bruce was a nice guy despite being a politician and an opportunist. As a concession to me he withheld *his* announcement of *my* retirement for about a month to allow me to attend a few upcoming conferences in my regular capacity. I upheld my part of the bargain by saying nothing, not even to my closest associates.

Ten weeks before my planned departure YB issued an announcement that I had "agreed to take on a new role as a 'Senior Advisor'" until I retire. As any career person knows, becoming a senior advisor is governmentese for being booted out with no place to go for a while. In reality, a senior advisor gets very few requests for advice.

Never trust a politician. I'm still waiting for that consulting work that was promised. Hence, I had the time to become an author.

Young Bruce went to Washington and resigned abruptly six months later because he had embarrassed the agency by, among other things, consorting in the wrong places. A day after he left he had a new job with a Washington lobbying firm, which suggested that he negotiated for that position while still on GSA's payroll. The latter offense skirted the agency's standards of conduct. As for the consorting, if a man is on a diet he can still look at the menu but he should have gone home to eat.

From the moment I went into my advisory capacity things started to crumble and all of the business laws applicable to exiled managers were activated. I wasn't invited to meetings that I previously chaired, I was off of e-mail lists and calls were unreturned. That was the least of my problems.

My deputy had taken over full blast. To make things more complicated, we were undergoing major renovations at the time and had to temporally relocate to another floor while our original space was renovated.

My deputy assigned his senior advisor an office of a size commensurate with my station in life but it was outside of the general work area which effectively put me totally out of the loop. I could have just as easily sat on the roof or at home. The only people who came to my office were either lost or were personal friends coming to reminisce. Few people saw me coming or going and since nobody sought me out in my advisor role I could have croaked in the office and I wouldn't have been found until the odor permeated the building.

I saw fit to have a grab bag of sorts of those office souvenirs which I either didn't want to bring home or would have no practical use. Each morning for about two weeks I sent an email to my former key managers to pass along to their staff, offering bits and pieces of my office to the first claimant. The things on the walls, desk contents, furniture accessories and so on were all up for grabs. Some things went fast, like my small piece of the Berlin Wall (compliments of my son's 1990 trip to Europe), my framed poster of Elvis at the Sun Studios (compliments of my visit to Memphis) and some gold shovels which were VIP gifts at groundbreakings. There were invitations to everything from courthouse dedications to self serving award ceremonies. I had *particles* (Liz is long gone from GSA but I remember her use of the word.) of GSA logo clothing, pens, briefcases, paperweights and as a special bonus, a few "letters of counseling" which I had the honor of receiving during my career.

When the parade of souvenir pickers ended I spent my time cleaning out my files, both hard copy and electronic, copying to disks any data which I thought I might need in the future, and dispensing some favors for a few deserving people who wouldn't get their due after I leave.

While all of this was happening my disenchantment with the establishment was building. I was always a straight shooter and I was getting miffed that some to whom I was loyal in the past had short memories. I was beginning to think that the organization to which I had been so loyal and which had been so good to me over the years had forgotten me before the body even got cold. It was a rude awakening but a fact of life and business.

*   *   *

When I left the government, the profile of government employment had changed dramatically from my early days. The women named Mary were gone, as were their typewriters and adding machines. Now the women were named Jennifer or Stacey, had advanced degrees, could negotiated blood out of a stone and could do magic with a computer. They drank apple martinis at happy hour. The Jims and Johns were augmented by Jasons and Michaels who wore designer shirts, never heard of polyester sport jackets and enjoyed a Samuel Adams with dinner.

When we traveled we didn't have to justify air versus auto or train and we stayed at the Marriott or Ritz-Carlton instead of the local fleabags. We went to conferences at the Waldorf and yacht clubs instead of the basement of the federal building. We could purchase refreshments for everybody without having to ask people to throw a few bucks in the pot or bury the cost in some other accounting classification such as a bogus cab ride.

Our computers were state of the art and our offices were first class. The vinyl floors and bare ceilings were replaced by plush carpet and modern lighting which didn't need supplemental desk lamps. The old gray or wood desks were now ultra-sleek modular units.

Employees were empowered to make critical decisions and they were all literate enough to sign their own correspondence. Those that couldn't work the usual 8:30 to 5:00 day were allowed to be flexible in their hours or even work at home. People received transit subsidies, child care assistance and tuition reimbursement. Among the most ingenious workplace initiatives was leave sharing, whereby if someone faced a hardship and ran out of vacation time and sick leave, they could receive donations of leave from fellow employees. This saved many from financial disaster.

We carried cell phones and BlackBerrys before many in the private sector. It was a good place to work. Salary levels were commensurate, and sometimes better, than private industry. A government employee was far from the old downtrodden bureaucrat chained to a lifetime of servitude in the system.

On the flip side, as a manager I couldn't fire or discipline anyone without a paper trail and lengthy due process. Every dissatisfied employee or unsuccessful contractor had multiple forums to seek justice. This took up an incredible amount of supervisory, legal and human resources time.

If I used one of my salty expressions at the wrong time I could get hit with an EEO complaint or be charged with creating a hostile work environment. Ditto if I innocently patted an employee, male or female, on the shoulder for good work.

We had to be careful of what we committed to writing because almost every document was subject to public review under the Freedom of Information Act or discovery in litigation. Likewise, any controversial project required public input, often a good idea but more often a forum for every super liberal or anti-government scholar who wanted to delay a project.

*   *   *

One of the hazards of being in a high profile position in government is that you are vulnerable to legal action. The government provides for a cheap and easy forum for every malcontent and incompetent who has a gripe. Unfortunately this ties up management's time mercilessly, which is often the complainant's real objective.

It was not unusual to be named in litigation instituted by contractors or our own employees. Most litigation was routinely handled by our regional counsel. On rare occasions if a government employee at any level is sued privately, the United States attorney would provide legal defense so long as the complaint concerned an act in the course of one's official duties. Here is where things got just a little bit murky.

My final days were marred by frivolous litigation brought against me personally by a disgruntled employee. It all started when I conveyed a message through our labor relations experts to the employee's attorney in response to a ridiculous offer to settle an EEO case in which she claimed age, sex and nationality discrimination. "You tell her lawyer that if they hung me by my dick from the Empire State Building I wouldn't settle this case." The Equal Employment Opportunity Commission was pushing for a settlement as they always do because it negates the need to make a decision and reduces their open case load.

The case involved an employee who was not selected for a merit promotion into a job for which she was clearly not qualified. She filed an unsuccessful grievance, followed by an EEO compliant. When those venues failed, she paid a nominal fee and filed an action in the Supreme Court of the State of New York against me personally, contrary to her attorney's advice, claiming I slandered her and damaged her reputation because in a conversation with her boss on the plaza someone overheard me saying something like, "Too bad we can't just fire the bitch." What the person with the big ears didn't realize was that I was paraphrasing a classic line from the movie and Broadway show, *Nine to Five*.

Her self representation was an offense to the court and the English language. I was accused of demonstrating "a lack of disrespect." She added that my behavior was "surprising for a man of his *statute*."

This is a person I had tried to fire for insubordination and incompetence but because she filed a complaint about non-selection for a job the other actions were suspended until resolution of this one. This was a great stalling tactic. After one of the informal hearings on her proposed dismissal I mentioned to our female attorney that we had the employee sweating in there, to which she replied, "Naw, it was just the Botox leaking from her forehead." Girls will be girls.

She further put GSA on the defensive by claiming in a separate grievance that GSA created an unsafe working condition by placing a fax machine in the office "which emitted toxic fumes" and caused her to have nausea attacks.

The same individual wrote letters to the president of the United States, the GSA administrator and an assortment of congressmen and senators, all of which came right back to our office to answer. It gave her another forum for action because she routinely claimed that our attempts to fire her were retaliatory for the letters.

I was not amused by these events because my name alone was on the court document. The complaint called my action "unconscionable and slanderous." Months earlier I had warned our legal establishment that unless we were more aggressive in our attempts to dismiss this person for gross incompetence or for many disciplinary issues, not only will we be stuck with an albatross but we would be left open to never ending legal action. I expressed my concern for personal litigation against me because in one of the EEO hearings, which should not have even taken place, the hearing examiner found in favor of the Government on the merits of the case but made a vague reference to his indecision on the slander issue since it was out of EEOC's purview.

After much badgering on my part both the legal and human resources experts went along with the dismissal. Her multitude of cases went on for years but at least while it was happening she was no longer on the payroll.

The scenario in this type of litigation is that GSA counsel requests representation from the Department of Justice which it did formally in a letter to Attorney General Janet Reno. The case was assigned to the United States attorney for the Southern District of New York. An assistant U.S. attorney did his due diligence by submitting a successful motion to substitute *United States of America* for myself as defendant, and asking that the case be moved to federal court. At that point the case was effectively lost by the plaintiff because you cannot sue the United States for slander, but as Yogi said, "It ain't over 'till it's over."

I tried to get it out of my mind but it took six months beyond my departure before the district court issued a decision in the government's favor. For some inexplicable reason, the employee then dug into her personal savings to pay another fee to appeal the decision.

A year after my retirement the U.S. Court of Appeals for the Southern District of New York issued a short decision, without discussion or debate, upholding the decision of the lower court to dismiss the case. At that point my own attorney was willing to initiate countersuits against the original plaintiff but I was just as happy to drop the issue and concentrate on being retired.

One week before my intended departure I journeyed to Washington to say my goodbyes and formally submit my papers. While there, I made a courtesy call to Young Bruce in his new office. He wished me well and thanked me for my loyal service, with a half-hearted assurance that his prior commitment was still valid. "I spoke to Young Tiffany and discussed some possible consulting assignments for you." I thanked him, and then said my goodbye to his boss, Stephen Perry, who was the White House-appointed GSA administrator and a real gentleman.

This was my final official trip to the seat of government so before leaving town I took a stroll through the Mall and then visited the new World War II Memorial. I went back to Famous Luigi's, my favorite local restaurant, for a beer and a bowl of pasta for old times' sake and then took the Metro to Reagan Airport for the last shuttle flight of the day.

*   *   *

While all of the legal wrangling was going on the party makers were hard at work. My sendoff from GSA was shortly after the passing of President Ronald Reagan, and was dragged out as long and with almost as much pomp and circumstance as his funeral. Because of all of the preparatory work for my departure I would have felt guilty had I not actually left.

The formal retirement party preparation was launched by my deputy, now my boss and the one to whom I was senior advisor but to whom I provided no advice. He designated a committee to begin the preparation. A smooth transition to retirement obscurity would accelerate appointment of my replacement. The eventual party was almost like a mob funeral with all of the proper respects being paid, except that the guest of honor was still alive.

The committee was headed by a close friend who volunteered for the task. I will call her "BT." I had insisted that any festive sendoff should not be costly to the attendees and I did not want any gifts. People who worked for me should not be obligated to contribute to a gift for the boss. I had designated a charity for those who insisted on spending for a gift and for those who actually gave me anything other than a gag or sentimental gift, I contributed like value to the designated charity.

The on again, off again, nature of my retirement drove BT a bit bonkers but when she got the final OK it was full speed ahead. One of my favorite New York restaurants, The Barking Dog, on East 34th Street, was contacted for a catering proposal. Former associates who had since retired were invited. A few outside contractors with whom I had done business came, too. New York City's commissioner of buildings also put in an appearance.

The party was held, appropriately, in the conference center of the Ted Weiss Federal Building at 290 Broadway. This property was part of my legacy and I was pleased with the choice. Much of my sweat and blood was in that building. My successor, who said he "felt crisp" that evening, emceed the event. Young Bruce was conspicuous by his absence. Young Tiffany, who had been in the job all of nine weeks, showed up for a few politically correct words and quickly left.

After the obligatory political flattery, a good time was had by all. There were touching tributes and a roast. My family and a few life-long friends were there. BT knew my priorities in life and decorated with a sports theme. She also posted some old photos of me as a long-haired up-and-coming youngster which provided a few laughs.

While the party was going on I couldn't help but recall that about midway through my career, during one of my many trips to purgatory, I used to say, "If I survive to retirement and the organization gives me a party, I will get up and first thank everybody for attending, and then proceed to say, 'And now I would like to name the ten biggest pricks I have known in my career.'"

Fortunately, when it came time for my speech I avoided that temptation. The only surprise I pulled was to resurrect a variation of the old award which I used to present for infamous achievements. Since I foresaw that the new regional administrator was apt to make decisions based on emotion and irrational judgment, I had a plaque prepared, called the "Bayonne Bleeder Award" in honor of a former prize fighter named Chuck Wepner, who had a reputation for going against the best, getting beat up and then getting right back in the ring.

I designated this as an annual presentation, to go to a deserving individual who took a hit for the team. The first award went to my associate, Alan Berman, a highly skilled engineer who was arbitrarily moved from his position because he dared to provide accurate information, rather than what the politically influenced regional administrator wanted to hear. He eventually was moved back when the RA realized that accuracy was more important than fluff. I was told that she continued to move people around who rubbed her the wrong way.

It was a fun sendoff. When the litigation was resolved I faded into the Sunbelt to a tranquil retirement.

EPILOGUE

Life changed dramatically after retirement.

The biggest trauma came in the hours immediately before and after my exit. On my last day I turned in my cell phone, BlackBerry, laptop and Smart Card (an ID coded to allow me 24/7 access to virtually every federal property in the region). Now, if I entered property during off hours the rent-a-cops would put the cuffs on me. I was stripped naked.

Within 24 hours I was cut off from the e-mail system and access to GSA's internal website. When I went back into the building a week later to turn in some additional paperwork I stood on the security line and went through a pat down, just like the people coming to apply for citizenship or to visit their parole officer.

I quickly subscribed to my own wireless service but the new cell phone seldom rang, except for my wife reminding me to pick up a container of milk. The visits and calls with the inevitable "by the way" came to a screeching halt, as did the invites to dinners, luncheons, groundbreakings and holiday parties. When I traveled, Marriott and Ritz-Carlton gave way to Super 8 and Days Inn.

These subtleties continued long after my career ended. Those who coveted my business now ignored me. I had traveled so much with US Airways that I got bonus points, priority boarding and free upgrades. Two years after retirement I received a terse e-mail from them stating that due to inactivity my frequent flier miles will be forfeited.

The consulting assignments which two regional administrators promised amounted to a few small tasks.

When I see people in suits and holding iPhones in hotel lobbies or airports, while I'm wearing my T-shirt and jeans, I do get wistful for the old days. The hotel conferences, banquet dinners and an array of logo souvenirs were replaced by an occasional pencil from Off Track Betting and accessories from the flea market. The closest equivalent to a conference lunch is a trip to Applebee's with my tennis buddies.

I was saddened that my successor succumbed to the whims of the new political administration by doing the inevitable massive regional reorganization. Although my successor and his political boss, as well as those they chose to surround themselves with, heard what they wanted to hear and convinced themselves that reorganization was good, my close confidantes told me that this was nothing shy of total disaster and a major morale destroyer. There were an inordinate number of retirements and resignations during this time. There was also more than a million dollars in fees to a major consulting company to validate this fiasco. Reorganizations generally do nothing but feed consultants and support the hospitality industry because of the number of meetings generated.

Perhaps the biggest disappointment that I felt was that the organization took to filling key positions with outside hires rather than qualified people within. This was sending a negative message to the loyal employees. They were also disheartened by the fact that my successor relied so much on the advice of the outsiders who knew little about our organization or the nature of the work we do. This was another slap in the faces of every conscientious employee in the place. But, like everything else, people and organizations adjust and life goes on.

After spending some time catching up with my family, surgically repairing a few body parts and doing an occasional minor consulting assignment for others, I eventually headed to sunny Florida where I now reside. I went from the city that never sleeps to a city that always sleeps.

When I moved to Florida I resurrected a sports writing avocation after a near twenty year hiatus. I am the world's oldest intern, covering the Florida Panthers of the National Hockey League for a northern based publication.

Before heading south I had the opportunity to check a few items off of my list of "places to go before I die using my government frequent flyer mileage." You don't get too many perks working for the government but the frequent flier miles are a residual payment for past services. I used the freebies to get to a few places I just had to see, including; Tombstone, Arizona for a re-creation of the gunfight at OK corral; Eveleth, Minnesota to pay homage to the United States Hockey Hall of Fame; southern Utah to visit an old Brooklyn buddy who retired to a county with a population density of 1.5 people per square mile; Jackass Flats, Nevada just to say I was there; Mount Rushmore to run a marathon and enjoy the scenery; Wrigley Field in Chicago, which I consider the ultimate Mecca for every baseball fan; and a bunch of presidential libraries across the country.

The frivolous litigation was like a case of crabs, annoying but not life threatening. It hung over my head for a year after my retirement before it was dismissed by the appellate court. My name remains in Public Buildings Service in perpetuity, at least for now, by the annual presentation of the Bayonne Bleeder Award to a deserving candidate who takes a hit for the team.

When I still lived in New York, and when I now visit the big city, I frequently meet some of my GSA friends for lunch or a brew, although I do not visit the office. I have been told by some former colleagues that both loyalty to the troops and a sense of humor are missing from management since my departure.

The Brooklyn projects were completed and the claims were settled on the Islip project; the two Foley Square buildings remain as showpieces of the region; the Mission to the United Nations has since been demolished and a modern replacement is being be erected on the same fertile site; a new Buffalo courthouse is under construction; the lobby at 26 Federal Plaza has been modernized to go along with my upgraded restrooms. I still get agitated when I look at the 290 Broadway cornerstone, which bears the name of the GSA administrator who threw us to the wolves.